Principles of American Journalism

In a rapidly changing media landscape, what becomes of journalism? Designed to engage, inspire and challenge students while laying out the fundamental principles of the craft, *Principles of American Journalism* introduces students to the core values of journalism and its singularly important role in a democracy. From the First Amendment to Facebook, Stephanie Craft and Charles N. Davis provide a comprehensive exploration of the guiding principles of journalism—the ethical and legal foundations of the profession, its historical and modern precepts, the economic landscape, the relationships among journalism and other social institutions, and the key issues and challenges that contemporary journalists face. Case studies, discussion questions and field exercises help students to think critically about journalism's function in society, creating mindful practitioners of journalism and more informed media consumers.

With its bottom line under assault, its values being challenged from without and from within and its future anything but certain, it has never been more important to think about what's unique about journalism. This text is ideal for use in introductory Principles of Journalism courses, and the companion website provides a full complement of student and instructor resources to enhance the learning experience and connect to the latest news issues and events.

Stephanie Craft is Associate Professor of Journalism Studies at the Missouri School of Journalism. Before earning a doctorate in Communication from Stanford University, she worked as a newspaper journalist in California, Arkansas and Washington.

Charles N. Davis is Professor of Journalism Studies at the Missouri School of Journalism and is the former executive director for the National Freedom of Information Coalition (NFOIC), headquartered at the School. In 2008, Davis was named the Scripps Howard Foundation National Jour-

Principles of
American Journalism

An Introduction

Stephanie Craft
University of Missouri

Charles N. Davis
University of Missouri

Routledge
Taylor & Francis Group

NEW YORK AND LONDON

Please visit the companion website at www.routledge.com/cw/craft

First published 2013
by Routledge
711 Third Avenue, New York, NY 10017

Simultaneously published in the UK
by Routledge
2 Park Square, Milton Park, Abingdon, Oxon OX14 4RN

Routledge is an imprint of the Taylor & Francis Group, an informa business

Library of Congress Cataloging in Publication Data

Craft, Stephanie.
Principles of American journalism : an introduction / Stephanie Craft and Charles N. Davis.
 p. cm.
 1. Journalism—United States. 2. Press—United States. I. Davis, Charles N. II. Title.
PN4855.C84 2013
071'.3—dc23   2012029860

ISBN: 978-0-415-89016-8 (hbk)
ISBN: 978-0-415-89017-5 (pbk)
ISBN: 978-0-203-08191-4 (ebk)

Typeset in Warnock Pro
by Apex CoVantage, LLC

Editor: Erica Wetter
Development Editor: Mary Altman
Editorial Assistant: Margo Irvin
Senior Production Editor: Gail Newton
Copyeditor: Gail Welsh
Proof-reader: Christine James
Cover Design: Gareth Toye

Printed and bound in the United States of America
by Edwards Brothers, Inc.

Dedicated to
Principles of American Journalism students past, present and future.

Contents

Preface

This book results from the process of co-teaching the Principles of American Journalism course at the Missouri School of Journalism—the task we were hired for and the course that continues to challenge us and change our thinking on so many issues, day after day.

In our daily conversations as we took turns teaching the course, we concluded that the many fine "Introduction to Mass Media" texts on the market did not meet the needs of a course designed to introduce students not to the entire world of mass communication, but to the central role that journalism plays within that broader world. What if we created a text that not only introduced students to journalism as a practice, but also highlighted its values and the many forces promoting and hindering journalism's ability to act in accordance with them? What if, in other words, we could teach students why journalism matters?

We, like so many others, were deeply influenced by *The Elements of Journalism*, Bill Kovach and Tom Rosenstiel's elegant testament to what makes journalism unique and important. It fundamentally changed the way we thought about teaching the course, and underscored the importance of a course that focuses singularly on the news media.

Of course, much has changed and continues to change since we began teaching the course and since Kovach and Rosenstiel published *The Elements*, changes that are reflected in this book's contents. We believe that much of what Kovach and Rosenstiel set forth stands the test of time—indeed, the ferocity and pace of change make taking a clear stance about journalism's values all the more important. We hope this book does credit to Kovach and Rosenstiel's work and pursues, even if it never quite reaches, the goal of making the case for journalism's essential role. In the end, we do feel we have a text that matches the goals of the course.

Chapters 1 and 2 trace journalism's role in democracy and ways of defining journalism that have implications for what we expect journalism to do. Chapter 3 takes a look at the changing tides of journalism, making the argument that while tools change, the principles underlying journalism don't (or at least shouldn't). Chapters 4 and 5 attempt to make sense of the economic context for journalism and the ever-present tension between profit and public service that has new urgency with the collapse of traditional revenue models. Chapters 6 and 7 address the ethical and legal underpinnings of journalism practice as well as offering practical information to help students understand what they *can* do and whether they *ought* to do it. Finally, Chapter 8 concludes the book with a spirited discussion of independence, the element of journalism that is central to journalism's ability to fulfill its democratic function.

Acknowledgments

A book is a collective effort reflecting the labors of many people. We'd be remiss if we failed to recognize the many fine colleagues, former students and friends who have added their expertise to the book through the many sidebar features you'll read. They add a depth and breadth to the text, as well as a fresh new voice.

We also would like to thank the thousands of students who have marched in and out of Principles of American Journalism over the past 13 years. To say that we could not do it without you all is trite, maybe, yet so true. Your feedback, your questions in class, your responses to the discussions we've had are all reflected in this book.

And this book also reflects one of the greatest joys of teaching Principles of American Journalism at Missouri: the many wonderful graduate students who have worked with us through the years. Many appear in these pages as contributors to the sidebars, but many, many others played a role in this book through discussions, comments and occasional cajoling. We thank you all.

We'd also be remiss if we didn't thank the faculty and staff of the University of Missouri School of Journalism, who prove daily that the "Missouri Method" continues to be the finest way to train young journalists ever devised.

And finally, our families and friends and colleagues, who have made countless adjustments to their own lives so we could get this book written. As for the Davis side of the writing partnership: thanks to my dear wife Julie, and my kids, Charlie and Mamie Davis—your father does nothing without you in mind. Bernie and Art Craft—the very definition of "supportive"—have their daughter's deepest gratitude.

1

The Mirror, the Watchdog and the Marketplace

Navigating the rush-hour traffic on his way to work in January 2009, Sri Lankan newspaper editor Lasantha Wickramatunga was gunned down by two assassins on motorcycles.

He knew it was coming.

For years his newspaper, *The Sunday Leader*, had exposed government corruption and questioned its conduct of the war against the separatist Tamil Tigers—reporting that had already subjected Wickramatunga and his family to beatings and no-holds-barred intimidation. Just days before his murder, he received a message scrawled in red ink on a page of his newspaper: "If you write you will be killed."

So why did he do it? Why did he keep writing in the face of such threats? In an editorial he wrote anticipating his assassination and published three days after his death, Wickramatunga offers a compelling answer, describing how he saw his role as a journalist and the role of a free press in society:

The free media serve as a mirror in which the public can see itself sans mascara and styling gel. From us you learn the state of your nation, and especially its management by the people you elected to give your children a better future. Sometimes the image you see in that mirror is not a pleasant one. But while you may grumble in the privacy of your armchair, the journalists who hold the mirror up to you do so publicly and at great risk to themselves. That is our calling, and we do not shirk it . . . We have espoused unpopular causes, stood up for those too feeble to stand up for themselves, locked horns with the high and mighty so swollen with power that they have forgotten their roots, exposed corruption and the waste of your hard-earned tax rupees, and made sure that whatever the propaganda of the day, you were allowed to hear a contrary view.

(Wickramatunga, 2009)

That Wickramatunga would put himself in harm's way—and ultimately pay with his life—for the "calling" of journalism demonstrates a singular kind of courage. But the very idea that simply doing journalism put him at risk might be a little difficult to understand from the vantage point of the United States, where journalists can generally report on and even criticize the actions of government without fear of violence. That freedom is easy for us to take for granted, but was grimly elusive for Wickramatunga. In that final editorial, he offered this blunt prediction: "When finally I am killed, it will be the government that kills me."

What can we, separated by thousands of miles and great historical and cultural differences, learn about American journalism from the assassination of an editor in Sri Lanka? A lot. In fact, if you substitute "pounds" for "rupees" in the quotation above, you could easily believe you were reading something penned by a patriot during the American Revolution. (OK, so you'd have to substitute "powdered wigs" or something for "styling gel" too. But you get the idea.) Why do these ideas sound so familiar to us? Because they echo a widely shared understanding of what democracy requires of journalism, and of the kind of freedom necessary for journalism to do what democracy requires.

▶ **THE HISTORICAL BACKDROP**

In the United States, that widely shared understanding has its roots in American colonial experience and the subsequent revolution, particularly in the background and mindsets of the group of men who would become the framers of the U.S. Constitution. The colonists' reasons for revolt largely centered on what was considered to be the tyranny—economic and political—of their British rulers. An ocean away from the Crown, the colonies wanted to shake off the inequity of taxation without representation and the indignity of being forced, after a long period in which the government practiced a hands-off policy toward them and they began to develop a distinct, "American" identity, to resubmit to British authority. (We are skipping over a ton of really interesting history here in the name of brevity. Promise us you'll read up on press history on your own.) But once they managed to successfully break free, they would still need to come up with a system of government to manage their affairs. What would it look like? Something completely different.

In addition to their personal experiences as colonists, the framers of the U.S. Constitution also were steeped in Enlightenment philosophy, particularly that of John Locke, which emphasized the power and authority of individual reason over other—arbitrary—sources of authority, such as the state. In very oversimplified terms, this emphasis assumes that individuals are free to exercise reason and that reason is the source of truth. Perhaps you can begin to see where all this is heading: A basic idea that people, exercising reason, are best equipped to govern themselves, to make sense of the competing "truths" in the marketplace of ideas, and the related conclusion

FIGURE 1.1 English philosopher John Locke (1632–1704) was a key Enlightenment figure whose ideas were very influential on the founding fathers of the United States.

Georgios Kollidas/ Shutterstock

▶ **DEMOCRACY:**
A system of government in which the people govern themselves. Typically characterized by free elections in which every adult can participate, freedom of expression, and an independent judiciary, this kind of self-governance stands in contrast to monarchies, dictatorships, theocracies and other forms in which an unelected person or small group of people hold power.

that government power must be harnessed in the service of the people, not the other way around.

So, how might a free press assist in that self-governance? By acting as a check on government power and by creating a space in which claims about truth could be debated. This notion of the press contradicts a tenet of English common law during colonial times that sounds, well, tyrannical. It's called "seditious libel." A libel is a statement that harms someone's reputation. The "seditious" part refers to a libel about government authority. In England, this was a crime punishable by life imprisonment.

It gets better. (Or worse.)

"The greater the truth, the greater the libel." This feature of the law essentially said that the truth of whatever libelous thing you dared to say against the government didn't matter. In fact, the more true the criticism, the bigger trouble you would be in for voicing it. Imagine what a law like that can do to the marketplace of ideas. Shut it down altogether, that's what.

When the framers turned their attention to drafting the founding documents of the United States, they saw vestiges of English law such as seditious libel to be contrary to what their experiment in democratic government would require. Not only did it violate Enlightenment notions of reason, but it also ran contrary to more practical concerns about how to check tyranny and discuss and debate public affairs. (Seditious libel, sadly, crops up again and again in American history, typically during times of war. You can take some comfort in the fact that it has been repeatedly beaten back.)

DISCUSSION QUESTIONS

American democracy today differs in many ways from the structure laid out by the founders. For example, virtually all citizens—not just rich, white, landowners—now have the right to vote. Further, those running for office appeal directly to the general public, rather than to an elite group of electors. In this new environment, is the role of journalism more or less important than it was more than two centuries ago?

Among those founding documents is the Bill of Rights, drafted by James Madison, which declares freedom of speech and of the press to be basic rights. (You'll learn much more about the First Amendment in Chapter 7.) The need—or lack of need—for a document to enumerate such basic rights was the topic of much debate. In fact, some colonists didn't want to ratify the U.S. Constitution without such a list. Nevertheless, if a list were to be drawn up, certainly freedom of expression would have to be on it. As Madison (1822) later wrote, "A popular Government, without popular information, or the means of acquiring it, is but a Prologue to a Farce or a Tragedy; or, perhaps both."

In his overview of the twists and turns the discussion about the Bill of Rights took, scholar Rodney Smolla (1992) gives us a sense of the magnitude of the framers' accomplishments:

> America had, for the first time in world history, put the people before
> the state. . . . In the Declaration of Independence and the grandiloquent
> opening of the Preamble to the Constitution, in which "We the People"
> asserted their ultimate authority, America reversed the flow of power.
> (p. 39)

▶ WHAT DEMOCRACY NEEDS FROM JOURNALISM

Now that we've got some background into why a free press is so intertwined with democracy, we will delve more deeply into just what, specifically, the press can or ought to do to support democratic governance. Interesting that the thinking of 18th Century American revolutionaries is echoed in the thinking of a 21st Century Sri Lankan newspaper editor, isn't it?

Notice the three metaphors for the role of the press Wickramatunga's editorial contains: First, the mirror, where society can see itself, warts and all. Second, the watchdog that is supposed to start barking when those in power become corrupt, forget their roots and waste the people's hard-earned money. Third, the marketplace of ideas, the space where even unpopular causes and contrary views can get a hearing. These metaphors for the press come up again and again, so it's worth spending time here to examine them in some depth.

First, let's compare those metaphors with how scholars talk about what democracy needs from the press. Five commonly discussed needs are: information dissemination, accountability, representation, deliberation and conflict resolution. **Information dissemination** is probably the easiest one to understand: Democracy requires some method for distributing all the information people need to make decisions and govern themselves. That means the press has to make decisions about what we need to know to do our jobs as citizens in a democracy, decisions that require exercising editorial judgment. Not

FIGURE 1.2 Sri Lankan media rights activists shout slogans and hold up posters bearing the picture of the disfigured face of journalist Keith Noyhar in Colombo on May 23, 2008. Noyhar, a deputy editor and defense analyst with the English-language weekly The Nation, was abducted outside his house on the night of May 22 by a group of unknown persons. He was badly beaten up and dropped off outside his residence. Media rights groups say the attack was motivated by Noyhar's criticism of the government's war efforts against the Tamil Tigers.

Lakruwan Wanniarachchi/AFP/Getty Images

all information is necessary for democracy to function, but without access to the essential information about governance, we can't begin to make decisions in a complex global marketplace of ideas. **Accountability** refers to democracy's need for some way to hold those in power responsible for their actions—actions that can affect all members of society. The value of accountability is as a corrective influence on government, which on its own is loathe to revisit mistakes and concede error. **Representation** means that in a democratic system, all people, not just those with the most education, money or influence, are visible to others and have the chance to be heard. The news media have a responsibility to ensure that those without an army of spokespeople still have a voice, that they can counter the voices of institutional power that might otherwise crowd them out of the marketplace of ideas. **Deliberation and conflict resolution** address democracy's need for a forum in which the interests of the public can be aired and debated and conclusions can be reached. The press exists, at least in part, so that a diversity of ideas find their way to the public conversation about the best course of action on the issues of the day.

What Wickramatunga knew—and what everyone from the framers and their Enlightenment philosophical forebears to 21st Century press critics have understood—is that when those needs go unfulfilled, democratic life is jeopardized. A free press is at the vanguard of all other liberties people in democracies enjoy. Without it, it's difficult to have freedom of pretty much anything else. The 1947 Commission on Freedom of the Press (known as the Hutchins Commission) put it this way:

> Freedom of the press is essential to political liberty. Where men cannot freely convey their thoughts to one another, no freedom is secure. Where freedom of expression exists, the beginnings of a free society and a means for every extension of liberty are already present. Free expression is therefore unique among liberties: it promotes and protects all the rest.
>
> (p. 6)

WHO AND WHAT WAS THE HUTCHINS COMMISSION?

Officially known as the Commission on Freedom of the Press, this group of 13 leading public intellectuals (but no journalists) was launched in 1942 "to examine areas and circumstances under which the press in the United States is succeeding or failing, to discover where free expression is or is not limited, whether by governmental censorship, pressures of readers or advertisers, the unwisdom of its own proprietors or the timidity of its managers," its chair, University of Chicago president Robert Maynard Hutchins, told the (*New York Times*, 1944).

The group met several times over the course of a couple years, interviewed many witnesses, and read lots of reports and documents. They didn't like what they saw.

Freedom of the press was in danger of failing, the Commission concluded. But that danger was largely due to the press's own poor performance and not some threat of government censorship. The evidence? Sensationalism, an emphasis on the trivial and stereotypical, the "scoop" mentality, the blurring of lines between advertising and news, and (significantly, as you'll see in later chapters) increased concentration of media ownership.

Commission members wrangled over the final report, some wanting to offer rather shocking prescriptions for government regulation of the press, others preferring to focus on improving the press by voluntary means. In the end,

the 1947 report cautioned the press that, unless it ramped up its own accountability, regulation of some kind would come.

The report was a call to journalists to consider themselves "professionals."
It also marked the birth of what is known as "social responsibility theory"
in journalism. That theory is based on the idea that with freedom comes responsibility. So, while journalism must be free from constraints on its actions,
it still must act in ways that serve the public.

Journalists at the time hated the Commission report. No surprise there. But
it has had an enduring influence on how people think about the role of journalism in society. That's why you'll see it pop up again and again throughout
this and other books on American journalism.

Read more:

Stephen Bates, *Realigning Journalism with Democracy: The Hutchins Commission, Its Times, and Ours* (Washington, DC: The Annenberg Washington Program in Communications Policy Studies of Northwestern University,
1995).

www.annenberg.northwestern.edu/pubs/hutchins/default.htm

So where do those metaphors fit in? The mirror, watchdog and marketplace of ideas metaphors describe the functions a press performs to meet
those democratic needs. We can match up the mirror metaphor with the
needs for information dissemination and representation. The watchdog is
all about accountability—monitoring power—and includes information dissemination as well. And the marketplace of ideas metaphor addresses representation, deliberation and, ideally, conflict resolution.

Taken together, these functions and the metaphors often used to describe
them paint a picture of the press as a key player in democratic life. How can
people be self-governing if they lack the information to make good decisions or a public forum in which to debate their options or a way of figuring
out if their leaders are doing what they're supposed to be doing? The answer
seems to be that without the press (and, importantly, a *free* press, which
we'll discuss below), they can't. If that sounds like an awful lot of responsibility to place on the press, well, it is. And whether and how well the press
performs those functions is the subject of thousands of books, editorial columns and shouting matches on television.

Take CNN's Anderson Cooper, for example. His methods are state-of-the-art, his tools squarely Information Age, yet it was his reportage from the flooded streets of New Orleans that served as the catalyst for a lively discussion of the journalism of outrage and its role in society. In 2005, as Hurricane Katrina bore down on New Orleans, Louisiana certainly needed a journalist. It needed its story told, but more importantly, it needed it told in a tone befitting the disaster unfolding before its citizens.

> ## DISCUSSION QUESTIONS
>
> Legal scholars have argued that democracy needs a press that provides information dissemination, accountability, representation, deliberation and conflict resolution. Are some of these needs more important than others? Again, does the dominant need vary based on time period and state of the country?

Jonathon Van Meter (2005) told the story of Cooper's reporting best, in *New York* magazine just a few weeks later:

> But it was on the fourth day of coverage, at the most dire and terrifying moment of the crisis, that Cooper came unhinged. He was interviewing Mary Landrieu, the senator from Louisiana, who had a big, sweet, southern smile spread across her perfectly made-up face. In a non-answer to one of Cooper's questions, she thanked President Bush for his "strong statements of support and comfort." Finally, Cooper boiled over. "I got to tell you," he said, "there are a lot of people here who are very upset, and very angry, and very frustrated. And when they hear politicians . . . thanking one another, it just, you know, it kind of cuts them the wrong way right now. Because literally there was a body on the streets of this town yesterday being eaten by rats, because this woman had been laying in the street for 48 hours. And there's not enough facilities to take her up. Do you get the anger that is out here?"

Riveting television. And it certainly looks like the mirror and the watchdog in all their glory. But was it good journalism? Was it the kind of reporting democracy needs? Cooper's comments pushed right up to the line between tough questioning and "confrontational advocacy journalism," as the *New York Times* described it, but viewers responded immediately to the reportage. It was outrage—pure, unvarnished outrage—and it reflected the moment and the powerlessness of the people on the ground and the lack of any coherent government response.

Asked later about the Landrieu interview, Cooper had this to say:

> Yeah, I would prefer not to be emotional and I would prefer not to get upset, but it's hard not to when you're surrounded by brave people who are suffering and in need. I feel like the people here deserve to have some answers.
>
> (Van Meter, 2005)

Demanding answers of those we elect to do our business represents the cornerstone of what makes journalism, well, journalism. Controversy about Cooper's tough questioning centered on his emotional response, his flash of anger while practicing journalism, how he saw himself as an advocate for the victim—just like Wickramatunga.

None of these metaphors—the mirror, the watchdog or the marketplace—makes mention of a specific medium such as print, broadcast or online, so

FIGURE 1.3 While the tools of early 20th Century journalists are a bit different from today's, much of the work and the values behind it remains the same.

Everett Collection/Shutterstock

let's separate out the practice of journalism from the final form it might take. And it's not all public officials and government meetings, either—not by a long shot. One of the amazing things about the rapidly changing media landscape is that wherever those with questions in need of answers gather to demand those answers, something akin to journalism emerges. It could be a website dedicated to a medical condition, a dog breed or a football team, but once its proprietor begins asking questions and posting the results on behalf of a readership, seeks and demonstrates independence, and exhibits transparency of method, it's hard to call it anything but journalism.

Standing as we now do in the thick of a seismic shift in how people get information makes it sometimes difficult to see just how and by whom our democratic needs will be fulfilled. Partly that's because the available media have shaped our traditional understanding of the press in society. Certainly the Founding Fathers had only newspapers in mind when they thought about press freedom, and those Colonial newspapers bear little resemblance to the newspapers of today. What does seem certain is that democracy's needs don't change even though the method for delivering journalism does. In fact, as the delivery platforms change, it's more important than ever for us to have a shared understanding of the values that make journalism an indispensable part of civic life.

◀ **THE PRESS:** Originally a term referring to printed newspapers and magazines, the term now includes journalism outlets spanning all types of media, from television and radio to the Internet. The term is often—as it is in this book—used interchangeably with "news media." Also, it is a collective noun, referring to journalism outlets as a group, or even an institution in society.

▶ HOW DOES THE PRESS FULFILL THOSE DEMOCRATIC NEEDS?

So, we've detailed five communication needs in a democracy. Let's flip those around now to examine how the press can/should/does fulfill them. The press performs at least five core functions in a democracy:

1. Journalism informs, analyzes, interprets and explains.

2. Journalism investigates.

3. Journalism creates a public conversation.

4. Journalism helps generate social empathy.

5. Journalism encourages accountability.

This is not an exhaustive list, but it's awfully close. A press that is performing these five functions is a press that improves the civic health of a democracy.

We'll return to each time and again throughout the book, but a quick look at each is in order.

Journalism Informs, Analyzes, Interprets and Explains   But first, it informs.

As self-evident as this may seem, it's worth noting that while the news media's role is informational, information does not necessarily equate to news. What? Information is the stuff of life, conveyed to us in a rich stream of stimuli, from the conversations we have with our roommates to the apps on our phone to the billboard we pass on the highway.

When you arrive at your home tonight, you may let your roommate in on some hot piece of gossip you picked up at work. That's information, certainly, but is it news? No, it's information. We are awash in it, veritably drowning in it, and that's precisely why news is so important, so endangered, so in need of saving. News is more than mere information; it is the result of processes and judgments constructed through institutions devoted to newsgathering. These institutions matter, for they convey value, judgment and professional norms on the process of news construction.

Think the distinction between information and news doesn't matter? Let's talk about the weather. Turn on the Weather Channel—one of our favorite cable destinations—and you'll see a ton of weather-related information: temperature, humidity levels, five-day forecasts and pollen counts. If you catch an anchor doing a standup, you'll no doubt see news as well—a tornado warning in Alabama, a hurricane brewing in the Caribbean. Why those two events, and why not the gentle rain landing in Topeka at the very same moment? Decisions have been made, about that which is newsworthy—unusual, or in the matter of that hurricane, potentially threatening. The decisions were journalistic in that their impetus was to inform, but also to bring meaning and context to the information. Not to persuade anyone of anything, and not to sell anything, but to bring meaning to the day's events, as the Hutchins Commission famously said.

It's not that news doesn't sell things, or persuade people to do things. But that is not the goal. The goal of the news is to share that information with others under the assumption that when citizens are properly informed, they will make sound decisions.

There are two concepts to take away from this information-versus-news discussion. First, news is a product, created by journalists, who happen to be human beings with all the promise and pitfalls of the species. Second, because news is a product, it is constructed. Its value lies in the fact that it is created to inform, first and foremost, by bringing meaning and context to what happened today. No similar institution exists in democracies.

1.1 THE VIEW FROM THE PROS: JOURNALISM INFORMS

A Tip, a Document and a Mountain

The call came in sometime on the afternoon of July 23, 2001, from a contact on my beat—science and the environment. I can't remember the exact words, but they were something like, "Check the Federal Register for Ameren."

It didn't sound like much, but in the end a major electric utility company withdrew its plan to build a huge hydroelectric facility on a pristine mountaintop in the Missouri Ozarks.

I hung up the phone and spent a few minutes on the Web searching the Federal Register, a public document in which government rules, notices and other business are published daily. Bingo. Buried in the complex language of law and technology, was a request filed by the St. Louis-based electric utility Ameren Corp. with the Federal Energy Regulatory Commission.

Ameren wanted to build its largest hydroelectric power plant ever—a $642 million, 770-megawatt facility with two dams. Filing its plan with the commission was the first legal step.

The key detail was the "where." The plant would be built on Church Mountain, considered by outdoor-conscious Missourians one of the gems of the Ozarks' gorgeous labyrinth of green mountains and clear floating and fishing streams.

This story *had* to get in the next day's paper, and I had only three hours till deadline. After telling my editor about the story and writing a summary he could use in the budget meeting a few minutes later, I called Ameren, the Missouri Coalition for the Environment and the Missouri Department of Natural Resources.

It's important to note that I was a journalist, not an environmental advocate. And my simple, straight, hard

news scoop—citing just the facts—ran the next morning on page one of the B section, the Metro section, with this lead:

"Ameren Corp. wants to build a hydroelectric power plant atop Church Mountain in the Ozarks, one of Missouri's most scenic areas."

What happened next? Nothing. No calls, no letters, no e-mails. I moved on. I had plenty of other stories to do.

A few weeks later I got another afternoon call. The politicians were weighing in, presumably having measured public opinion on the Ameren plan. This call came from the Missouri attorney general's press aide. The AG was announcing he planned to file suit against the company.

Another story that *had* to be in the next day's paper. I told my editor and wrote the budget line. I interviewed the AG, the Ameren spokeswoman, the governor's spokesman, the director of the environmental coalition and a few others. The AG said, "We are opposed to blowing off the top of Church Mountain and replacing it with a limestone bathtub." (You've got to love the rhetorical artistry of politicians who've figured out where they stand on an issue.)

The next day, Aug. 30, the story ran, this time on page one of the A section. Here was the lead:

"Citing public opposition, Ameren Corp. on Wednesday pulled out of its plan to build a hydroelectric power plant and two dams on Church Mountain in the Ozarks. The company's announcement came shortly after Missouri Gov. Bob Holden and other state officials attacked the plan." (A governor's words generally trump an AG's.)

How did this turn of events happen? Was my first story the trigger? After all, I broke the story, and my newspaper was the most powerful and respected source of information in that region. The public was informed. Elected officials responded. The company's plans changed.

Whoa! First, I can't take credit for "breaking" this story. C'mon. A guy called me. I just did what a professional journalist does: vet and report an interesting story that was going to come out sooner or later anyway.

Nor can I take credit for bringing about that change in Ameren's plans. Yes, I reported the facts to the readers of my newspaper, and the media echo chamber magnified the story. But how can you trace back the definitive moment in that scrum of stories, ideas, influence and decision-making that lead to such changes?

Even so, there's no denying the role journalists play in shining a light on activities of the powerful is important, no matter who gets the credit.

But is it ever fun finding and chasing such stories! And participating in that sometimes awesome marketplace of ideas.

The Church Mountain episode reveals many lessons.

Lesson 1: The power of producing a simple, short news story about something way under your audience's radar.

Lesson 2: The amazing changes that can happen when the public is informed about seemingly routine events.

Lesson 3: The objective journalist's role as a reporter of straight news.

Lesson 4: The value of setting up a beat and getting to know sources who may contact you with tips.

THINK ABOUT IT: Allen lists four lessons from this series of events. Can you think of others? Could beginning reporters on other types of beats (sports, fashion, food or health) have this kind of impact? Why or why not?

_____

Bill Allen is Assistant Professor of Science Journalism at the University of Missouri, and a former science writer for the *St. Louis Post-Dispatch.*

Journalism Investigates   It hasn't always, you know.

In fact, the investigative press we know today is a late-20th Century creation, but one with roots in its muckraking past. The "watchdog press" revered by journalists is not nearly as all-encompassing as we'd like to think, but it is a vital function of journalism.

From award-winning project teams at some of the United States' larger news outlets looking into topics of national import to the community newspaper editor filing a public records request for the contract that the school board signed at its last meeting with a consultant, journalism's investigative function takes on many forms.

James S. Ettema and Theodore L. Glasser, in their book, *Custodians of Conscience: Investigative Journalism and Public Virtue,* put it this way: "the work of these reporters calls us, as a society, to decide what is, and what is not, an outrage to our sense of moral order and to consider our expectations for our officials, our institutions, and ultimately ourselves" (1998, p. 3).

Documents, verified facts, eyewitnesses: these are the stuff of investigative journalism. Note also that there is an adversarial tone at the heart of

1.2 THE VIEW FROM THE PROS: JOURNALISM INVESTIGATES

Why do we investigate? We do it because power and corruption so often go hand-in-hand. We do it because we care, almost to a fault, about the people at the edge of society. We care about the little guys and want to make sure "the system," in all its incarnations, works as it should.

Doing this kind of work is antagonistic. It's oppositional. It requires you to ask questions no one wants to ask and get things people don't want to give.

Its nature dictates that investigative reporting can't be done on word of mouth alone. A good investigation can change laws. A good investigation can get people fired, freed or locked up. To put power like that in the hands of hearsay alone would be irresponsible.

For that reason, more and more reporters turn to documents. "Documents," in this sense, is a shorthand. It means traditional dusty paper records, sure. But it also means e-mails, text messages, databases and maps. It means meeting minutes, letters and forms. In short, documentation means evidence that speaks for itself.

Interviews have their place. But using documents and independent analysis as the backbone of my reporting changes the entire tenor of the interview process. Rather than a means to find information, interviews have become a way to get reactions or explanations. If I've really done my job, the interview is a time for people to give excuses.

Investigative reporting is some of the hardest, most time-consuming work we do. But it's increasingly necessary. In the new information economy, people in power increasingly have "message" people on staff. They call them "public information officers" or "spokesmen." I call them flaks. Their job is to dictate the news of the day, and they're good at what they do. Daily e-mails of story ideas, phone calls during breaking news—if we aren't doing the independent research required by investigative reporting, we allow ourselves to be used.

Perhaps that's the best way to describe the role. Too often, journalism is reactionary and forgetful. A shooting happens, we report who got shot, where, when and what weapon was used. A person gets convicted, we answer the same basic questions.

Investigative reporting allows us to turn the tables and focus on the "Why"? and "How"? we rarely get to answer with breaking news. It allows us to tell our audience more substantive truths about the things we cover. It allows us to do what, at its best, journalism is meant to do.

LEARN MORE: To get a feel for the types of documents that can be used in reporting, go to the Public Records page of the Journalist's Toolbox, a site produced by the Society of Professional Journalists (www.journaliststoolbox.org/archive/public-records/).

Matt Wynn, 27, is a reporter at the *Omaha World-Herald*. He has worked at the Springfield (MO) *News-Leader* and *Arizona Republic* since graduating from the Missouri School of Journalism in 2007.

investigative journalism, as reporters are cast as challengers to the concentrated power of government and of the corporate state. As Ettema and Glasser (1998, p. 64) put it, "the notion that the press should be a relentless adversary of the powerful" has always animated American journalism.

Detached, independent observation, or impassioned adversarial watchdog: which is it? Well, a bit of both, if journalism is to flourish.

Journalism Creates a Public Conversation   Scholars long have agreed that democracy requires a public forum where people can speak freely about government without government interference. For decades, the press together with its broadcast colleagues performed this role: people read the news, wrote their editors, and television contributed news and public affairs programming.

Today's mix of news, opinion, outright spin and the rich social conversation that is the online medium's great strength make it difficult to point to any one civic conversation as the "public sphere" deemed so crucial to the life of a democracy, yet it's clear that one of the things journalism must provide is that public sphere.

1.3 THE VIEW FROM THE PROS: JOURNALISM CREATES CONVERSATION

One of my first columns was about a creative land deal the city of Tucson was pushing.

The city planned to sell a prime piece of real estate to a struggling, but well-connected, developer for $250,000. That developer would then flip it for $1.4 million. The column hit, and outrage followed. The public was outraged about the deal. And, in turn, mayor and council were outraged about the column. At their next meeting, they excoriated me and the column. It was unfair, they said. I didn't understand the deal. The developer wasn't really going to profit from the flip. Man, they were really steamed.

And then, finally, one councilman said regardless of what they thought about the column, questions had been raised in public. The city, in turn, would now have to answer those questions in public.

I had done my job. The community conversation had started.

One of the big lessons I've learned in journalism is not to identify with outcomes. Some stories spur change, others don't, and the world keeps turning just the same. The best a reporter can do is tell a compelling, accurate and truthful story. Or put another way, it didn't matter if the council killed the land deal. But it did matter the community knew about it.

Put the information out there, and let the public respond. Sounds so simple, but it's powerful stuff. Forget about the labels—investigative, watchdog, beat reporting,

whatever—at the end of the day, good daily journalism is a conversation starter. And that conversation shapes communities, spurs accountability, defines values and, sometimes, leads to big change. The only place this happens is in the daily news cycle.

With blogs and social media, it's a brave new world out there in information land. But journalism isn't information. Journalism is the process that makes information relevant to the public—from school board meetings all the way up the chain to the Wikileaks Iraq war diaries. Sure, it's an imperfect and messy process. But so is democracy. And the two don't exist without one another.

Here's a link to the column I'm referring to: http://bit.ly/bYhrHm.

THINK ABOUT IT: Go online and look at the blog or column by a popular columnist for your local newspaper (hint: sports columnists usually attract large numbers of followers). Read the column and then read the comments (either at the bottom of the story, posted to Facebook or shared on Twitter). How closely do the comments follow the issues raised in the column? How often does the conversation veer off topic? Are comments informed or based solely on gut reaction? Did the columnist succeed in starting a conversation?

Josh Brodesky is a Metro Columnist for the *Arizona Daily Star*.

If, as Bill Kovach and Tom Rosenstiel explained so simply in *The Elements of Journalism*, the principles of American journalism are defined by the role of journalism in the lives of people, then the more things change, the more they stay the same: to provide citizens information in a context in which they can govern themselves. Media scholar James Carey put it this way: "The role of the press," he once said, "is simply to make sure that in the short run we don't get screwed, and it does this best not by treating us as consumers of news, but by encouraging the conditions of public discourse and life" (cited in Mindich, 2008).

Journalism Helps Generate Social Empathy   The Hutchins Commission report points to the importance of the news media as inculcators of tolerance and pluralism:

> The truth about any social group, though it should not exclude its weaknesses and vices, includes also recognition of its values, its aspirations, and its common humanity . . . If people are exposed to the inner truth of the life of a particular group, they will gradually build up respect for and understanding of it.
>
> (p. 27)

A cursory review of the media landscape today could lead one to question whether the members of the Hutchins Commission would recognize the place, until we stop and revisit the notion of democratic self-governance.

Self-governance means far more than being informed voters. It is not only about bills and laws and votes. Our democracy, after all, is a social compact in which we collectively regulate all of society through what academics call "public norms"—the formal rules of the road, sure, but also the conventions and expectations that shape everyday life. We socialize one another, in other words, and in doing so we set the boundaries of societal behavior. The news is a major engine for the creation of public norms, which, along with laws, are one of the ways in which we govern ourselves.

Journalism Encourages Accountability   It's worth noting that accountability—the oversight of the functions of an institution—ought to

Can you think of any group in society more deserving of empathy than parents whose children have died? What if the parents are responsible, unintentionally, for their children's death? Do they still deserve your empathy?

Those were the questions *Washington Post* writer Gene Weingarten explored in a heart-wrenching story of children who died of hyperthermia after their parents forgot them in the backseat of a car.

Winner of the 2010 Pulitzer Prize for Feature Writing, this story is an excellent illustration of journalism's empathy function. In an online chat with Weingarten after the Pulitzer was announced, one reader said, "Your article made me think long and hard about these kinds of incidents. I am enormously judgmental by nature, but you definitely made me think twice about people like those profiled in your article. So thank you for giving them the humanity they deserve."

Here's an excerpt:

Fatal Distraction: Forgetting a Child in the Backseat of a Car Is a Horrifying Mistake. Is It a Crime?

By Gene Weingarten

Washington Post Staff Writer

Sunday, March 8, 2009; W08

The defendant was an immense man, well over 300 pounds, but in the gravity of his sorrow and shame he seemed larger still. He hunched forward in the sturdy wooden armchair that barely contained him, sobbing softly into tissue after tissue, a leg bouncing nervously under the table. In the first pew of spectators sat his wife, looking stricken, absently twisting her wedding band. The room was a sepulcher. Witnesses spoke softly of events so painful that many lost their composure. When a hospital emergency room nurse described how the defendant had behaved after the police first brought him in, she wept. He was virtually catatonic, she remembered, his eyes shut tight, rocking back and forth, locked away in some unfathomable private torment. He would not speak at all for the longest time, not until the nurse sank down beside him and held his hand. It was only then that the patient began to open up, and what he said was that he didn't want any sedation, that he didn't deserve a respite from pain, that he wanted to feel it all, and then to die.

The charge in the courtroom was manslaughter, brought by the Commonwealth of Virginia. No significant facts were in dispute. Miles Harrison, 49, was an amiable person, a diligent businessman and a doting, conscientious father until the day last summer—beset by problems at work, making call after call on his cellphone—he forgot to drop his son, Chase, at day care. The toddler slowly sweltered to death, strapped into a car seat for nearly nine hours in an office parking lot in Herndon in the blistering heat of July.

It was an inexplicable, inexcusable mistake, but was it a crime? That was the question for a judge to decide.

* * *

"Death by hyperthermia" is the official designation. When it happens to young children, the facts are often the same: An otherwise loving and attentive parent one day gets busy, or distracted, or upset, or confused by a change in his or her daily routine, and just . . . forgets a child is in the car. It happens that way somewhere in the United States 15 to 25 times a year, parceled out through the spring, summer and early fall. The season is almost upon us.

Two decades ago, this was relatively rare. But in the early 1990s, car-safety experts declared that passenger-side front airbags could kill children, and they recommended that child seats be moved to the back of the car; then, for even more safety for the very young, that the baby seats be pivoted to face the rear. If few foresaw the tragic consequence of the lessened visibility of the child . . . well, who can blame them? What kind of person forgets a baby?

The wealthy do, it turns out. And the poor, and the middle class. Parents of all ages and ethnicities do it. Mothers are just as likely to do it as fathers. It happens to the chronically absent-minded and to the fanatically organized, to the college-educated and to the marginally literate. In the last 10 years, it has happened to a dentist. A postal clerk. A social worker. A police officer. An accountant. A soldier. A paralegal. An electrician. A Protestant clergyman. A rabbinical student. A nurse. A construction worker. An assistant principal. It happened to a mental health counselor, a college professor and a pizza chef. It happened to a pediatrician. It happened to a rocket scientist.

Last year it happened three times in one day, the worst day so far in the worst year so far in a phenomenon that gives no sign of abating.

The facts in each case differ a little, but always there is the terrible moment when the parent realizes what he or she has done, often through a phone call from a spouse or caregiver. This is followed by a frantic sprint to the car. What awaits there is the worst thing in the world.

Each instance has its own macabre signature. One father had parked his car next to the grounds of a county fair; as he discovered his son's body, a calliope tootled merrily beside him. Another man, wanting to end things quickly, tried to wrestle a gun from a police officer at the scene. Several people—including Mary Parks of Blacksburg—have driven from their workplace to the day-care center to pick up the child they'd thought they'd dropped off, never noticing the corpse in the backseat.

Then there is the Chattanooga, Tenn., business executive who must live with this: His motion-detector car alarm went off, three separate times, out there in the broiling sun. But when he looked out, he couldn't see anyone tampering with the car. So he remotely deactivated the alarm and went calmly back to work.

* * *

THINK ABOUT IT: What long-term impact might this story have had on its readers? Would it have been as effective if it had been written more as a straight news story and less as a news feature?

You can read the entire story here: www.washingtonpost.com/wp-dyn/content/article/2009/02/27/AR20090227 01549.html.

be a two-way street in journalism. A central tenet of democracy is that it is a self-correcting mechanism; that is, it fixes itself on the fly. Key to that self-correction is the principle that no one is infallible and that no information is, either; that which we report as fact is always subject to validation and potential revision.

The concept of a Fourth Estate—a term borrowed from the Scottish satirist Thomas Carlyle, who saw the reporters in Parliament as a "fourth branch" of government, an independent arbiter of fact sitting just beyond the realm of government, yet very much involved in public affairs—begins with the recognition that government can't handle accountability left to its own devices. Other institutions must work to keep them honest.

Scholars write that accountability requires answerability and enforcement. In other words, there must be an obligation on the part of the institution to provide information about its decisions and actions, or answerability, and there must be some sort of sanction when the institution behaves badly.

There are two types of accountability: horizontal and vertical. Horizontal accountability refers to the capacity of institutions to check one another, such as the "checks and balances" enshrined in the Constitution or the requirement that state agencies report to the governor. It's one part of the institution checking up on another, and for that reason, it's fraught with political tension and potential cronyism and corruption.

That's where vertical accountability comes in, as citizens, non-governmental organizations and the press seek to enforce standards of performance on officials. Journalists provide vertical accountability every day, in countless ways. Sometimes simply showing up at a little-known, scarcely attended city meeting causes a bit of transparency that was about to be shoved into a dark corner. Other times, a well-timed, pointed question aimed at a candidate for public office reveals a shocking lack of knowledge on a vital topic. Journalists are key actors in what has been called the "chain of accountability."

1.5 THE VIEW FROM THE PROS: JOURNALISM ENCOURAGES ACCOUNTABILITY

Talk to Dana Priest about the role of accountability in journalism, and you come away from the conversation thankful there are journalists doing the hard work of unraveling official malfeasance, but also worried about the future of a craft so resource-dependent.

Priest, a two-time Pulitzer Prize-winning investigative reporter for *The Washington Post*, frequently covers stories that shine a light into the darkest recesses of government, including the government's use of extraordinary rendition and secret detention facilities. Some of her finest work uncovered the appalling conditions our wounded soldiers faced when shipped to the U.S. Army's flagship medical facility—Walter Reed Army Medical Center.

Here is Dana Priest and Anne Hull's lede from the Feb. 18, 2007, story that rocked the entire nation:

Behind the door of Army Spec. Jeremy Duncan's room, part of the wall is torn and hangs in the air, weighted down with black mold. When the wounded combat engineer stands in his shower and looks up, he can see the bathtub on the floor above through a rotted hole. The entire building, constructed between the world wars, often smells like greasy carry-out. Signs of neglect are everywhere: mouse droppings, belly-up cockroaches, stained carpets, cheap mattresses.

This is the world of Building 18, not the kind of place where Duncan expected to recover when he was evacuated to Walter Reed Army Medical Center

from Iraq last February with a broken neck and a shredded left ear, nearly dead from blood loss. But the old lodge, just outside the gates of the hospital and five miles up the road from the White House, has housed hundreds of maimed soldiers recuperating from injuries suffered in the wars in Iraq and Afghanistan.

The stories documented a system in which soldiers were warehoused in a labyrinth of cheerless wards, bound by red tape and met by apathy and bureaucratic buck passing. America's heroes, treated with borderline contempt. One of Priests's sources neatly summarized the situation:

"We've done our duty. We fought the war. We came home wounded. Fine. But whoever the people are back here who are supposed to give us the easy transition should be doing it," said Marine Sgt. Ryan Groves, 26, an amputee who lived at Walter Reed for 16 months. "We don't know what to do. The people who are supposed to know don't have the answers. It's a nonstop process of stalling."

Like many of Priest's stories, Walter Reed began with a tip.

"I became involved through a friend, who sent me to a friend, who had a loved one at Walter Reed," she said. "So we went to lunch and she told me a story that was just a tiny part of this world . . . she knew wives of soldiers who were not getting care. Simple things that just weren't working. I couldn't believe it was true, but hey, you check."

So she and Hull began calling, and "two names gave me four names, and then we got more names, and what started as a traditional story became so much bigger," she said.

Stop for a second and consider just how hard this story was to do. *The Washington Post* can't just walk into Walter Reed and start asking soldiers tough questions about the level of care they're getting—soldiers are inherently mistrustful of the motives of the press on a good day.

So Priest and Hull spent the better half of four months at Walter Reed talking to soldiers and their families, cultivating the relationships that eventually would yield the stories. Sources had to be convinced to go "on the record" (and speak publicly and for attribution), no small task considering that these were military men and women with families and careers at stake.

These soldiers, however, had tried, and failed, to get their superiors within the chain of command to do anything about conditions at Walter Reed, and so Priest and Hull represented real accountability, the kind of accountability that sometime requires publicity.

"These people had a lot at stake. They didn't know precisely what the story was, and they had to trust that our intentions were good, that we were there to see that they got help," Priest said.

That's the essence of accountability. It's an external force that people can turn to when the internal checks fail.

"The courts and the legislature through its committees, and inspector generals, are all supposed to be checks on Walter Reed," Priest said. "But you have times when the check must be external. Walter Reed is such a good example. High-ranking members of the executive branch and the military were being ushered through there on a regular basis, but it was a show. They had a 'VIP Room' all cleaned up to walk people through."

Priest recalled a moment in her reporting that makes the point for her.

"We were taken, like the senators and the military brass, to the VIP rooms and to the orthopedic ward, and the place was just gleaming," she said. "And then one of our sources took us right around the corner, and the floors were all grubby, and he said 'this is where the real hospital starts . . .'"

Peering around the corner. Asking the impertinent question at precisely the most awkward moment. Calling back, and calling again, and making it clear you aren't going away without answers. This is the essence of accountability. Messy? You bet. Unpopular? Often. Yet it is essential to a functioning democracy.

"We would not have known the unpleasant realities of a lot of things we were doing without journalism," Priest said.

THINK ABOUT IT: Investigative journalism as described in this example is time-consuming and expensive. Priest writes that the stories took nearly four months to complete. As news organizations struggle to make profits in an increasingly competitive information environment, is this type of reporting at risk? What is the danger to the profession if these types of investigative efforts go away? What is the danger to American democracy?

———————

Here is a link to the Walter Reed series: www.washingtonpost.com/wp-srv/nation/walter-reed/index.html.

▶ ## CAN JOURNALISM PROVIDE WHAT DEMOCRACY NEEDS?

Let's look at those democratic needs one more time, from yet another angle. Without diving too far into the deep end of democratic theory, let's just say that our views about the prospects for a robust democracy are shaped by our views of people—their nature, abilities and desires. (For now, we don't need to worry about the many specific forms democracy can take. We're just interested in the idea that in a democracy, generally speaking, the people are sovereign.) At a minimum, democracy takes as its starting point the idea that the people can and should govern themselves. That some people have been quite skeptical about the public's capacity to do so is, perhaps, not entirely surprising. And the implications of that skepticism for journalism warrant further exploration.

In the early part of the 20th Century, newspaper columnist Walter Lippmann was what we today would call a "public intellectual." More than just a journalist, Lippmann was part of the intellectual elite, an adviser to heads of state and even a player in the Treaty of Versailles negotiations. In 1922, he published the book *Public Opinion*, one of a series of three books he wrote about the relationship between democracy and the press. This one included a rather stunning and ultimately pessimistic view: People are too limited in their capacity to process the information of an increasingly complex world to effectively self-govern, and it is beyond the ability of the press, populated by similarly limited people and subject to other constraints, to help the public very much. Indeed, Lippmann seemed to express some concern that the press could make things worse. His argument wasn't that people are stupid, but that between the complexity of the information one is required to understand to be an effective democratic participant and the many "filters"—personal biases, education, background and so on—through which that information must travel, there was little or no chance of reconciling the "world outside and the pictures in our heads." If democracy depends on the "omnicompetent" citizen, it's in big trouble.

It might be understandable that Lippmann reached that conclusion, as he was writing in the aftermath of World War I, which had brought the power of propaganda and public manipulation fully into view. However, his grave prediction met with considerable resistance from John Dewey, another leading public intellectual and founder of the philosophy of pragmatism, who called Lippmann's book "perhaps the most effective indictment of democracy . . . ever penned" (1927, p. 337). Dewey's 1927 book *The Public and Its Problems* responded to Lippmann's critique with an acknowledgment that, while Lippmann might be right about the limited capacity of people, he was wrong about democracy. What was missing from Lippmann's account, according to Dewey, was an understanding that democracy is more about conversation than it is about information. Dewey was a strong proponent and scholar of education, so it is understandable that he saw democracy's prospects as intertwined with education and not just journalism. If one sees democracy as an ongoing process of education in how to deliberate and how to be a citizen, and not as the end result of the best information dissemination techniques, then the prospects for it are not so gloomy.

As Kovach and Rosenstiel so eloquently illustrate in *The Elements of
Journalism,* Lippmann and Dewey
represent not just different under-
standings of democracy, but different
ways of thinking about journalism's
role in democracy too. In terms of the
metaphors and functions we've been
discussing, Lippmann essentially was
arguing that the press could not ade-
quately act as a mirror or watchdog—
that it would have difficulty fulfilling
the informing and accountability
functions. Dewey's perspective was focused more on the potential for journalism to promote the marketplace of ideas, to create conversation and generate empathy. Whose view seems to have won out in journalism? Do we
see more of Dewey or of Lippmann in our current news media landscape?
Perhaps these aren't really fair questions. Certainly Wickramatunga saw his
newspaper performing all those functions, and he doesn't seem to have preferred or promoted one over the others. And Anderson Cooper was chan-
neling Dewey and Lippmann in the same breath, directing his watchdog ire
at slow-footed officials while simultaneously holding a mirror up to New
Orleans for all to see. That Cooper happened to be holding one of the biggest microphones in the marketplace ensured public attention.

> ## DISCUSSION QUESTIONS
>
> The title of the chapter lists three ways to look at
> the role of American journalism: The mirror, the
> watchdog and the marketplace. Which do you think
> best characterizes the role journalism plays in our
> society? Does the dominant approach change based
> on the time period and situation we face? For example,
> might one approach be more appropriate in wartime
> and another in peacetime?

Even though journalists' self-identity is arguably more bound up in the
watchdog/accountability roles—that is certainly the basis on which they defend their choice to pursue controversial stories—the range of content the
news media offers suggests a broad view of the roles journalism can play
in a democracy. But remember that we're talking about what democracy
requires, not all of the functions of the press. Does the press entertain us
at times? Sure, but unless you argue that democracy requires that the news
entertain us, it's a bit off topic.

▶ MUST JOURNALISM PROVIDE
WHAT DEMOCRACY NEEDS?

Even as they describe different functions that the press can and should perform in a society, the mirror, watchdog and marketplace metaphors share

some assumptions. They all assume, for example, that the press's key allegiance is to the public, the citizens of a society, and not necessarily to those who wield power. These metaphors likewise seem to start from the premise that the press can and should act as the public's representative. Finally, the metaphors assume the press is free to act in all those ways. But free from whom and for what, exactly? The "from whom" part usually refers to the need for the press to be free from government control, though as we will find out in Chapter 4, that's not the only kind of control the press needs to worry about. The "for what" part gets us back to this idea of responsibility. Some argue that because the press is uniquely positioned to be the mirror, watchdog or marketplace, it is therefore obligated to act in certain ways.

Certainly the Hutchins Commission we mentioned earlier believed that. Note the title of its very influential report—*A Free and Responsible Press*—and its chief conclusions that the media should: "1) provide a truthful, comprehensive and intelligent account of the day's events in a context which gives them meaning; 2) serve as a forum for the exchange of comment and criticism; 3) project a representative picture of the constituent groups in the society; 4) present and clarify the goals and values of the society; and 5) provide full access to the day's intelligence." The kicker is that the Commission believed if the press didn't do those things, if it failed to meet its obligations, it risked losing its freedom altogether.

▶ **ACCOUNTABILITY:** Think of it as oversight. There are two kinds: horizontal and vertical. One of the chief functions of journalism in a democracy is vertical accountability— reporting on what the powerful do and say as a way of making them answerable to the people for their actions. Journalism that promotes such accountability is often referred to as "watchdog journalism."

It might not surprise you to know that the reaction of the press to the Hutchins Commission report was, well, indignant. After all, where did the Hutchins Commission get off essentially threatening an institution whose freedom is constitutionally protected? And you might also have noticed, 60+ years later, that the press often fails to do those things, but still looks and acts pretty free. Even if the "threat" didn't amount to much, *A Free and Responsible Press* became an important part of an ongoing conversation about journalism—what it is and, perhaps most important, what it is expected to do.

To consider journalism as entirely and solely responsible for meeting the needs of democracy is unreasonable, some scholars have argued. Such a view seems to ignore the role of other important institutions in democratic society, such as political parties, social groups and elements of civil society, like public schools, that all play a role in informing people and facilitating discussion and debate. These scholars also point to the economic pressures the news media face, pressures that can put the news media in the position of having to choose between providing a public service and producing profit. Finally, the traditional understanding of the press's democratic role seems too focused on politics and not enough on other kinds of media content, even entertainment, which can serve important democratic functions. These are important

DISCUSSION QUESTIONS

Are the concerns raised by the Hutchins Commission still present today? Are they even more problematic than they were more than 60 years ago? How would you respond to people today who make threats similar to those made by the commission—that media risk losing freedoms if they do not fulfill their functions?

arguments to keep in mind as we explore the tension between what the press can do and what it should do that has defined the history and practice of journalism in the United States and will be the focus of later chapters in this book. First, though, we'll need to be clear about what we mean by "journalism" in the first place. That's the question we'll take up in the next chapter.

Chapter One Review

Chapter Summary

Suggested Activities

Read More

▶ CHAPTER SUMMARY

Journalism is essential to democratic self-governance, for several key reasons. First, because it serves as an essential check on power—the power of the state, the power of the corporation, and the power of the majority. The press serves society by creating a space in which claims about truth can be debated.

The press performs at least five core functions in a democracy:

1. Journalism informs, analyzes, interprets and explains.
2. Journalism investigates.
3. Journalism creates a public conversation.

4. Journalism helps generate social empathy.

5. Journalism encourages accountability.

Each is a core function of the press in the United States, and each can be viewed through the three metaphors for the key roles the press plays in our system: as a mirror, as a watchdog and as a marketplace. Each starts with the proposition that the press's key allegiance is to the public, the citizens of a society, and not necessarily to those who wield power.

▶ SUGGESTED ACTIVITIES

1. To examine how the press performs its five core functions in a democracy, examine a local or national media outlet (newspaper, website, newscast, etc.). Find at least one example of content that illustrates each of the functions (Informs, analyzes, interprets and explains; Investigates; Creates a public conversation; Helps generate social empathy; Encourages accountability). This could be done as a small group activity in class (especially if you have copies of newspapers you can bring to class) or as an independent homework activity. Share your findings with the class. Did you find content that performed multiple functions? Were any examples harder to find?

2. Although the functions played by the press in a democracy are not dependent on delivery format, a specific medium might be better suited for one function or another. Split up into different groups within your class (print, broadcast, online/digital). Each group should examine the functions their medium is best suited for and which ones might pose more of a challenge. Discuss the following with the whole class: Will the functions change as our delivery system of news and information changes in the country?

3. Watch Associated Press officials talk about "accountability journalism" and the watchdog role of the press (www.youtube.com/watch?v=Sxf90TXThY8). How does this differ from the type of journalism that we see on a day-to-day basis? Watch a clip of the first five minutes from a recent local newscast. Would any of that be "accountability journalism"? Why might local news stations and local newspapers be limited in playing this role? Next, as an example of how smaller news organizations can fill this role with limited resources, look at The Cold Case Project (http://coldcases.org/). One small-town newspaper editor, Stanley Nelson of Concordia, LA, has been able to work with the non-profit group to help bring unprosecuted civil rights violations to light and hold officials accountable (you can see one story here: www. concordiasentinel.com/news.php?id=4263).

4. In an era of digital delivery of information and social networks, where everyone is a publisher and average citizens can attract tens of thousands of followers on Twitter, does American democracy need journalists to provide information dissemination, accountability, representation, deliberation and conflict resolution? Some could argue that the role of traditional journalists in fulfilling these needs has become even more important—others could argue that it's become less important. Write down the five needs, and write next to each whether the role of traditional news outlets has become more important, less important or stayed the same. Consider the results across the whole class. Why did people vote the way that they did?

5. To learn more about journalism history, read the article "Early American Newspapering" from history.org (www.history.org/foundation/journal/spring03/journalism.cfm). How does the historical context relate to the roles the founders expected journalism to plan in their new form of government? Using the information in the chapter about the functions of journalism in our society and the historical information from the supplemental reading, post a 350–500 word response on the class discussion board on this topic.

▶ READ MORE

Commission on Freedom of the Press (Hutchins Commission), *A Free and Responsible Press: A General Report on Mass Communication: Newspapers, Radio, Motion Pictures, Magazines, and Books*, Chicago: University of Chicago Press, 1947.

John Dewey, *The Public and Its Problems*, New York: Henry Holt, 1927.

James S. Ettema and Theodore L. Glasser, *Custodians of Conscience: Investigative Journalism and Public Virtue*, New York: Columbia University Press, 1998.

Elizabeth Jensen, "An Anchor Who Reports Disaster News With a Heart on His Sleeve," *New York Times*, September 12, 2005.

Bill Kovach and Tom Rosenstiel, *The Elements of Journalism: What Newspeople Should Know and the Public Should Expect*, New York: Three Rivers Press, 2007.

Walter Lippmann, *Public Opinion*, New York: Free Press, 1965. Originally published in 1922.

James Madison, Letter to W.T. Barry, August 4, 1822.

David T.Z. Mindich, "Journalism and Citizenship: Making the Connection," *Nieman Reports*, Winter 2008. www.nieman.harvard.edu/reports/article/100678/Jour nalism-and-Citizenship-Making-the-Connection.aspx.

New York Times, "Commission to Make 2-Year Study of All Phases of Press Freedom," February 29, 1944: 11(A).

Rodney A. Smolla, *Free Speech in an Open Society*. New York: Random House, 1992.

Jonathon Van Meter, "Unanchored," *New York* magazine, September 11, 2005. http://nymag.com/nymetro/news/features/14301/.

Lasantha Wickramatunga, "And Then They Came for Me," *The Sunday Leader*, January 11, 2009. www.thesundayleader.lk/archive/20090111/editorial-.htm.

World Bank Institute, "Social Accountability in the Public Sector." Washington, DC: WBI Working Paper No. 33641 (2005).

2

What Is Journalism?

"Michael Jackson Dies"

The headline, posted to the TMZ website at 2:20 p.m. Pacific Daylight Time on June 25, 2009, was simple and to the point. The rest of the item offered what few details were known at the time: The 50-year-old King of Pop had suffered cardiac arrest at his home, and neither the paramedics called to the house nor the doctors at UCLA Medical Center were able to revive him. The King of Pop was dead.

It looked and read like the kind of item any number of news organizations might have posted to their websites. But most didn't post it right away. The *Los Angeles Times* waited nearly an hour, and CNN's confirmed report came an hour after that. That's weird, isn't it? Jackson's death was huge news. Why not post that news while it's fresh? It's not like telling readers or viewers about the stories other news organizations have broken is unprecedented. So why, then, did it take awhile for others to post the story?

Hold that question while we consider another high-profile death that prompted a different—and more disastrous—response.

A State College, PA, student news site, Onward State, tweeted news of legendary Penn State football coach Joe Paterno's death at 8:45 p.m. on Saturday, January 21, 2012. Its tweet was short and authoritative:

> Our sources can now confirm: Joseph Vincent Paterno has passed away tonight at the age of 85.

And, as we learned a day later, it was false. Paterno did not pass away until the next day, a fact confirmed by his family.

By that point, Onward State's erroneous tweet had spread to a report on a local FM radio station, then to CBS Sports, which published an obituary on its site, declaring that Paterno "has died," seemingly based on the Onward State report, but without direct attribution. The Huffington Post followed minutes later with its own report, again passing along the Onward State version of the truth, unattributed (Huffington Post later acknowledged in a correction that it "did not properly attribute the source").

Twelve minutes after the initial, erroneous report, the *New York Times'* Mark Viera tweeted:

> Dan McGinn, the Paterno family spokesman, at 8:57 p.m. on reports about Joe Paterno's death: "Absolutely not true."

In 12 minutes, a story of national importance ricocheted across the Internet, putting into stark relief the promise and peril of journalism in the age of instantaneous publication.

▶ "ACTUAL REPORTING"

Both the Michael Jackson and Joe Paterno stories contain clues about why, in the chaos and uncertainty of breaking news events, the conventions of journalism matter more than ever. In a world of TMZs, of Onward States and 70 million WordPress blogs, it's more confusing—and more important than ever—for journalists to have a sense of what makes the profession unique. And in both instances, what journalists did with the information at hand is instructive.

In both the Jackson and Paterno stories, notice that none of the key information is attributed to a specific, named person. That means the reader has no way of knowing how believable that source might be. The source could be someone close to the action, such as a nurse at the hospital or a family member of the deceased, or it could be no one at all, as far as the reader knows. In each instance, readers had to trust that the messenger's sources were good.

But the use of anonymous sources can't completely account for the difference between the reporting TMZ and Onward State did and what more traditional news outlets did with that reporting. After all, the *Los Angeles Times* waited to confirm Jackson's death on its own, while CBS Sports and others didn't bother to confirm Paterno's death before posting the news. And traditional news organizations use anonymous sources fairly regularly, so there had to be something else going on.

Actually, there were probably at least two things—one philosophical and one technological—going on. First, the Jackson story was broken by TMZ, a celebrity gossip site; the Paterno story by a student sports site. The reputation and credibility of the sites themselves probably influenced how other news organizations acted. Gossip site? Maybe sketchy. They'll post anything, right? But a news site run by Penn State students? Perhaps not as sketchy, especially if CNN and the like believed the students might have better sources than news outlets outside the Penn State community. The philosophical thing going on here, the perceptions of each site's credibility, is how people see *journalism*.

◀ **CREDIBILITY:** The combination of trustworthiness and expertise that makes us more or less likely to believe or rely on what a source of information tells us.

Perhaps Paul Colford, the director of media relations for the Associated Press, said it best, when he told the Poynter Institute in an e-mail, "At no time did AP report or imply Paterno's death on any platform. AP was relying upon actual reporting."

That may seem a bit simplistic, but let's first lay out what we see as a starting point: a definition of journalism.

> *Journalism is a set of transparent, independent procedures aimed at gathering, verifying and reporting truthful information of consequence to citizens in a democracy.*

The second, technological, point is that Twitter wasn't quite the juggernaut in 2009 that it had become by 2012. Would the *Los Angeles Times* or CNN have retweeted TMZ's report of Jackson's death? Of course we don't know for sure. But this example shows just how easy it is for technological change to put pressure on that definition of journalism, to encourage a focus on the gathering part while leaving the verifying part to fend for itself. We'll be thinking about those kinds of tensions throughout the book.

One more thing. The issue here isn't whether Jackson's or Paterno's death is news. They are, or at least it's pretty easy to argue they are, depending on your definition of news. We'll get around to defining "news" a little later in this chapter. The issue also isn't whether information you find on the Web can be trusted, though you should be wary of lots of stuff you see there. The issue is what distinguishes journalism from other kinds of information, entertainment and commentary you might find on the Web or anywhere else. What goes on behind the scenes at a place like the *Los Angeles Times* that makes many people more comfortable relying on the *Times*' report of Jackson's death than on TMZ's?

This chapter explains how we arrived at our definition of "journalism" from a few different directions—by examining common definitions that fall short of capturing the whole picture; by identifying activities often mistaken for journalism and explaining why they are not journalism; and by laying out what we believe are essential features of anything that can rightfully call itself "journalism."

▶ DEFINITIONS: PLENTIFUL BUT LACKING

If you enter "definitions of journalism" into Google—come on, you know you want to!—you'll discover a lot of stuff like this:

> *The periodical collection and publication of current news; the business of managing, editing, or writing for, journals or newspapers; as, political journalism.*
>
> (brainyquote.com)

*The collecting, writing, editing, and presenting of news or news ar-
ticles in newspapers and magazines and in radio and television
broadcasts.*

(answers.com)

And from the Merriam-Webster Dictionary website, you'll notice a few different meanings:

*1a: the collection and editing of news for presentation through the
media; b: the public press; c: an academic study concerned with the
collection and editing of news or the management of a news medium.*

*2a: writing designed for publication in a newspaper or magazine; b:
writing characterized by a direct presentation of facts or description of
events without an attempt at interpretation; c: writing designed to appeal to current popular taste or public interest.*

According to these definitions, "journalism" is an activity that involves collecting, writing, editing and publishing, and/or it is a certain kind of writing
and/or an area of study. While there's nothing particularly wrong with any
of these definitions—they do reflect the way people often talk about journalism—there's nothing particularly useful about them either. The first one
seems to suggest that journalism happens only in newspapers and magazines. The second includes TV and radio, but doesn't have anything to say
about the Internet. The third includes all media, but seems to count only
writing as journalism. The definitions contain some ambiguous terms too.
What is "news"? What are "facts"? What is the "public interest"? In the end,
even if we had answers to these questions, these definitions still don't help
us understand the difference between what TMZ and the *Los Angeles Times*
are doing—whatever it was that made TMZ report the news of Jackson's
death first, while others like the *Times* waited.

The question of who counts as a journalist and, therefore, what constitutes
journalism has even been tackled by the courts in the United States in cases
that involve things like whether a journalist must reveal the source of sensitive information included in a story. But coming up with airtight definitions
is not something judges have been very excited about doing, in large part
because any criteria can seem pretty arbitrary or quickly become outdated.

The U.S. Supreme Court said as much in its 1972 decision in *Branzburg v.
Hayes*:

> The administration of a constitutional newsman's privilege would present practical and conceptual difficulties of a high order. Sooner or later, it would be necessary to define those categories of newsmen who qualified for the privilege, a questionable procedure in light of the traditional doctrine that liberty of the press is the right of the lonely pamphleteer who uses carbon paper or a mimeograph just as much as of the large metropolitan publisher who utilizes the latest photocomposition methods. (p. 703)

Indeed, the "latest photocomposition methods" the court referred to have long been left in the dust. And things like blogging and Twitter mark a sort of return of the "lonely pamphleteer" (though without the carbon paper) the Court said has the same rights as the professional news media. So now what? As time went by, the courts, instead of creating "categories of newsmen," started to focus on the activity in which a person was engaged as the primary indicator of whether he could be called a journalist. That means journalism is mostly defined in terms of its purpose and content, and not whether the person creating or doing it makes a living at *USAToday*.

For example, in the 1993 *Shoen v. Shoen* case, the Ninth Circuit Court of Appeals said, "What makes journalism journalism is not its format but its content" (p. 1293). The kind of content the court mostly had in mind was "investigative reporting." But what is investigative reporting? A good question, which comes up again in a case called *In re Madden* decided by the Third Circuit Court of Appeals a few years later. In that case, the court created a three-part test for whether to consider someone a journalist: the person had to be:

1. engaged in investigative reporting;
2. gathering news; and
3. have had the intention from the very beginning of making that news public. (p. 130)

Here, as in the dictionary definitions mentioned earlier, we have "journalism" (or "journalist") defined in terms

DISCUSSION QUESTIONS

Unlike physicians, lawyers, teachers and electricians, journalists do not need to be licensed or pass a test to practice their profession. Is this good or bad for journalism? Good or bad for U.S. democracy? If journalists had to pass one test to enter the profession, what kinds of things would they be required to know? What kinds of skills would they need to have?

of other things that need defining themselves, such as "news" and "investigative reporting." Also notice how the intent of the person to make the reporting *public* matters in this definition. That will be a key point, as you'll see a bit later on.

▶ DEFINITIONS HAVE CONSEQUENCES

The *Branzburg, Shoen* and *Madden* cases aren't the only ones where these issues about who counts as a journalist have been discussed. But they do offer a glimpse into the kind of thing the courts have wrestled with as well as highlighting just how difficult but important all this definitional business is. That is, thinking about what "journalism" means isn't just something people brainstorm about on long roadtrips when their MP3 player dies. The answer actually has some consequences for how free people are to do journalism and how the public interprets and responds to what they read and see.

At a time when the way "traditional" journalism has been financed is under challenge, the answer might even have consequences for the survival of journalism itself. Time.com writer James Poniewozik addressed this issue a couple years ago and almost immediately ran into the definitional problem. In the post below, he mentions what he wrote and how some people, on a journalism blog called "Romenesko," responded. Pay particular attention to the parts we've put in italics.

> You can't open a newspaper—or read a newsmagazine website—these days without seeing a report wondering if X, Y or Z "can save journalism." Maybe that's the wrong question.

> Let's assume, for the sake of argument, that nothing saves journalism. *"Journalism," that is, as a profession and as currently constructed: a full-time job paid for by newsgathering entities through a combination of subscriptions and advertising.*

> [Update: Some commenters at Romenesko argue *this is a narrow definition of journalism. Agreed. That's the point.* It is the narrow definition implicit in all those articles about "Will _____ save journalism?" But. *However you do define journalism—a term I generally hate anyway but have no substitute coinage for—it will still be practiced by human beings who need to pay rent and purchase food.* Where will they get that

money? And thus, how will the activity of journalism be enabled, if not
by the presently-constituated [*sic*] profession of "journalism"? Especially
if "unnamed model that someone else will invent later" is not an allow-
able answer? That's the question of this post.]

(2009)

Poniewozik's definition focuses on journalism as a profession, something
people are not only paid to do, but paid enough to make a full-time job of
it. It is, as the commenters noted, a pretty narrow definition that excludes
everyone from freelance photographers to people who blog about local res-
taurants or what's going on in their neighborhoods. So what, if any, value is
there in defining journalism this way? What Poniewozik wants to highlight
is that the activity of journalism as traditionally practiced by people with
full-time jobs at particular kinds of news outlets is expensive in both money
and labor—but that expense is necessary if one hopes to have the kind of
journalism democracy requires. He doesn't really think journalism *ought*
to be defined in terms of where somebody works or how much someone is
paid. He is worried about saving the practice of journalism, not necessarily
the traditional news organizations that have undertaken that practice. No,
he doesn't define that practice. But his distinction between practice and or-
ganizational structure is useful for our purposes here. The big picture is that
the contexts—economic, as well as political and social—in which journalism is defined are critically important. We'll continue the discussion of the
economics in Chapter 4.

What we might begin to conclude from these varying definitions, not to
mention the sheer difficulty in defining journalism at all, is that to call something "journalism" seems to mean having some sort of expectations about it
that go beyond whatever its format or distribution channel might be. As the
Pew Research Center's Project for Excellence in Journalism puts it: "Journalism is storytelling with a purpose."

The Missouri School of Journalism gets us a little closer to some answers
with a definition of journalism discussed in its introductory courses: "a
current, reasoned reflection, in print or telecommunications, of society's
events, needs and values." But even that definition is better at defining news
than journalism. A reflection of society's events, needs and values describes
a product of some kind, the actual content or information or "stuff" that is
disseminated by the media. It says little about the process by which that reflection was produced except to say that it is "reasoned."

FIGURE 2.1 Even though people often talk about "news" and "journalism" as meaning essentially the same thing, distinctions in their definitions do matter.

Aaron Amat/ Shutterstock

As it turns out, "reasoned" is pretty important. It means that the content/ information/stuff that constitutes "the news" has been the subject of some kind of reasoning process, of someone thinking things through, exercising judgment, and making decisions. It's that notion of a process—and one with distinct, essential features—that's missing from most definitions of journalism.

◀ **NEWS JUDGMENT:** How journalists determine which events and information—and which aspects of those events and information—are important enough to cover as news and how to cover them.

The way we think about the difference between journalism and news in this book is that "journalism" describes the process through which "news" gets made. Pretty straightforward, right? Well, before you get too excited about how simple that sounds, consider the implications of thinking about news and journalism that way. First, it means that "news" doesn't just exist out in the world waiting for someone to trip over and report it. News is constructed by people who are selecting and confirming and explaining those things out in the world. (If this raises the notions of bias and objectivity in your mind, you're on the right track to understanding this implication. More on that later.) Second, but related to the first implication, is that "news" can mean different things in different places. That is, what's considered news

DISCUSSION QUESTIONS

Are standards of journalism the same for newspapers, magazines, radio, television and the Internet? If not, should they be? What about journalists and news outlets that use Twitter—should they be held to journalistic standards of verification, transparency, accuracy, etc.? Why?

in Indonesia might not be considered news in Italy or Ivory Coast. Third, it suggests that treating "news" and "information" or "journalism" and "media" as synonyms—something you'll notice happens all the time in regular conversation—is flat-out wrong. Information might be part of the raw material of news, but it's not the whole thing. And journalism might be conducted by people working in or for the media, but there are lots of media folks who don't "do" journalism at all. Finally (for now!), it means that the definition of "journalist" could apply to anyone who engages in that distinctive journalistic process of selecting, confirming and explaining. In other words, you don't have to work for *The Arkansas Democrat-Gazette*, the NBC Nightly News or CNN.com to do journalism.

Before we go any further with these implications, let's turn our attention to describing in detail what we argue are the essential features of the process called "journalism"—those things that most people believe distinguish TMZ from the *Los Angeles Times* and Onward State from ESPN.com, or at least part of ESPN, some of the time.

▶ THE ELEMENTS OF JOURNALISM

We—and you!—are indebted to Bill Kovach and Tom Rosenstiel for laying out a vision of journalism that highlights its distinctive features. Their book, *The Elements of Journalism*, starts from the premise that journalism really only makes sense in the context of democracy. That means journalism is defined in large part by the role it plays (or is meant to play) in aiding self-governance—all the stuff you learned about in Chapter 1. The first two "elements" Kovach and Rosenstiel describe—journalism's first obligation is to the truth and its first loyalty is to citizens—emphasize that role. Journalism treats people as *citizens* undertaking the challenging job of self-governance. To do that job, those citizens need truthful information they can rely on.

Notice that Kovach and Rosenstiel *don't* say journalism's first obligation is to facts, even though lots of people seem to think journalism is all about sticking to the facts. So what kind of truth do they have in mind? Journalists

THE ELEMENTS OF JOURNALISM

Bill Kovach & Tom Rosenstiel's *The Elements of Journalism: What News-people Should Know and the Public Should Expect* distills the underlying principles of journalism practice into nine elements essential to journalism fulfilling its democratic function. Those elements are:

1. Journalism's first obligation is to the truth.

2. Its first loyalty is to citizens.

3. Its essence is a discipline of verification.

4. Its practitioners must maintain an independence from those they cover.

5. It must serve as an independent monitor of power.

6. It must provide a forum for public criticism and compromise.

7. It must strive to make the significant interesting and relevant.

8. It must keep the news comprehensive and proportional.

9. Its practitioners must be allowed to exercise their personal conscience.

aren't necessarily looking for big, philosophical truths like the meaning of life or the nature of time as much as they are the practical truths necessary to gaining a perspective on what's going on in the world and figuring out what, if anything, requires change or attention. This kind of truth starts with gathering facts, but it certainly doesn't stop there. Those facts have to be put in some context that gives them meaning.

Here's an example: Suppose Senator Slackjaw claims his new bill will make it easier for people to get student loans. It's certainly a fact that he introduced the bill and another fact that he claimed it will simplify getting a loan. But would the proposed law really make it easier to get a loan? Is the senator's claim actually true? That's a question the journalist might pose to bankers, people trying to get loans, people who already have loans, consumer groups, college financial aid administrators, etc. The senator's announcement about the bill is just one of many facts a journalist would gather to get at the truth. Beyond verifying those facts and claims, a journalist would seek to put the facts in context. It might be important to know, for example, that Senator Slackjaw represents a state where the largest student loan processing company is based. Or that the National Association of Really Cheap Student

FIGURE 2.2 Verifying information, not just gathering or distributing it, is a key part of what sets journalists apart from other mass media communicators.

Picsfive/Shutterstock

Loan Issuers donated a large amount of money to the senator's last election campaign. Or that his state has the lowest percentage of people who can afford to go to college. Any or all of those things might have a bearing on how the average citizen hearing about the senator's proposal interprets it. The journalistic process, then, produces a kind of actionable truth by offering citizens tools for understanding what's going on around them. That truth—unlike the immutable truths of space and time—has a way of changing and adapting as new information becomes part of the narrative.

The second important thing to notice about Kovach and Rosenstiel's description of journalism is that journalists don't seek truth just because they feel like it or it's interesting to them (though that wouldn't hurt). Kovach and Rosenstiel describe truth seeking as an obligation of journalists—an obligation they owe to *citizens*. Thinking of people as citizens instead of as, say, an audience or consumers shapes how journalists do their work, both the kinds of stories they pursue as well as how they pursue them. For example, citizens need to know if the local sewer system is failing, even though knowing that isn't particularly entertaining. And while you might, as a consumer, be happy to hear all about which store has the best price on Your Favorite Brand of soda, as a citizen you probably also need to know Your Favorite Brand has been accused of engaging in unfair trade practices that harm companies in other communities. Journalists from the Kovach and Rosenstiel perspective act in certain ways and pursue certain kinds of news and truth because they think of their readers, viewers or listeners as citizens who might need to act on the information, not merely as an audience that wants to be entertained.

So journalism is a truth-seeking endeavor, addressed to citizens. Now what? While these first two elements lay the groundwork for distinguishing journalism from other kinds of communication, such as the stuff meant primarily to entertain you or persuade you to buy something, the third element begins to describe what it is that people who practice journalism actually do. Kovach and Rosenstiel write: "The essence of journalism is a discipline of verification." This follows logically from the first element. Journalists have a basic obligation to truth; getting the truth involves engaging in a strict process of verifying evidence and claims. That process goes beyond simply repeating what others say—the kind of "he said, she said" practice that Kovach and Rosenstiel dismissively call the "journalism of assertion"—to subjecting what others say to some scrutiny. What's involved in that process? Let's have a look at an example.

DISCUSSION QUESTIONS

Think back to the Michael Jackson example at the start of this chapter. What pressures might the journalists have felt to run the story? Who might be pressuring them to go with the information and why? What would the harm have been to go with the story, which did turn out to be correct? How does this example differ from the Joe Paterno story?

▶ BECAUSE I SAID SO? NOPE

In a series of articles that won him a Pulitzer Prize in 2004, *Wall Street Journal* reporter Daniel Golden demonstrated how white students benefited from a form of affirmative action in college admissions. Rich people donate to universities, and those universities let their rich children—whether actually qualified or not—into their elite schools. That's not news, so what's the big deal, right?

Well, as Golden's stories pointed out, this kind of affirmative action actually bears some similarity to the other kind of affirmative action—the legal kind, which at the time was before the U.S. Supreme Court, which was considering a case filed by several white applicants rejected by the University of Michigan.

Think for a second about what it takes to get to the truth of a story like this. First, Golden had to determine whether preferences that overwhelmingly favor some white college applicants actually exist. He couldn't just say, "Well, *everybody* knows this happens," nor could he just quote a few people who believe that to be true, though no doubt there wouldn't be any shortage of people willing to offer such an opinion. Golden had to verify—to get some actual confirmation—that some students receive preferred treatment because of their parents' status or how much money they have. But does that sound like something Harvard or Yale would be delighted to discuss? How about those who benefit from such preferences? Would they be willing to talk?

Here's one approach Golden took, as he describes in the story, "For Groton Grads, Academies Aren't Only Keys to Ivy Schools":

> Groton doesn't reveal class rankings, even to students. But a document from Groton's college-counseling department that was reviewed by *The Wall Street Journal* provides details of class ranks (for sophomore year through the first semester of senior year), test scores and college-application results for all of the school's 1998 graduates.
>
> William M. Polk, Groton's headmaster, says the document, titled "Groton School Class of 1998: College Acceptances/Rejections/Wait-Listings by Class Rank," is not an "official school record." But 20 Groton graduates whose names appeared on the list said their test

scores and college-admission outcomes listed on the document were accurate.

(Golden, 2003)

So, to find people who might have received preferential treatment, Golden looked to Groton, an elite college preparatory school. He managed, somehow, to get hold of Groton's own records showing students' grades, scores, class rank, and college application status. The document confirmed that children of influential parents were accepted to some schools when their better achieving but less wealthy or influential Groton peers were rejected. And then, when the school insisted that the document wasn't an official record—basically, trying to deny that Golden could or should rely on it—he verified the document's contents by individually contacting 20 of the listed students. Golden went far beyond assertions, denials and reluctance to get to the truth.

Think about any science classes you've taken in which you conducted an experiment. Let's say one experiment was meant to determine whether a person's ability to taste flavors is linked with his or her gender. To test that claim, you would follow a set of procedures—establishing a hypothesis, recruiting subjects of different genders, having those subjects sample a variety of test papers with different kinds of flavors on them, recording how many flavors each subject could taste and so on. In the end, you would compare how many flavors subjects of each gender could taste. To make your results stronger and more credible, you would need to use more than one or two subjects, right? And even if you were really sure ahead of time that your hypothesis was correct, you would have to be open to the possibility that the data might not support you. Either way, you would report your experimental procedures and results so that future researchers could learn from and build on them.

What does that super-basic overview of the scientific method have to do with Golden's story about affirmative action? More than you might think. Golden, after all, started with a sort of hypothesis that some kids received preferential treatment in college admissions because of their parents' wealth or influence. To test that claim, he located a set of "subjects"—the graduates of an elite high school—and looked at their academic qualifications and which colleges admitted them and then compared where the wealthy and less wealthy students were admitted. He even could take into account grades and scores and see that some students were admitted over students whose grades and scores were better. Golden couldn't just rely on one or two anecdotal cases. And he had to be open to the possibility that the hypothesis wouldn't be supported by the data. Whatever his "experiment" showed, he would have to report it.

That's what Kovach and Rosenstiel are getting at with the discipline of verification. Similar to the scientific method, the verification process in journalism is transparent. That means journalists are open about whom they talked to, what documents they consulted—all the evidence they gathered—and what that evidence says. Also similar to the scientific method, the journalism of verification doesn't just rest on what one or two "subjects" say, especially without trying to determine whether what those one or two folks said is true. One final similarity with the scientific method is that the journalistic "method" of which the discipline of verification is a key component is objective. Oh boy. Now, before your head starts to explode, notice that we've said the *method* is objective. The *method*, people! We'll tackle the thorny, complicated, head-exploding concept of objectivity in greater depth later. For now, try to focus on verification, especially how it is different from assertion (the "he said, she said" thing) as well as how it works to distinguish journalism from lots of other things that might look like journalism, but aren't. Are the people offering their opinions on Fox News or CNN doing journalism? Not if they aren't offering some verification along with those opinions, they're not. Verification is handy that way—it offers a clear way to think about what sets journalism apart. And where does all of this leave TMZ and its ilk? At best, in a gray area. Even if you put aside the issue of whether knowing about Michael Jackson's death is important to citizens in a democracy, the reporting process that brought you those stories is neither transparent nor very heavy on verification. That's why the *Los Angeles Times* and others weren't eager to just repeat what TMZ reported. Journalists needed to verify it according to their own standards.

Of course there are still many open questions. What (or who) counts as credible evidence? For example, what if Golden had just interviewed his friends and their children for the college admissions story? What if he was a graduate of one of the elite universities in question and didn't want to make his alma mater look bad?

DISCUSSION QUESTIONS

What do journalists mean by "transparency"? Is it simply crediting sources or something more? Why is transparency important in journalism?

▶ INDEPENDENCE AT THE CENTER OF IT ALL

Enter element 4: "[Journalism's] practitioners must maintain independence from those they cover." By now, you are probably starting to see how all these elements fit together. Part of what makes the discipline of verification (element 3) work is a commitment to finding the truth (element 1) that citizens (element 2) need. For verification to be the transparent and

2.1 THE VIEW FROM THE PROS: INDEPENDENCE

Walter Williams, founding dean of the world's first school of journalism and a newspaper publisher himself, understood the central importance of independence. He insisted that the best way to teach the principles and practices of journalism was by means of a media outlet produced by students under faculty direction that would be both editorially and commercially independent.

The school's teaching newspaper, then called the *University Missourian*, began publication on the school's first day of classes in September 1908. Within months, its independence was under assault, not from those it covered but from those who had been the school's strongest supporters, other publishers.

The objection was to the dean's decision to have the Missourian sell advertising, of course in competition with nearby newspapers. The objections were so strong, and the publishers' political clout so powerful, that the Missouri legislature quickly wrote into law a prohibition against the use of state funds by "any newspaper which solicits, receives or accepts paid subscriptions or which prints or publishes advertising." The university's governing body immediately translated that ban into rule.

The independence of not only the newspaper but the school, and by implication the principles it taught, appeared to be doomed.

But Williams, demonstrating his own independence from his nominal superiors, set up a non-profit corporation, the "University Missourian Publishing Association," turned over ownership of the paper to that group and moved the publication temporarily off campus.

Advertising sales and independent coverage continued, and continue more than a century later. The *Columbia Missourian*, as the community daily is called today, is still owned by the Missourian Publishing Association, which contracts with the School of Journalism to produce it.

The continuing importance of structural separation and courageous leadership were on display again in the late 1970s, when another chancellor ordered another dean to restrict the Missourian's commercial competitiveness. Dean Roy Fisher responded by enlisting prominent alumni and members of the Publishing Association board to lobby the chancellor's superiors, the university Board of Curators.

After hearing from the managing editor of the *New York Times*, the editor of Missouri's biggest newspaper and others, the curators ordered the chancellor to rescind her order.

Journalistic independence, like democracy itself, requires repeated defense. Another assault, this one directed at the school's television station, came shortly after terrorists struck America in 2001.

The news director of KOMU-TV, a member of the faculty, forbade his on-air staff, student and professional, from wearing the flag pins or ribbons that had suddenly become the popular symbol of patriotism. "Our news broadcasts are not the place for personal statements of support for any cause – no matter how deserving the cause seems to be," he wrote. "Our job is to deliver the news as free from outside influences as possible."

The television station, unlike the newspaper, is owned directly by the university, which depends on the state legislature for funding. Legislators reacted with outrage. The House of Representatives adopted a $500,000 cut in the university budget, "to send a message to the School of Journalism."

Actually, the sponsor of the cut told reporters, he'd have preferred to punch the news director in the nose.

In response, faculty colleagues sent to the state's newspapers a statement that sought to make clear what was really at stake. The statement read, in part:

It would be easy to dismiss this latest flare-up as just another episode of the stupid legislative tricks Missourians have come to expect this time of year.

However, the attitudes expressed by legislators are probably widely shared by their constituents. Certainly, university administrators appear to believe that's true.

That's why the faculty of the Editorial Department of the School of Journalism believe it necessary – not just for the school, or even for journalism, but for the public – to emphasize that this abuse of legislative power illustrates both the importance of journalistic independence and its fragility.

It was no accident that the First Amendment to the United States Constitution guarantees protection for our freedoms of religion, speech, press, assembly and petition. The founders, even as they launched their unprecedented experiment in democracy, understood that these freedoms were inextricably linked, that they were essential to the democracy and that they would certainly come under threat. History has demonstrated that they were right on all three counts.

The most important moment to defend freedom is when it is most unpopular. The most important quality of a free press is that it be independent, both from the powerful whose acts it monitors and from the people to whom it reports.

In the end, the budget cut was reduced to $100,000. The "message" was received and rejected. The policy stood. Independence, one more time, was preserved.

THINK ABOUT IT: The *Columbia Missourian* is a unique community newspaper produced by the School of Journalism at the University of Missouri, but most campuses have a student newspaper, website and broadcast outlet (radio or television). What is the reporting structure of those student media outlets? Are they under the journalism program, student affairs, student government or another group? Is this transparent to readers and viewers? How might the reporting structure affect content?

George Kennedy, now a professor emeritus at the Missouri School of Journalism, was managing editor of the *Columbia Missourian* for nearly 12 years.

objective process necessary to meet those commitments, it can't be easily manipulated by people who might have a stake in the story—including the journalists themselves. Independence, in the way Kovach and Rosenstiel talk about it, means that journalists' loyalties cannot be divided. Nothing should come between a journalist and the truth or between a journalist and the citizens for whom she works.

The notion of independence can apply to the press more generally, not just individual journalists. Consider, for example, a column the (now former) executive editor of the *Seattle Times*, Mike Fancher, wrote a few years back. In it, Fancher says, "Independent, as we use it, means freedom from control or influence of others. It applies whether we're talking about the relationship of the press to government or the ability of journalists to do their work without pressure from any special interest" (2005).

All those things to which someone might be loyal or have an interest in promoting or protecting are called "factions." So a political party might be a faction, but so might a church or a charitable organization or a sports team or a company or even The League of People Who Love Starbucks, for that matter. If your love of Starbucks would spur you to write or not write something about the company regardless of what's best for citizens, then you are not acting independently. You've let your factional loyalty overtake your primary loyalty, in which case you aren't doing journalism, you're doing public relations or advertising, or merely cheerleading for your favorite coffee. Independence from faction, then, helps us define journalism by specifying one way in which it is different from other information-related activities that are frequently confused with it. Someone doing journalism is loyal to citizens first; someone doing public relations is loyal to the client first. That client might be Starbucks or the Libertarian Party or the Sierra Club. Or, in Golden's case, a faction might be the college he attended (if it's among those the story focuses on). And while what's good for that client might also be good for citizens more generally, that coincidence doesn't change the basic difference in approach to gathering and reporting information someone doing journalism and someone doing PR takes. Think back to the experiment analogy, where we discussed the transparency and objectivity of the scientific method. Scientists who deviate from this by, for example, skewing the results of their experiments to please someone who might benefit from those results are harshly criticized and their work dismissed as lacking validity. Independence, then, is necessary for the discipline of verification to work.

Oddly enough—at least at first glance—this doesn't mean that journalism (or journalists) should be neutral. Consider that journalism is a necessary component

FIGURE 2.3 Comedian and television host Stephen Colbert waves a Chilean flag after arriving onstage from a capsule similar to the one used to rescue Chilean miners alongside Jon Stewart (R) prior to speaking as thousands gather for the "Rally to Restore Sanity and/or Fear" on the National Mall in Washington, DC, October 30, 2010.

Saul Loeb/AFP/Getty Images

▶ **NEUTRALITY:**
Taking no position
on an issue. While
such detachment
can be beneficial
in journalism, it
also can get in the
way of journalists'
truth-telling mis-
sion if it reduces
journalism to
merely reporting
what each "side"
of an issue says.

of democratic life, so it will always be partial in some sense—that is, non-neutral—regarding what democracy requires.

But this independent-but-not-neutral business is tricky, not just for journalism students, but for journalists too. Just consider the confusion and criticism surrounding National Public Radio's decision to prohibit its employees from attending the "Rally to Restore Sanity" (and/or the "March to Keep Fear Alive") in October 2010. Sure, the journalists *covering* the rally put on by comedians Jon Stewart and Stephen Colbert could attend. But other employees couldn't, even on their own time.

In a memo to the staff, NPR's then senior vice president for news, Ellen Weiss, referred to the network's already established ethics code and social media guidelines. (You can find the full text of both documents here: www.npr.org/about/aboutnpr/ethics/.)

▶ NPR journalists may not run for office, endorse candidates or otherwise engage in politics. Since contributions to candidates are part of the public record, NPR journalists may not contribute to political campaigns, as doing so would call into question a journalist's impartiality.

▶ NPR journalists may not participate in marches and rallies involving causes or issues that NPR covers, nor should they sign petitions or otherwise lend their name to such causes, or contribute money to them. This restriction applies to the upcoming Jon Stewart and Stephen Colbert rallies.

▶ You must not advocate for political or other polarizing issues online. This extends to joining online groups or using social media in any form (including your Facebook page or a personal blog) to express personal views on a political or other controversial issue that you could not write for the air or post on NPR.org.

▶ NPR journalists may not serve on government boards or commissions.

These guidelines have "independence from faction" written all over them, don't they? The admonition against contributing to political campaigns or participating in rallies or advocating for causes is meant to guard against a collision of loyalties a journalist might face. We're guessing it seems rather bizarre and extreme to you that joining a Facebook group is considered just as problematic as joining an anti-war demonstration, according to NPR's guidelines. Rest assured, a lot of it seems weird to us, too. But let's not lose sight of the principle before we start nit-picking about the details of how journalists try to follow it. To call something "journalism," according to Kovach and Rosenstiel, is to say that the procedures that produced it were as free of competing interests as possible. Given the public nature of what journalists do and the transparency the verification process requires, most journalists try to avoid even the *appearance* of a conflict of interest or competing loyalties. The NPR guidelines (and the guidelines of many other news organizations) are basically saying that even if it were possible for a journalist to advocate for the League of People Who Love Starbucks on her own time and still impartially cover that league when she's on the clock as a journalist, the appearance of a conflict would raise too many questions that get in the way of the public's ability to trust her reporting.

2.2 THE VIEW FROM THE PROS: INDEPENDENCE OUTSIDE THE UNITED STATES

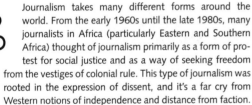

Journalism takes many different forms around the world. From the early 1960s until the late 1980s, many journalists in Africa (particularly Eastern and Southern Africa) thought of journalism primarily as a form of protest for social justice and as a way of seeking freedom from the vestiges of colonial rule. This type of journalism was rooted in the expression of dissent, and it's a far cry from Western notions of independence and distance from faction.

It is a pity that many practicing journalists are not impartial about either the government or those who oppose it. It is not in the DNA of many African journalists to be as fair and impartial on matters such as human rights protection, responsible national governance and socioeconomic equality. It is also pretty clear that the universal ethical standards—such as truth or accuracy or responsibility—in Africa's journalism have different meanings under oppressive governments. For instance, many young journalists chronicle the activities of state actors and simply promote state propaganda. That is their understanding of journalism, which they define as *developmental journalism*. These journalists might think of themselves as being truthful when they accurately report on government business, but in most cases they are providing little more than public relations for the state instead of reflecting good checks and balances.

But an even more significant difference lies in the state of investigative journalism in many African nations. Even privately owned media never report corruption in top government offices that are closely connected to the presidency. They only investigate and expose junior politicians and mid-level civil servants. Thus, the media report what is principally "truthful" and "accurate," about African governments. But it is also irresponsible journalism because their coverage of news tends to favor government leaders and friends of media owners and the government.

I should point out here that the challenge is that journalists fear retribution from some of the dictatorial governments. Yet, it is the independent media (media that are neither owned/controlled by the government nor a government official) which are more crucial to mobilizing and politically energizing citizens to de-legitimize dictatorships. It is my contention that government leaders try to tear down the adversarial role of the press when coverage is aimed at state institutions because such coverage gives citizens the information they need to make the right decisions in a democratic society.

Even in this new millennium, independent journalists in Africa can easily be co-opted by their governments or national leaders due to the culture of state patronage.

Throughout the 1990s and the 2000s, governments appointed journalists they patronized or compromised in order to destabilize independent voices in the news media. For instance, I write in my book *African Media and Democratization* (2011) that, in the mid- to late 1990s and 2000s, independent journalists were ferried in and out of police detention on weekends so regularly in parts of Africa that their wives automatically recognized a peculiar jail scent.

Here are a few examples of why the concept of journalism and journalism practice is a daunting challenge in many African nations:

- In late 2007, journalist Mathias Manirakiza, director of Radio Isanganiro was detained for the third time in five years on charges of authorizing his station to broadcast information capable of breaching national security.
- In Ethiopia, two editors and countless journalists were also prosecuted simply for writing about non-threatening topics such as music that exposes government corruption. For example, Amare Aregawi, the editor-in-chief of the *Reporter*, Ethiopia's leading independent newspaper, was imprisoned in connection with published stories addressing criticisms about the management of a brewery linked to the government.

Journalists can be charged with treason in many African nations for inciting "disaffection with the government" for their reporting. The risk of going to prison poses the greatest threat to independent journalists. A few independent newspapers also face financial constraints that prohibit them from managing a news organization. For instance, the state-run *New Times* is the only daily newspaper in Rwanda. Just like the other East African nations, the Rwandan government does not advertise with any independent news organization that is perceived to be criticizing the regime and its government. The list of problems for the practice and understanding of journalism in Africa is endless! Yet the courage and energy of African journalists is astonishing under such difficult conditions.

LEARN MORE: Students in the United States often take for granted the First Amendment freedoms of press, speech, religion, assembly and petition. Visit the website for the Committee to Protect Journalists (www.cpj.org) and read more about the challenges faced by journalists in Africa and other parts of the world.

———————

Yusuf Kalyango Jr. is a faculty member at the E.W. Scripps School of Journalism at Ohio University.

▶ SO WHAT IS JOURNALISM, ANYWAY?

If nothing else, this chapter has illustrated how difficult but important the task of defining "journalism" is. It's pretty easy—too easy—to wind up with a definition that includes or excludes too much, or that defines "journalism" using *other* terms that are also ambiguous, such as "news" or "information." Scholars Erik Ugland and Jennifer Henderson point out one further complication: People seem to assume that a question like "Who is a journalist"? is a single question, and not a number of different questions, depending on the context in which one is asking. If one is considering how to define "journalist" for the purpose of deciding who may qualify for a privilege like a White House press pass, then certain kinds of elements will be important. If, on the other hand, one is considering the definition for the purpose of distinguishing good or credible practices from less credible ones, the focus of the definition will be very different. Ugland and Henderson (2007) refer to the first context as the legal domain characterized by "an *egalitarian model* that emphasizes equal access to rights and privileges," and the second context as the professional ethics domain characterized by "an *expert model* that emphasizes the unique proficiencies and duties of media professionals" (p. 244).

> In the law domain, fundamental rights are at stake, so the consequences of defining protections for newsgathering and expression too narrowly (especially when the party drawing the line is the government) are substantially greater than in the professional ethics domain where the debate is more about virtue than freedom. In the legal domain, there is an element of coercion—the exercise of government power to restrain behavior. That is not true in the professional ethics domain. There, it is about a private dispute among communicators regarding whose work is more valuable.
>
> (Ugland and Henderson, 2007, p. 259)

What we learned earlier in this chapter about legal definitions is that the courts have been far happier to define journalism in terms of its content or the type of activity that produced that content than in terms of its format or mode of distribution or, even worse, where someone works. What Ugland and Henderson are suggesting refines this point further. Even if we agree that journalism ought to be defined in terms of content and practices and not format, distribution or whatever, we might still disagree about whether the definition ought to focus on *what* a person does or *how* he does it. That kind of disagreement seems to be at the heart of skepticism about "citizen journalism"—essentially, news content produced by people who don't work full-time as journalists but who might, nevertheless, engage in reporting practices that look an awful lot like the journalistic method. Columnist Leonard Pitts (2010) put it this way:

> Journalism is hours on the phone nailing down the facts or pleading for the interview. Journalism is obsessing over nit-picky questions of fairness and context. Journalism is trying to get the story and get it right. "Citizen journalism," we are told is supposed to democratize all that, the tools of new technology making each of us a journalist unto him or herself . . . If some guy had a wrench, would that make him a citizen mechanic? If some woman flashed a toy badge, would you call her a citizen police officer? Would you trust your health to a citizen doctor just because he produced a syringe?

Pitts' skepticism seems to rest, at least in part, on his view that *standards* are an important defining feature of journalism—a view that shares some similarities with the expert model Ugland and Henderson describe. Even if citizen journalists would meet the definition of a journalist put forth under the egalitarian model, Pitts is saying they wouldn't (or shouldn't) meet the definition under the expert model.

We happen to disagree with Pitts that the work of citizen journalism can be dismissed so easily. If, in fact, a citizen journalist spends "hours on the phone nailing down the facts" and engages in the kind of independent verification process aimed at offering a truthful account of events that citizens need, then how is that NOT journalism? Even so, we acknowledge the difficulty in separating "professional"—connoting adherence to a certain set of standards—from "journalism"—which we think refers to a set of procedures. What we, Kovach and Rosenstiel, and many others in journalism have in common is a tendency to slide back and forth between the egalitarian and expert models and an inclination to talk as much about what journalism *ought* to be or do as what journalism is. (Notice, for example, that elements 5–9 on Kovach and Rosenstiel's list are framed in terms of what journalism "must" do.) One thing is certain: As the opportunities and technical capabilities for more people to do journalism outside of traditional news organizations grows, standards and expectations will change in ways we can't fully anticipate. Some of those changes might even be positive.

In late 2003 and early 2004, the Anuak tribe in Ethiopia lost 425 of its members in a massacre by the Ethiopian military. No one would know about this terrible event if it weren't for The McGill Report, a website run by former *New York Times* reporter Douglas McGill. How he came upon the story and reported it is a fascinating tale (see www.mcgillreport.org for more) that begins with a student in his English as a Second Language class telling him about receiving cellphone calls from friends and family in his village in which he could hear shooting and screaming, and eventually leads to McGill traveling to Ethiopia to interview witnesses and survivors. Even with the accounts of dozens of people and a separate investigation by Genocide Watch confirming many of the details, McGill could not get more traditional news organizations to publish information about the massacre. Why not? Without the confirmation of high government officials, McGill's story didn't meet the demands of those news organizations' verification processes or, really, their definition of "journalism."

▶ ENOUGH ALREADY! WHAT'S THE ANSWER?

Ultimately, who gets to say what journalism is? The power to define is, indeed, power. Scholar Andrew Cline comes down on the side of the public, saying that who counts as a journalist "should arise primarily from the experiences of a public that uses journalism as a civically important text" (2007, p. 295). That means that journalists alone don't get to decide what journalism is; the public is part of any defining process. As Cline goes on to say, "Journalists produce journalism for citizens, and citizens use journalism for public purposes" (p. 295). That relationship creates obligations for both journalists and for the public. Those obligations and the ethical issues arising from them will be discussed later. For now, let's reprise our definition of journalism:

> *Journalism is a set of transparent, independent procedures aimed at gathering, verifying and reporting truthful information of consequence to citizens in a democracy.*

It's not perfect, and it's only the beginning of the story. We have a lot more refining and elaborating to do in the rest of the book.

Chapter Two Review

Chapter Summary

Suggested Activities

Read More

▶ CHAPTER SUMMARY

Defining what is—and is not—journalism is a difficult task indeed, but an important one. While scholars, journalists and even the courts offer a variety of definitions, it's best to focus on the unique values that distinguish journalism from other forms of mass communication. The work of Kovach and Rosenstiel provide a great foundation for a working definition by declaring initially that journalism is a truth-seeking endeavor, addressed to citizens in a democracy. In order to perform such democratic truth seeking, journalism requires verification and independence. Each value forms a key part of a working definition of journalism:

> *Journalism is a set of transparent, independent procedures aimed at gathering, verifying and reporting truthful information of consequence to citizens in a democracy.*

▶ **SUGGESTED ACTIVITIES**

1. Parking on campus. On virtually every campus, students think it's too expensive, too inconvenient and too limited. Gather into small groups to discuss this project. Using Kovach and Rosenstiel's elements as a guide, half of the groups should tackle this problem: How would you get at the "truth" if assigned to write this story? What facts would you gather and from whom? Which facts, if left out, would compromise the truth? The other half of the groups can examine the issue using the discipline of verification. Are the students off base in their thinking? How could you verify whether student opinion is correct? Discuss your ideas with the class.

2. To illustrate the confusing mix of news, punditry and advocacy, select a hot-button topic in your community (one example was a debate over a proposed "fair tax" in Missouri) and search online for information. This activity works well with pairs or small groups. First, make an unfiltered Google search for the information on the issue. Critically evaluate the content that you find. How much of it is true journalism? How much of it masquerades as journalism, but is really advocacy? What role do social networks play in the discussion? Next, limit your search to the "News" results from Google and then carry out a directed search on a local newspaper online archive or a news database such as LexisNexis. How do the quality, tone and structure of the information differ based on limiting the search to established news outlets? Post your thoughts in a discussion board (online) or share with the class (group discussion).

3. Invite a journalist and a local newsmaker (politician, official, etc.) to class and interview them about how they define journalism and journalism's role in democracy. Read this chapter and prepare questions for each about journalistic independence, verification, transparency and truth-seeking. How do their perceptions of these journalistic conventions and role of the profession differ? How are they similar?

4. Find the NPR ethics guidelines at http://ethics.npr.org. Under "Impartiality," several guidelines talk about journalistic independence and the appearance of objectivity. Choose one (one good suggestion: Don't sign, don't advocate, don't donate) and discuss your reactions to it in small groups for about three to five minutes. Discuss amongst the class whether the policy goes too far, not far enough or is just right. Why might the NPR guidelines be tougher in this area than those of other U.S. news outlets? Now consider reporters covering sports, fashion or entertainment. Should they be held to the same standards as those covering politics? Does a one-size-fits-all policy work?

5. Find a breaking news story online on a major news outlet (CNN, a national newspaper, ESPN.com). Note the attribution (sources quoted or paraphrased) used in the story. How many sources are used? What percentage of the story is attributed? Now find people writing about the same story on Twitter, Facebook or on a general blog site. Does the attribution differ on these posts from the writing for the traditional news outlets? Post your findings to the class discussion board, then examine what others have posted. Be sure to also discuss how attribution is related to the definition of journalism discussed at the start of this chapter.

▶ READ MORE

Branzburg v. Hayes, 408 U.S. 665 (1972).

Andrew R. Cline, "Death in Gambella: What Many Heard, What One Blogger Saw, and Why the Professional News Media Ignored it," *Journal of Mass Media Ethics* 22 (2007): 280–299.

Michael Fancher, "What Independence Means to this Paper," *The Seattle Times*, January 30, 2005, accessed June 21, 2012. http://seattletimes.nwsource.com/html/localnews/2002164845_fancher30.html.

Daniel Golden, "For Groton Grads, Academics Aren't Only Keys to Ivy Schools: A Look at Who Got in Where Shows Preferences Go Beyond Racial Ones," *The Wall Street Journal*, April 25, 2003, accessed June 21, 2012. http://online.wsj.com/public/resources/documents/golden1.htm.

In re Madden, 151 F.3d 125 (3d Cir. 1998)

Bill Kovach and Tom Rosenstiel, *The Elements of Journalism: What Newspeople Should Know and the Public Should Expect*, New York: Three Rivers Press, 2007.

Pew Research Center's Project for Excellence in Journalism, "Principles of Journalism," accessed June 21, 2012. www.journalism.org/resources/principles.

Leonard Pitts, Jr., "Why Citizen Journalism Doesn't Measure Up," *The Dallas Morning News*, October 6, 2010, accessed June 21, 2012. www.dallasnews.com/opinion/latest-columns/20101006-Leonard-Pitts-Why-citizen-1722.ece.

James Poniewozik, "If the Journalism Business Fails, Who Pays for Journalism?" Time.com, June 8, 2009, accessed June 21, 2012. http://entertainment.time.com/2009/06/08/if-the-journalism-business-fails-who-pays-for-journalism/.

Shoen v Shoen 5 F.3d 1289 (9th Cir. 1993).

"This is NPR. And These are the Standards of Our Journalism," accessed June 21, 2012. www.npr.org/about/aboutnpr/ethics/.

Erik Ugland and Jennifer Henderson, "Who is a Journalist and Why Does it Matter? Disentangling the Legal and Ethical Arguments," *Journal of Mass Media Ethics* 22 (2007): 241–261.

3

How Is News Made?

Ron Sylvester, a veteran reporter now at the *Las Vegas Sun*, spent years at the *Wichita Eagle* covering the court system. He's a lifer, the sort of journalist you can build a newsroom around.

He's also a blogging, tweeting, video-taking machine.

Sylvester began his career on an IBM Selectric typewriter; today he rolls around a briefcase that holds a digital camcorder, a wireless microphone, a MacBook Pro with Final Cut Express, and a grab bag of wires and A/V accessories. He taught himself every tool he uses.

Today Sylvester covers gaming, the biggest show in Vegas and one that breaks news 24/7. One minute Sylvester is headed to a casino for some press event or another, and the next he is attending a high-level meeting on the tourism trade or interviewing a high-rolling member of the Vegas jet set. It's a huge change from his days in Wichita scouring court dockets, but the way in which he produces news is in many ways the same.

LEARNING OBJECTIVES

▼
Examine the ways news is made, and note how newsgathering is changing.

▼
Identify newsgathering in the broader world of mass communications.

▼
Think about what changes in news processes are doing to the principles of good journalism.

▼
Reconcile newsgathering with current forces shaping the media economy.

News, to Sylvester, is no longer is a series of finite, deadline-driven events, but a stream of posts, tweets and, finally, stories.

Sylvester began blogging as an extension of his judicial reporting, and began Twitter feeds shortly after its launch. Watching TV coverage of trials, he began to wonder if he couldn't begin to add video as well. With the help of colleagues in the *Eagle*'s photography and Web departments, Sylvester patched together some equipment and started learning.

Today, you're likely to find Sylvester tweeting live from a news event, then shooting some video and compiling a blog post. He says he uses multimedia in much the same way that he once used a reporter's notebook, compiling information that might find its way into the print edition.

"I'm a reporter," Sylvester said. "I'm just taking advantage of the tools available to me to tell stories, but I'm still reporting, at the end of the day."

Nate Skid, a multimedia reporter for *Crain's Detroit Business*, also utilizes a deep reservoir of digital tools to cover Southeast Michigan's business scene. His job evolved along with his skill set; even today, he finds himself picking up new roles as the de facto staff photographer.

"I shot a little in school, but when I got here, I saw that I would need to get a lot better at it, so I just began to experiment, and now, when colleagues need an environmental shot for a feature story, I am the go-to guy," he said.

Skid's day is a hodgepodge of assignments, enterprise stories, long-form interviews and breaking news pieces. Some hit the blog, others go to *Crain's* website, and still others to the weekly print edition. He gathers audio and video, writes and edits, and monitors an endless stream of incoming information from a host of digital sources for news on his beat. At the end of the day, though, Skid says he remains a writer.

DISCUSSION QUESTIONS

Do you think it's challenging for journalists to attune to all aspects of their jobs while mastering new reporting and delivery tools? Is it easier or harder for journalists who have been out of school for several decades to adapt to this change? Is this a function of age or personality?

"I am willing to try things that better tell the story, and that sometimes means I will grab a new tool, but when it all comes down to the story, I am practicing journalism, just like I did when all I had was a pen and paper," he says. "The questions that are asked, and the documents that are relied upon, and the sources I use, none of that changes."

▶ TOOLS CHANGE. AUDIENCES CHANGE. THE WORK DOESN'T

OK, so Skid and Sylvester are picking up new skills and advancing their careers by embracing the newest techniques in newsgathering—and that is great. The tools of the profession do change—the School of Journalism at Missouri once had a thriving linotype program, after all—but it's important to think about where journalism has come from in order to understand where it might be headed.

In speaking with scores of journalists, young and old, tech-savvy and just learning, a few trends emerge about the way news is made these days. Journalists tell us that the more things change, the more they need the basics: persistence, enterprise, a love of fact, and the willingness to dig and to ask tough questions of those in power. Whether on Twitter or through a

FIGURE 3.1 New ways of gathering and delivering information are threatening to take over the old. Whether and how printed newspapers will survive in the online era is a topic of great speculation and anxiety in the industry.   .

Helder Almeida/ Shutterstock

crowdsourcing site, on video, the Web or in print, journalism retains its first principles. In other words, even while the form of journalism changes fundamentally, the process changes only slightly—and its values don't change at all.

Recall the definition we came up with in the previous chapter:

> *Journalism is a set of transparent, independent procedures aimed at gathering, verifying and reporting truthful information of consequence to citizens in a democracy.*

It's comforting to think that while digital media certainly have sped up the process of newsgathering, increased opportunities for transparency and widened the possibilities as far as distributing news, those in the business of making news stress that the purpose of journalism and, therefore, the fundamental principles underlying it haven't changed—and if they *have* changed, that should sound alarm bells. Could it be possible for an industry in the throes of such cataclysmic change to keep its soul intact?

We believe the answer is yes. And not just because we are wishful thinkers who believe it's essential to democratic society for the answer to be yes. We see "yes" in the work Sylvester and Skid and scores of other journalists are doing. We see "yes" in the way those journalists are making sense of the flood of news and information, not getting washed away by it.

▶ INFORMATION, NEWS AND JOURNALISM

Notice how we just said journalists make sense of news and information. That implies that news and information are two different things. Notice also how we describe what journalists are doing as sense making. That sounds like some sort of process, doesn't it? When we talked briefly about news in the last chapter, we pointed out that it is *constructed*; it's not just like a penny on the sidewalk waiting for someone to walk by and pick it up. We'll expand on that construction idea a bit here and throw "information"—sort of the raw material for news—into the mix for good measure. The basic idea is this: Information, news and journalism are not synonyms. News might bear a striking resemblance to information sometimes, and journalism might get talked about as though it's news. But journalism must be understood as distinct from both. That distinction is all in the process and the principles.

Let's try to begin making some distinctions through an example. Take this Reuters story that ran May 21, 2012:

> A suicide bomber in army uniform killed more than 90 soldiers in the heart of the Yemeni capital on Monday and an al Qaeda affiliate threatened more attacks if a U.S.-backed campaign against militants in the front-line state did not stop.

That's information: It gives us details about events on the ground as they happen. Back when journalists were the major providers of news, particularly about faraway events, that sort of information came almost exclusively from news organizations. In today's world of information surplus, that which we perceive as news comes from a rushing flood of sources, from our Twitter account to our Facebook page to an incoming text. And that includes information from around the world, not just around the corner.

FIGURE 3.2 Yemeni soldiers ride on top of a pick-up truck near the town of Jaar, a jihadist stronghold north of the Abyan provincial capital Zinjibar, on May 30, 2012 as Yemeni forces continue their offensive against al Qaeda loyalists in the south.

AFP/Getty Images

No longer owned or even significantly controlled by media organizations, information has become a commodity—a product that news consumers don't want to pay for because they can get it free from so many different channels. Information transmission is what the Internet perfected.

▶ **COMMODITY:**
A product, usually produced and/or sold by many different companies that is uniform in quality and thus driven entirely by price.

There's also a way in which that Reuters story is news. How so? Because Reuters took some facts—some information—and put them together in a specific way. They (and other news organizations) decided that what was happening in Yemen was important, so they reported it. They *decided* it was news. The journalistic process transformed the raw information into news.

Is that really necessary? Couldn't people just put all that information swirling around the Internet together for themselves? Theoretically, of course they could (and sometimes do). But practically? That's quite a lot to do, because information alone tells us very little. The Yemen story is a perfect example: In the weeks before the May 21 attack, there were pitched battles between the terrorist organization and domestic troops. That is, the battles and suicide bombings that happened before May 21 were important context—bits of information put together in a certain way—for what happened on that day.

Let's turn to a May 21 story in the United Kingdom's *Telegraph*, and see what we mean as we begin to see the pieces come together:

> Washington is increasing its military support for Hadi's government and the U.S. military has targeted militants in Yemen with drones, which have frequently killed civilians and are deeply resented by Yemenis, even the many who abhor al Qaeda.
>
> (Baron and Spencer, 2012)

And a bit later, the British Broadcasting Corporation (BBC) ran its own story, including this information:

> Monday's attack comes 10 days after the military launched an offensive against Islamist militants linked to al-Qaeda in the Arabian Peninsula (AQAP) in the southern province of Abyan . . .
>
> Ansar al-Sharia, or Partisans of Islamic Law, was founded in response to the growing youth movement in Yemen, which has marginalised Salafi jihadists who advocate the violent overthrow of the government.
>
> In November, protesters forced President Saleh to hand over power to Mr. Hadi, then his vice-president, as part of a deal brokered by the Gulf Co-operation Council.

Mr. Hadi was elected president in February and immediately said one of his most important tasks was the "continuation of war against al-Qaeda as a religious and national duty."
(British Broadcasting Corporation, 2012)

DISCUSSION QUESTIONS

Information, news and journalism are not synonyms. But how do they differ? Do audiences understand this distinction?

See how information becomes breaking news, and those fast-moving, seemingly random events on the ground begin to take shape as the procedures of journalism are applied to information? Journalists pointed to events in Yemen as news and then gathered information—facts and context—to make sense of those events for their audiences.

◀ **BREAKING NEWS:** A sudden, compelling news event covered immediately by reporters.

In an age of information surplus—of news as commodity—journalists must become the processors of news, and in that process, they must take that news flood and organize it, synthesize it, digest it and make it engaging as well as informative. Wow, that's some task! But it's always been journalism's core job to get it right, to bring meaning to the day's events. It's just that now journalists no longer need worry themselves with who got the news first, because it most likely was not a media actor at all. The origination of news, so important in the rise of the mass media, no longer matters as much. In a world in which news travels the world in the blink of an SMS message, journalism, fueled by reporting, takes on added importance.

Don't be fooled by the volume and accessibility of information. It's tempting to see a cascading Twitter feed as a substitute for journalism, but it's not. Without journalism, what we have is lots of information vying for dominance, untested, unvetted and, often, coming from people wishing to persuade, rather than inform. That's why it's important to think about the process of news: so you can start to understand how and why it differs from other forms of communication.

▶ **SO WHERE DOES NEWS COME FROM?**

There's still a missing piece in our discussion so far: How does something get called "news" in the first place? How and why did journalists "construct" the events in Yemen as news? Ask a non-journalist and you'll likely hear something sort of clichéd, like "If it bleeds, it leads," or "Sex sells." Ask a journalist the same question and you'll likely get an equally simplistic response: "Because it's news." Indeed, perhaps the greatest source of misunderstanding between journalists and their critics lies in the selection of news. Arguments abound over whether the news includes too much of this or too little of that.

Newsworthiness defies simple explanation, yet if we cannot tell our audience what constitutes news, how can we expect to defend where our news judgment takes us? We'll start by harkening back to what you learned in Chapter 1 about the functions journalism performs. Informing, investigating, creating conversation and so on suggest a set of criteria journalists use to make news judgments—the kinds of information and events that self-governing people need will (or ought to) make the cut as "news," right? But those functions don't offer a complete description of the criteria.

Scholars, critics and long-time observers of the news have identified a number of factors that seem to influence what becomes news. Journalists' reliance on these "news values," as the factors are called, offers us a way to discuss the first step in how news is made—its selection as news. It's not surprising, really, that the way journalists select news is not so different from the way the rest of us perceive and discuss the world. Keep in mind, though, that while the list below does a good job of *describing* the factors that make up news judgment, it isn't necessarily meant to *prescribe* them. In fact, a couple of the items on the list are a bit problematic, as you'll discover in later chapters. But let's not get ahead of ourselves. In no particular order, the news values are:

▶ *Timeliness* (immediacy): News isn't news, we often are told, if it is not of recent vintage. In today's 24/7 media landscape, it's stressed more than ever before. It also underscores the tyranny of the deadline: less and less time to acquire different viewpoints from multiple sources, to verify, to fact-check.

▶ *Impact*: Impact describes an issue's effect on the public. The number of people affected by a news event can be an important part of the equation, but it's more than mere numbers—it's more of a judgment call on how many members of the audience are likely to be interested in the story.

▶ *Currency*: Articles with currency describe ongoing issues, using the ongoing nature of the story to maximum advantage. If it happened today, it's news. If the same thing happened last week, it's no longer interesting, unless people can't stop talking about it.

▶ *Conflict*: Perhaps the most common news value, conflict appears in nearly every imaginable story as reporters question who benefits or suffers and who is involved. Conflict often provides action, villains and heroes . . . the stuff of storytelling!

▶ *Novelty/Emotions*: Don't underestimate the power of human interest in news selection. An unusual aspect to a story often gets coverage. In fact, human interest stories often cause news organizations to disregard the main rules of newsworthiness: for example, they don't date as quickly, they need not affect a large number of people, and it may not matter where in the world the story takes place.

▶ *Prominence*: Behold the power of fame. Prominent individuals, such as politicians, celebrities and athletes, often receive coverage by virtue of their position in society.

▶ *Proximity*: News events in areas close to the audience are considered to be more relevant than events further away. The emphasis on geographic proximity is being challenged by the borderless nature of online communication, but local news still drives much of the news agenda.

Just as reporters use news values to select news, editors use news values to determine where and how prominently news will be played. Typically, articles containing multiple news values are more likely to appear in more prominent roles in the news product.

This list is not used as a checklist, and journalists exercise a great deal of independent judgment when selecting news events for coverage. Still, much that appears in daily journalism ticks off one or more of these values.

DISCUSSION QUESTIONS

Are certain media better at conveying stories with certain types of news values? For example, is emotion easier to convey through words or moving images? Is timeliness best suited for online? As media organizations converge, how might delivery format affect the types of information conveyed through each format?

▶ THE NUTS AND BOLTS OF NEWSGATHERING

▶ **PSEUDO EVENTS:** A term popularized by the historian Daniel J. Boorstin, describing events or activities that serve little to no purpose other than to be reproduced through advertisements or other forms of publicity.

Much of what becomes today's news originates with press releases, government press conferences, legislative hearings, court hearings and the like—far too often, with what the historian Daniel Boorstin called "pseudo events." At newsrooms across the country, journalists monitor these developments and select from an ever-growing pile of press releases, notices, incoming e-mails and phone calls alerting them to potential news. So journalists are culling through mountains of information, choosing the best bits and passing them along.

Journalists also produce what are called **enterprise stories**—stories that rely upon sources they have developed through their area of coverage, or beat, to keep them informed and pass along news items to create original works of journalism.

▶ **BEAT:** A specific topic area of news coverage, such as the police beat or the local government beat.

Stories—the currency of journalism—are either assigned by supervisors (editors in the print world; producers in broadcasting, although job titles are fluid these days) or originated by journalists as enterprise stories. Assignments vary wildly according to medium, beat, reporter expertise or even the time of day, for that matter. If you're the night police reporter, and a crime suddenly hits the scanner in the newsroom, guess whose assignment it is?

The life of a story, from origination to distribution, depends as well on a number of things. If the story concerns what we call breaking news—a sudden, compelling news event such as a multi-vehicle accident on the main thoroughfare through town, a sports star's sudden departure for another franchise, or an unexpected hailstorm that tears through the city—things are moving fast and the process will be as short as a few hours.

On the other hand, enterprise stories and even some assignments require serious research and preparation, multiple interviews with several sources, time spent with a subject observing and follow-up interviews to nail the story down and get it straight.

Longer, more detailed stories may involve multiple drafts, and editors look for holes, logical problems and missing angles at each turn. Often, reporters are sent back to the field for additional reporting and fact-checking, before a story is deemed finished.

3.1 THE VIEW FROM THE PROS: CHANGING PLATFORMS

This year, *Sporting News*, the publication I've worked for since 2003, is celebrating its 125th anniversary. At a time when the best of magazines are folding and even the biggest names in print are fighting for their lives, that SN still exists is a testament to its ability to evolve. Since 1886, it has gone from the black-and-white "Bible of Baseball" to a seven-sport glossy to a multimedia company.

I joined SN right out of journalism school, where I had studied magazine editing. My online experience in school consisted of a one-hour class on coding; at that point, not a whole lot more web-focused coursework was even offered.

When I started at SN, though, it had already embraced the online revolution—in 2000, it beefed up the website, and shortly after I started, in an effort to boost our visibility, SportingNews.com announced a partnership with Fox Sports—but at that point, the majority of the company's talent and the resources were still focused on the weekly magazine. Most editors worked on the magazine, and the writers spent most of their time on mag stories; pieces filed for the website were more of an afterthought, sent in their spare time and with quotes and information left over from mag reporting. Writer travel and photo shoots were almost never arranged solely for online purposes. For younger writers, a byline in the magazine was a status symbol, something they coveted and worked hard to achieve.

Sporting News was bought by American City Business Journals in 2006, and in one of our first meetings with the new owners, they discussed the direction they imagined for the company—largely a digital one. Under ACBJ, SN embraced the concept of blogging; we contracted some of the biggest names in sports blogs to write for SN.com and poured a lot of resources into that. For Super Bowl 41, we sent more bloggers than magazine writers.

Around this time, talk across the country began to focus on the recession, and people started to speculate about the death of print, the result of a loss of advertising dollars combined with the loss of readers to Internet news. Born out of this trend was *Sporting News Today*, a digital magazine we launched in 2008. It is distributed daily to subscribers via e-mail; we wanted to combine our traditional reporting strengths with new web-based technologies, including smartphones and now the iPad. SNT is published seven days a week, and it's a massive undertaking; the average size is around 50 pages. To coincide with launching SNT, we cut the magazine's frequency in half. It now comes out just every other week.

While we were launching SNT, other magazines were shutting their doors, and there were massive newspaper layoffs—especially in sports—every time you turned around. More than once, I lamented the fact I hadn't fallen in love with a profession that was a little more recession-proof. Everyone at SN seemed to know someone who had lost his or her job. We didn't undergo any layoffs, but ACBJ did institute a 5 percent across-the-board pay cut (a number that seemed pretty forgiving when I heard about the double-digit percentages some of my friends had accepted) in addition to a hiring freeze. When people left the company, we didn't fill their spots. We had been a relatively small operation, anyway—we never had *Sports Illustrated* or ESPN-type staffing levels—but what we wound up with were a few editors and writers working a ton of hours, the majority of those on SNT. No one complained much because there was a feeling we ought to be happy just to have jobs.

To keep those hours down as much as possible, we had to move copy as fast as we could, so it was hard not to let editing standards slip. Despite the now, now, now mentality that comes with digital media, readers' expectations didn't change. They demand perfection just as they did when all the copy came on paper. For the tiniest mistake, we receive hundreds of e-mails, most punctuated with a statement like, "Are you guys a bunch of idiots?"

As all this was going on, and people's time became even more precious, writers started to fall behind in their magazine work. When we would ask why a piece hadn't made deadline, the response was always, "I have all this stuff to do for SNT first," which was certainly true. No longer was the magazine byline the status symbol it had once been.

In August 2010, we relaunched SportingNews.com, and in talks surrounding the event, our publisher said that we're turning SN's traditional model on its head. While we were once magazine, SNT, online, we are now online first, then SNT, then magazine. This is in terms of how we allocate our resources and how our writers should allocate their time—a sign of the times.

As we entered 2011, the company restored our 5 percent, handed out some raises and made a number of hires to support our increased copy flow. Advertising dollars are as good as they've ever been, and I'd say the same for office morale. But I don't see any signs our company model will ever change from the new 1-2-3 online, SNT, magazine hierarchy.

I still think my sans-online education was incredibly valuable—journalistic skills and principles are the same no matter the medium—and I don't think print, or my own magazine, is dying. I wouldn't discourage students today from going into journalism, either, although I would give them one piece of advice I didn't get: Be ready to change and change, then change again.

THINK ABOUT IT: In what ways might highly focused publications like *Sporting News* be better off in the changing media economic structure? How might they be more resilient than general-interest publications like metropolitan newspapers?

Corrie Anderson Gifford joined *Sporting News* after graduating from the University of Missouri with an M.A. in journalism.

But that's far from the end of the process. Copy editors then step in, reading microscopically to ensure clarity, grammatical and mechanical cleanliness and last but certainly not least, compliance with Associated Press style, the dominant style and usage guide in American newsrooms. Copy editors often also create headlines, photo captions and other news elements.

If the story concerns, say, the federal budget, there may be a need for a news artist to produce a compelling graphic representation of the budget, before the whole package is delivered to news designers, who maximize the layout of the piece within the news product.

Broadcasting's use of more extensive technology, and its dependence upon a finite time period, alter the way that news is gathered and presented. Television reporters, working with producers, often spend most of the day away from the station, getting footage shot on location for the stories that will appear that night.

▶ **PACKAGE:** An edited set of video clips for a broadcast news story.

Time dictates that broadcast news be written and edited down to the second, with no room for error. That makes for a lively, and at times chaotic, work environment, as producers and editors work on editing **packages** to fit, adding voiceovers and graphics as they go. News directors oversee the process, supervising reporters and producers and consulting with the news anchors on the upcoming show. The anchors await the completion of the packages before going on air to present the news.

We could move from broadcasting to radio and magazines, detailing the news production process, but at this point, you should know that the newsgathering process differs only in form, not in function. Sure, significant differences emerge between daily newspaper stories, radio stories and long-form magazine articles, for example, but did the process of originating the content for any of those stories vary drastically?

The process of magazine news production differs from other media forms, of course, as does radio news and online news, thanks to size and time constraints, audience segmentation, market, and a host of other variables, but we'd be remiss if we didn't instead turn our attention to the news here—because all of the various forms of news production have felt the changes ushered in by digital technologies to various degrees.

The actual process of creating news reflects many of the changes transforming the business of journalism these days. News organizations have been famously slow to grasp the extent to which digital media are changing the process, but signs clearly point to a long-awaited awakening on the part of the profession.

The question is whether it's too little, too late, and whether new technologies will strengthen or threaten traditional newsgathering. The early results are a mix of promise and peril. Much about online journalism can be seen as a beacon of hope, from its emphasis on

FIGURE 3.3 Mobile devices such as smartphones are among the newest platforms for reporting and receiving news.
Dragonian/iStock

innovation to the interactivity fostered between news consumers and audiences.

▶ NEWS: NOT JUST LIKE ANY OTHER PRODUCT

A prevailing myth underscores much of the discussion of journalism: that because news is the product of a predictable, replicable series of processes, it is "made" just like other consumer products. This reduces a craft to a factory line, and excuses a lot of behavior damaging to journalism itself. And as journalism's production and distribution models have come under evolutionary stress in recent years, many observers have looked at all that change and concluded that if the process has changed, then the values undergirding the profession must be changing as well.

While that's certainly possible, it doesn't have to be. *The Dallas Morning News'* series (see Sidebar 3.2) is a fine example: Much was different about the way the reporters and editors on the series did their jobs, until you drill down to the reporting itself. That reporting—from the identification and interviewing of a whistleblower reluctant to talk, to battles with the hospital over documents, to scores of interviews with officials and former patients— is the way journalism is "made." The process changes daily with each story, to say nothing of each new technology. Yet its core remains the work of reporters and editors—the shoe-leather reporting, the documents, finding the elusive eyewitness. Amidst all the change, some things remain unchanged.

From this myth about the news "product" streams other misconceptions about journalism, journalists and the news, some of which have done real damage to the craft. For if news is "made" like any other consumer product, its production can be forever streamlined, tightened, its processes refined by the technology available to it, with the goal of producing the news as cheaply and efficiently as possible. A journalism slave to the interests of a narrow class of corporate owners can be every bit as endangered as journalism captive to the whims of a totalitarian government.

The concept of news as product began, as the scholar Stuart Allan noted most precisely in *News Culture,* as a reflection of the economic interests of publishers intent on capturing an emerging working-class readership in the United States during the Industrial Revolution, and in Allan's United

Maud Beelman is a great interview, and a fine example of a journalist wrestling with what all of this change means, at the end of the day. Beelman is a deputy managing editor at *The Dallas Morning News*, where she directs a team of investigative and special projects reporters on major long-term news stories.

Beelman—who, as the founding director of the International Consortium of Investigative Journalists at the Center for Public Integrity in Washington, DC, won a George Polk, an Investigative Reporters and Editors, and a Society of Professional Journalists' award for investigative reporting—also spent 14 years reporting for the Associated Press in the United States and abroad. She's covered German unification, reported from Iran and Iraq on the aftermath of the first Gulf War and spent five years covering the wars in the former Yugoslavia. In short, she's a lifer—a journalist who has worked throughout all of the changes we are discussing in this book.

In a 2010 series for the *Morning News*, "First, Do No Harm," the newspaper demonstrated its embrace of all that is new in the delivery of journalism, while also demonstrating the craft itself, strengthened, perhaps, but otherwise unchanged by technology.

The story focused on a pair of venerable Dallas institutions: the University of Texas Southwestern Medical Center and Parkland Memorial Hospital. A renowned medical campus long known for world-class research and residency programs that have turned out generations of excellent doctors, Parkland is the main training ground for the school's new doctors. As a public hospital and major trauma center, it is also a safety net for the region's most vulnerable patients. In other words, it's a sacred cow, and a pretty important one, too.

The *Morning News* stories began as so many great journalistic projects do—with a tip from a source, pointing reporters to a lawsuit, from a whistleblower inside the hospital system upset with what he was experiencing.

"Fifteen stories later, we found a system that for decades had deceived virtually all of its patients, put many at risk and, by the hospital's own estimate, seriously and often needlessly harmed on average two people a day," Beelman said.

The "stuff" of the investigation came from the lifeblood of journalism: sources and records. Reporters obtained internal records from the two institutions, sworn testimony by current and former employees and records stemming from federal inquiries. The documents led the reporters to people—patients harmed by loosely supervised residents and what the newspaper described as "a class-based culture of care."

Among the stories' findings:

- Most of the patient care at Parkland was delivered by doctors in training—first-year interns and other residents. Some patient care was even handled by students who had not yet graduated from medical school.
- Patients were harmed during surgeries by resident physicians, including a young mother whose common bile duct was severed during a gallbladder operation and a former Parkland employee who eventually had her leg amputated after knee-replacement and post-surgical care provided, in part, by medical students.

It's a heavy-hitting, serious piece of journalism. Was it altered at all by the digital arena? Sure it was. Beelman said the entire package was produced with a Web-first mentality, which affected everything from the way the stories were approached to the deadlines to story length.

"We did not handle this as a traditional investigation," Beelman said. "Before the Internet, we would have done the research, then the reporting, then the writing, and then we would have dropped a huge Sunday piece on people's doorsteps," she said.

Instead, the *Morning News'* approach was to continually research, report, and when ready, write—then publish online and in print.

"The Web places a certain discipline on you," she said. "We knew we had to publish bite-sized pieces of this stuff, and we knew we needed video and accompanying documents online as the stories broke on print. So rather than wait for the whole package to go into one giant 'poodle killer,' as we always called those massive Sunday papers, we saw it evolve into this continual process of newsgathering."

THINK ABOUT IT: What are the downsides to reporting a story like this in small pieces as details emerge? Compare this approach to live television broadcasts of breaking news events. Does the information seem disjointed at times? What are the upsides to this approach? Do lengthy print versions of stories like this still matter? How?

Kingdom. To capture that mass market, both the "penny press" of the United States and the "pauper press" in the United Kingdom worked to reach the maximum number of readers. This led to the evolution of a press dedicated to notions of objectivity, which we'll turn to in greater detail later.

Many of the ways in which the American media landscape formed are in tension with each other. Capitalism has played a role in American journalism since its founding days, and much of what is laudable about capitalism supports democratic values: democracies tend to value openness, transparency of information and unrestrained discussion. On the other hand, when markets become an end in themselves, the technologies we hail as revolutionary can just as easily serve to monopolize information. In this revolutionary period, just like the others preceding it, decisions made about news systems will have much to say about journalism's future.

All this focus on the distribution model clouds the focus on what's really at the heart of this discussion. As we have discussed, journalism's core mission is informing the citizens in a democracy.

3.3 THE VIEW FROM THE PROS: WHO IS YOUR JOURNALISM FOR?

Let's think about that question on multiple levels. Why, and for whom, are you a journalist? To whom is your publication directed? For whom did you cover today's news event?

It's not for yourself, not for your colleagues, and not for your sources. It's for the audience. The community. The readers, viewers, listeners and users.

On the surface, that's no problem. Journalists tend to have a strong service ethic. Many would say they got into the business to make their communities, and democracies, better by providing needed information. If we're here to serve a need, it follows that we must identify a community's needs and have a sense of whether we're really meeting them. That requires the news processes and products to be audience-focused.

And today's audience is changing rapidly.

The days of news as a one-way broadcast are ending. Many people get their news not by tuning in to a specific channel, publication or website. Instead, the news comes to them, in e-mail and RSS feeds, in sound bites and channel surfing, and on social platforms such as Facebook, Twitter and YouTube. They consume snippets of information all day, in many locations and on multiple devices. In addition, they're often creating their own media, and documenting their own lives and stories. Forward-thinking journalists are finding new ways to be part of a rapidly changing, increasingly crowded media landscape.

The role of journalists is fundamentally shifting. We're not the only providers of information. Instead, we need to focus on being credible, authoritative voices in a noisy world. We need to figure out what we offer that no one else can, and make sure we're providing that service or content in a way that respects readers' habits and time. We need to harness the wisdom and power of the crowd, respecting how the community can contribute to telling its own story.

And we need to accept that, rather than deciding what information users have access to, we're instead helping them decide what to pay attention to.

One way we can do that is by amplifying other voices, not just promoting our own. Some news organizations are forming robust partnerships with local bloggers. Rather than assuming all other media are competitors, they're teaming up to cover stories. Their extensive linking back and forth leads to more audience for all involved.

Knowing that users' attention is what we (and advertisers) seek, we need to have the audience firmly in mind when we decide how, when and where to share our content. It's no longer enough to publish a story (regardless of platform or media type) and hope the audience finds it. Journalists have an obligation to identify the people who most want and need their content and make an effort to take the content to them.

When the staff of *Voice of San Diego* covered the story of a refugee who was deaf and unable to speak, they were shedding light on issues and problems they felt deserved attention. Rather than simply posting the story and moving on, they actively sought out audience, taking the links to the parts of the community they thought most needed the content. For the package to do the most good, it needed to be seen by those who could effect change.

So let's ask again: Who is your journalism for?

Journalism can't be just about the product—the *"what"* of the 5 Ws. *Who* is already talking about what you're covering? Can you take your information to that conversation, making it richer and more contextual? Can you picture *where* and *when* what you're providing will be most useful? Have you shown *why* and *how* it's relevant?

Journalists are great at the craft of storytelling and information providing. But without incorporating a focus on audience, we'll find ourselves talking to an empty room.

That's the real meaning of "social media." It's not about Twitter or Facebook. The news has always been social.

Clipping out an article and mailing it to a family member is a social act. If we recognize that people create and share media all day, how are we encouraging them to make our content and products part of their naturally social lives? And how can we best invite them to share their content with us, collaborating with us to tell the stories of their communities?

Journalists have long trusted their gut feelings about what news consumers want to read, view or listen to. But in the world of online media, we can know what people are reading. Not only that, we can know how far into the video users are watching, what time of day they like what kind of content, what search terms brought them to us, what kind of technology they're using—all information that will help us provide content they're likely to respond to.

We have the opportunity, in other words, to structure our time and resources to best cover the topics and stories our news consumers have shown us they most value. We have the ability to know what information needs we're trying to serve, and how well we're doing it.

We have a chance to adapt in exciting ways—to create a journalism that is truly focused on its audience. As we do that, we're faced with some key questions.

THINK ABOUT IT:

How do we preserve the journalism we find most fundamentally important while also responding to audience desires?

How can our storytelling be responsive to actual, demonstrated community information needs?

How do we make sure the work we're doing reaches the people who most want and need it?

And if a journalism tree falls in a forest and no one consumes it, does it do any good?

———————

Joy Mayer is an associate professor at the Missouri School of Journalism. She spent a year as a fellow at the Reynolds Journalism Institute studying audience engagement in journalism.

That has not changed, and will not change, no matter how quickly the wheels of modern technology spin. And it is easy to lose sight of that, with so much change afoot. That change, however wrenching and disruptive, is still external, process-oriented change—change to the way in which journalism is made in terms of the parts, the process even, but not the fundamentals.

Let us ponder the scope and breadth of the changes transforming journalism, then return to these fundamentals.

Until the turn of the century, news companies found the Internet a sci-fi novelty, a hobby for geeks but hardly worthy of serious journalistic attention. News executives felt that online content cannibalized the print editions of their newspapers and magazines, and television saw no potential for the new medium.

That attitude changed over time, and most news companies began posting content, first in an experimental, on-again, off-again way, then quite seriously, building online news staffs and launching stand-alone websites. The content began to flow online, and it was all-free, all-the-time—an oft-regretted decision by the industry, as we'll discuss in Chapter 5.

As audiences moved to the Internet for their news consumption, the industries that produce news—newspapers, magazines, radio and TV stations and a small band of newly emergent online-only properties—moved with them, although much more slowly and clumsily than the average teenager with a laptop.

Today we see a wild mix of models as news companies begin to revisit the decision to give away all their content, even as a seemingly endless stream of entrants start producing news online. Even though the Web contributes less than 9 percent of total newspaper advertising, and 5 percent of consumer magazine revenue, the argument over its centrality to journalism's future has concluded: get online or get lost.

Want a sign of just how fast things are changing? In a 2011 column on *New York Times* journalists' use of Twitter, public editor Arthur Brisbane recounted this exchange with the great Nicholas Kristof, one of the world's finest reporters:

> Nicholas Kristof, the Op-Ed columnist (4,242 tweets, 1,036,906 followers), tweeted, blogged and wrote columns inexhaustibly from various hot spots in the Middle East after the revolutions there began. Now, he said, he is planning a possible trip to Mauritania and has used Twitter to query his million-man follower group in search of expertise on the country—with good results.

He has used it also for something that blogs and columns just aren't appropriate for, he said: publishing a hunch.

"On Twitter in Libya, I tweeted something to the effect that I think people are a little too optimistic," he said. "That proved to be a useful caution. I didn't put it in my column. It didn't fit; I didn't have any evidence for it."

Is Twitter appropriate for "publishing a hunch?" Is any medium? Why is the relevance, the verification of information posted on a medium like Twitter somehow subject to a lower standard of proof, and should it be?

A return to Kovach and Rosenstiel seems a fitting way to conclude this chapter, for a reading of *The Elements of Journalism* certainly lends clarity to all this focus on technology.

Journalism that begins with an obligation to truth seeking, and whose first loyalty is citizens, they write, depends on an environment in which verification is "the essence" of journalism. Think about that a moment: If we start with the proposition that journalism begins at the moment of verification, what does that tell us about Twitter? Well, that's a tool for disseminating information once it's verified, and not as some high-tech shortcut for throwing stuff at the wall to see if it sticks.

And yet we see journalists trying to walk back information they've reported all the time. Instantaneous outlets demand greater emphasis on verification than ever before, not less. With information so free, it's never been more important for journalists to stake out the factual ground, to add meaning and context through their work, and to call attention to the best work of others. Today's journalist plays many roles— part reporter, editor or designer, part curator, part social networker, part thought leader. All of those roles can get confusing, but in the midst of all of these, two simple rules from Kovach and Rosenstiel must remain inviolable:

DISCUSSION QUESTIONS

What pressures might journalists have to use Twitter and other media platforms in the same way the general public does? If many people are reporting a rumor, what's wrong with retweeting it? Why should journalists be held to a higher standard?

1. Journalists always verify everything before reporting.
2. Journalists must remain fiercely independent.

To which we add:

3. Journalists must demonstrate their loyalty to citizens by (a) remaining committed to truth-telling and (b) exhibiting a commitment to elevating the discourse.

Much, much more about this as we progress, but for now, it's enough to note that if journalists fulfilled those missions, journalism would come much closer to serving its democratic mission.

Each remains central to journalism connected to democracy building. Each is core to the mission of helping a society govern itself. Each is being buffeted by changes to the form and function of newsgathering.

Chapter Three Review

Chapter Summary

Suggested Activities

Read More

▶ CHAPTER SUMMARY

The best journalists have always kept an open mind and embraced the newest techniques for gathering and presenting information. Today's journalist has more tools at her disposal than ever before. The gatekeeper model of journalism—that once-proud notion of the editor as arbiter of what's news—is long gone. The gatekeeper has yielded to the engagement editor, the digital curator, and the future of journalism looks a lot more conversational these days.

▶ SUGGESTED ACTIVITIES

1. When the Pulitzer committee awarded *The Tuscaloosa News* the 2012 prize for breaking news coverage of a devastating local tornado, it cited the paper's social media efforts as a factor in its decision. Read the Twitter feed submitted as part of the entry (www.pulitzer.org/files/2012/breaking_news_reporting/08tuscaloosa.pdf; note, you must read from the bottom up to see the story in correct chronological order). How does this type of reporting differ from more traditional reporting? How is it the same? Are the news values similar in this environment? Does this type of reporting enhance or limit our emotional connection to the news? Are the journalists more part of the story than they are in traditional print coverage?

2. Pick a news story that interests you and either bring it to class or keep it for homework (if this activity is an at-home assignment). Analyze the story for the presence of the seven news values (timeliness, impact, currency, conflict, novelty/emotion, prominence and proximity). Mark the words or phrases that suggest that these news values are at play in the story. Next, identify the dominant news value in the story (the main reason why the story is news). You can share your results with the class (in-class option) or bring a brief written summary of your analysis to class (homework option).

3. Invite a local journalist to class (or Skype with a journalist from another community) to talk about how he or she live tweets a breaking news event. What information should be included? What writing style is used? What consideration is given to the audience in writing these updates? How does he or she do the traditional parts of the job (interviewing and taking notes) while still having time to tweet? If a journalist is not available, you likely can find a journalist on twitter at virtually any point of the day live tweeting from an event. Follow that feed for a few minutes. Then discuss with the rest of your class the information included, the writing style and whether the journalist is considering his or her followers while posting.

4. Watch Jon Stewart's take on CNN's error in reporting the June 2012 Supreme Court decision on the Obama health care plan. (http://www.thedailyshow.com/watch/thu-june-28-2012/cnn---fox-news-report-on-the-obamacare-ruling). How might the rush to be first have played a part in this error? Why did it take CNN so long to correct the information (compared with Fox)? What are the implications for the credibility of the network? CNN issued an apology, saying: "CNN regrets that it didn't wait to report out the full and complete opinion regarding the mandate. We made a correction within a few minutes and apologize for the error." But that apology didn't stop the harsh criticism leveled by Stewart, other media outlets and the general public. Some have asserted that this error will become as well known as the "Dewey Beats Truman" headline.

5. Replicate the "Cover it Live" real-time reporting experience by covering a television event live on Twitter. Watch a television program (a football game, a speech, even a guest on a late-night talk show) and begin to "cover" the event. Create a hashtag and post at least three tweets during the event. What news values did you emphasize in this reporting? What writing style did you use? What thought was given to the audience? Reflect on your experience in a 400-word discussion post on what works well and what doesn't when covering an event with Twitter.

▶ **READ MORE**

Stuart Allan, *News Culture*, Berkshire, England: Open University Press, 2010.

Adam Baron and Richard Spencer, "Al-Qaeda Kills Nearly 100 Soldiers in Yemen Attack," *Telegraph*, May 21, 2012. www.telegraph.co.uk/news/worldnews/middleeast/yemen/9280543/Al-Qaeda-kills-nearly-100-soldiers-in-Yemen-attack.html.

Daniel J. Boorstin, *The Image: A Guide to Pseudo-Events in America*, New York: Vintage Books, 1987.

Arthur Brisbane, "A Cocktail Party With Readers," *New York Times*, March 12, 2011. www.nytimes.com/2011/03/13/opinion/13pubed.html?_r=1.

British Broadcasting Corporation, "'Al-Qaeda Attack' on Yemen Army Parade Causes Carnage," May 21, 2012 broadcast. www.bbc.co.uk/news/world-middle-east-18142695.

Reuters, "Suicide bomber kills 90 in Yemen, al Qaeda vows more attacks," May 21, 2012. http://www.reuters.com/article/2012/05/21/us-yemen-suicide bomb-deathtoll-idUSBRE84K0O720120521.

"The Changing Newsroom: What is Being Gained and What is Being Lost in America's Daily Newspapers?" www.journalism.org/files/PEJ-The%20Changing%20Newspaper%20Newsroom%20FINAL%20DRAFT-NOEMBARGO-PDF.pdf.

4

Who Pays for Journalism?

Back in 2008, the *Orlando Sentinel*'s new owner, Sam Zell, paid a visit to the newspaper. Zell had made his billions in real estate and decided to enter the world of media by acquiring the Tribune Company—publisher of the *Chicago Tribune* and *Los Angeles Times* newspapers, in addition to the *Sentinel* and other media properties—in a deal that saddled the company with a ton of debt and eventually forced it into bankruptcy. Getting into the newspaper business in 2008, just as an historic recession and wave of technological change were creating havoc with newspapers' viability as a business, took some serious guts and/or a healthy ego. Zell had both, along with a very particular vision about how journalism and business mix.

In his remarks to the *Sentinel* staff assembled in the newsroom, Zell talked about innovation and giving readers what they want, which all seemed fine until one of the journalists in the room, photographer Sara Fajardo, asked about how, you know, *journalism* might fit into this plan.

Things got a bit awkward.

Zell's response: "I want to make enough money so that I can afford you. You need to in effect help me by being a journalist that focuses on what our readers want that generates more revenue."

When Fajardo dared to point out that what people want and what they need might be pretty different—people might like stories about puppies more than, say, the Iraq war—Zell called that suggestion "journalistic arrogance" and finished off the cringeworthy encounter by uttering an obscenity at Fajardo, who shook her head and walked away.

FIGURE 4.1 The Comcast Center building, which houses the headquarters of Comcast Corp., stands in Philadelphia, Pennsylvania. On Thursday, December 3, 2009 Comcast Corp., the largest U.S. cable-television operator, agreed to form a $37 billion joint venture combining General Electric Co.'s NBC Universal with its own media assets, strengthening a push into programming.
Bradley C. Bower/Bloomberg via Getty Images

Just another day at the office, right? Thankfully, no. But while Zell's obscenity made this incident a minor YouTube sensation, it's the back and forth between Zell and Fajardo that is of key interest to us. Their exchange is an excellent illustration of a fundamental tension in American journalism: the pull of profit in one direction and of public service in the other. In a commercial media system, those interests compete more often than they complement each other, so finding the balance between them (if there is one) is pretty tricky. Look at Zell's quote again. He is putting profit-making ahead of public service, operating on the logical premise that without money, a news organization wouldn't have the means to perform public service anyway. Fajardo, meanwhile, is rightly concerned that the profit-making motive will take precedence over and even get in the way of the public service mission of journalism. What Zell saw as arrogance, Fajardo saw as duty.

Who's right? They both are. That's what we're going to explore in this chapter: Who pays for journalism and what are the implications of paying for it that way? The tension between profit and public service isn't new, but the amount of tension on the rope has perhaps never been greater than it is now. The Zell incident illustrates that and also offers a great example of how a media that enjoys so much freedom from government intrusion is not all that free when one considers the demands that profit-making imposes on it.

▶ "THIS NEWS IS BROUGHT TO YOU BY": THE COMMERCIAL MEDIA

So, let's begin at the beginning. The American media system is a commercial one, which means that mass communication is conducted by and through businesses that are owned by individuals, families, or groups of people, perhaps even millions of them (through stocks and mutual funds). Maybe it seems a little simplistic to you to begin at such a basic level. The media are businesses—big surprise. What else would they be? Well, look around the world, and you'll get all kinds of answers. The point is that a commercial media is neither natural nor inevitable. It's also worth noting that there are different types of businesses.

Newspapers got their start as businesses mostly because they were one of many products or services that someone running a printing business offered. This was before the development of reporting and journalism as we

**TABLE 4.1
Summary of
Media Models**

	Market model	*Public sphere model*
How are media conceptualized?	Private companies selling products	Public resources serving the public
What is the primary purpose of the media?	Generate profits for owners and stockholders	Promote active citizenship via information, education and social integration
How are audiences addressed?	As consumers	As citizens
What are the media encouraging people to do?	Enjoy themselves, view ads and buy products	Learn about their world and be active citizens
What is in the public interest?	Whatever is popular	Diverse, substantive and innovative content, even if not always popular
What is the role of diversity and innovation?	Innovation can be a threat to profitable, standardized formulas. Diversity can be a strategy for reaching new niche markets	Innovation is central to engaging citizens. Diversity is central to media's mission of representing the range of the public's views and tastes
How is regulation perceived?	Mostly seen as interfering with market processes	Useful tool in protecting the public interest
To whom are media ultimately accountable?	Owners and shareholders	The public and government representatives
How is success measured?	Profits	Serving the public interest

Source: David Croteau and William Hoynes, *The Business of Media: Corporate Media and the Public Interest,* Pine Forge Press, 2001, p. 37.

know it today. As for broadcasting, consider our friends and former colonial rulers in the United Kingdom. In both the United States and the United Kingdom, the invention of radio was hailed as a great step forward in communication, but one that very quickly demonstrated the need for some sort of regulation to deal with all the battles over who got to use which frequency, etc. So the question was how to treat this new invention. Was it like the telegraph or telephone? How should frequencies be doled out? What sort of expectations could the government place on the folks who got a frequency? They were, after all, going to be using something everyone considered to be a public resource: the airwaves.

Almost immediately, the U.S. and British paths diverged. Both were (and are) democracies with capitalist economic systems. Both were considering what to do with radio at pretty much the same time. Debates in both countries centered on which structure—private or public control of media—would best serve the public interest. But in the United States, those favoring a market-based approach prevailed over those who wanted to keep this resource public, that is, more under government control. And in the United Kingdom, just the opposite happened: public (government) ownership and control of media won out over the private ownership, market approach.

Those approaches formulated in the early part of the 20th Century continued through the invention of television. The dawn of the Internet sparked another "what is it"? debate, with some people arguing that it makes the most sense to treat the Internet, regulation-wise, like the telephone, and others arguing it bears more resemblance to broadcasting or cable television, and still others saying it's a whole new thing and ought to be treated as such. But let's not get bogged down in that, at least not yet. We first need to think about the advantages and disadvantages of each approach. Is more government involvement better or worse than more market control? Well, that's going to depend on some things, like how you view government and what it is you expect media to do.

In Chapter 1, you read about journalism's unique and important role in democracy and the ways in which that special role is thought to place certain responsibilities for public service on the press. You might also remember that one of the things journalism needs to do what democracy requires of it is independence. The First Amendment to the U.S. Constitution guarantees press freedom from government intrusion. (You'll learn more about that in Chapter 6.) There's no guarantee in the Constitution or elsewhere, however, that other things won't inhibit press freedom. Does the need to make a profit sound like something that might constrain freedom? To be sure,

DISCUSSION QUESTIONS

Some say that profits and good journalism are constantly in conflict. Do you agree? Can they co-exist in the U.S. market-driven journalism structure?

any arrangement involves some sort of constraint. The question is what's the source of the constraint and what does it force or prevent journalism from doing?

In the United States, what we might call the "market" group was able to successfully argue that having the government in control of the media could threaten independence and that the government had no business interfering with or depriving individual entrepreneurs from creating a vibrant broadcasting industry. So unlike nations with significantly less press freedom, say North Korea, the government can't control the information people get. That's a big advantage however you slice it.

In the United Kingdom what we might call the "public sphere" group successfully argued that leaving mass communication (at least broadcasting) to market forces would not serve the public interest at all. The media would be so busy meeting the demands of business that it would be unable to focus on public service goals. In owning the media, the government could assure that it lives up to its public interest obligations. That's a huge advantage too.

And where does all of this leave us? Right back at the doorstep of the fundamental tension—the Zell/Fajardo exchange—again.

What's interesting to note here is that, in some sense, both "sides" in the radio debates ended up being right *and* wrong about the best structure for a media system in a democracy. The press in the U.S. media system manages to fulfill its public service mission at least some of the time, in spite of market demands to do otherwise. Meanwhile, the press in the British system likewise manages to fulfill its public service mission without a load of government interference. In saying that both were right and wrong, though, we risk oversimplifying the outcome. There is growing and sustained dissatisfaction with press performance in the United States, which is largely absent in Great Britain. And the dissatisfaction stems almost entirely from byproducts of a private ownership, market-oriented system: news that is focused on trivial matters that are entertaining and cheap to cover but do not provide citizens with needed information, and under- and mis-representation

THE BBC TRUST

On the BBC Trust's website, you'll find the six "public purposes" the BBC defined in its Royal Charter. They are:

1. Sustaining citizenship and civil society.

2. Promoting education and learning.

3. Stimulating creativity and cultural excellence.

4. Representing the UK, its nations, regions and communities.

5. Bringing the UK to the world and the world to the UK.

6. In promoting its other purposes, helping to deliver to the public the benefit of emerging communications technologies and services and, in addition, taking the leading role in the switchover to digital television.

Check out more information here: www.bbc.co.uk/bbctrust/governance/tools_we_use/public_purposes.html.

of certain groups in society. The journalism produced by the British Broadcasting Corporation (BBC), which now operates as a quasi-government trust, is of very high quality and exhibits fewer of these problems.

Let's examine the market approach more closely to see why it sometimes produces such undesirable results.

▶ WHO OWNS THE MEDIA?

Here's one thing you know from this chapter so far: In the United States, the media are (almost entirely) privately owned. In other countries around the world, the ownership picture is more mixed, involving government and private actors.

But let's take a step back briefly. People tend to talk about "the media" as though it's a single, monolithic thing. Every now and then, you might see a "don't trust the media" bumper sticker on a car; far more often, you hear people complaining about "the media" being biased or sensationalistic or immoral or whatever. But are all these people complaining about the same thing? Or are some referring to "Dateline NBC," while others are thinking

▶ **MEDIA OWNERSHIP:** Who owns the media—whether an individual, a corporation that issues stock, or the government—has a big impact on how the media operate, particularly the kind of content an outlet produces as well as expectations about how much profit (if any) the outlet is expected to make. The vast majority of media in the United States is commercially owned, meaning they are for-profit businesses owned by individuals or, more typically, corporations.

about "Family Guy" or something else? It's hard to say. The lines between news and entertainment aren't exactly neon yellow and blinking. But that's a problem for another day and another chapter.

For now, let's define "the media" as all the entities sending and receiving messages on a mass scale—the mass media. That includes television, radio, magazines and newspapers (the printed and online kind), websites, individual blogs, movies, books, etc. Even with just this list, you begin to see how complaining about "the media" doesn't make much sense, unless one really wants to argue that all media—whether books or blogs—are producing biased, sensationalistic and/or immoral garbage.

More useful for us is to define "*news* media," which may be what people who complain about "the media" have in mind anyway. "News media" would include any of those entities listed above that, on a mass scale, send and receive a particular kind of message: news. That definition helps narrow things down a bit, though you might still think that it doesn't make much sense to criticize a television newscast in the same way you would a magazine profile of a politician or commentary about the local school system on a blog. Point taken. And we'll get to that.

People who have complaints about products—the shirt shrank the first time you washed it, the package arrived damaged—might reasonably seek out the owner of the store or company to register their displeasure. So following that logic, where would people with complaints about the news media go? If I don't like something that appeared in my local newspaper, I can call the publisher, though he or she might not be the ultimate owner. What if I don't like what a correspondent on "20/20" had to say? It would be a little more difficult, but I could eventually track down the names and contact information for that correspondent's boss and maybe even the head of the news division at ABC, which broadcasts "20/20." But if I wanted to talk to the owner? I'd need to track down the number for The Walt Disney Company, which owns ABC, ESPN, a bunch of radio stations and book publishers, along with its film and theme park businesses. And if I really wanted to split hairs, I'd need to contact all the people—millions, maybe—who own stock in Disney.

In fact, just a handful of corporations—six at the time this book was published—own the vast majority of broadcasting, cable and book publishing companies in the United States, and a few newspaper chains, including the Tribune Company Sam Zell led into bankruptcy, own a good chunk of the nation's 1,400 newspapers. (See *Columbia Journalism Review*'s "Who Owns What" for details.) This situation when ownership rests in only a few hands is called concentration of ownership. Over the past few decades, ownership of mass media in the United States has become increasingly concentrated.

DISCUSSION QUESTIONS

Are media businesses owned by families more immune to market pressures than publically owned companies? How might their pressures be different than those companies who answer to shareholders?

▶ CONCENTRATION OF OWNERSHIP

From the owners' perspective, one of the main advantages of concentration of ownership is dealing with a relatively small number of competitors. Fewer competitors means it's easier to get a bigger piece of the pie. From the consumers' perspective, such reduced competition is one of the chief *dis*advantages of ownership concentration. Fewer competitors means there's little reason for companies to be innovative or keep prices low.

Concentration of ownership in the media industry also offers opportunities for horizontal and vertical integration—again, things that look good from the owners' perspective, but may have less than good outcomes from the consumer perspective. Horizontal integration describes the situation when a single large media corporation owns a number of different kinds of media products or outlets. Vertical integration describes the situation when a media corporation owns companies involved in different phases of the media production process—creating media products, distributing them, showing them, etc. A media corporation can be both horizontally and vertically integrated.

The Hearst Corporation, which owns newspapers, magazines, television and radio stations, cable channels, a book publisher and a number of websites, is a good example of horizontal integration. The arrangement allows Hearst to cross-promote its media products by, for example, using its A&E cable network to promote books published by Hearst, or to take content from *Cosmopolitan* magazine and turn it into a book. To remember that this

▶ **INTEGRATION:**
How the many businesses within a media conglomerate work together to create advantages within a market segment. Horizontal integration refers to a conglomerate owning a number of media outlets across the marketplace. Vertical integration refers to a conglomerate owning companies up and down the chain of production and distribution of media products. A media company can be horizontally integrated, vertically integrated, or both.

is the *horizontal* kind of integration, just think of all the media products as different boxes of cereal lined up on the same grocery store shelf. They are all cereal, but differ greatly in terms of who mostly eats them—say, All Bran for older people, Count Chocula for kids. If the same company owned both All Bran and Count Chocula, it might offer a coupon for Count Chocula on the All Bran box so that grandparents can stock up on the good stuff for when their grandkids visit. That would be a kind of cross-promotion (and a reason for grandkids everywhere to rejoice!).

Comcast Corporation's 2011 purchase of NBC Universal from General Electric offers a good example of how a corporation can increase its vertical integration. Comcast had been primarily in the distribution business, with its group of cable companies. Buying NBC means that Comcast is now in the creation/production and exhibition business too. It has all the steps on the ladder covered (a ladder is vertical, get it?), from creating a media product to selling it, which helps Comcast manage costs and compete. It also provides what economists call "economies of scale"—the cost advantages that a business obtains due to expansion. The bigger the potential market, the lower a producer's average cost per unit, so for media owners, bigger is better.

So what's the big deal about whether and which way a corporation is integrated? It's all about risk and responsiveness. Heavily integrated corporations have, in a very real sense, integrated themselves out of risk. Let's take an example from the world of entertainment. The Walt Disney Company, which is both horizontally and vertically integrated, is known for animated films. But for every *Toy Story 3* or *The Lion King* that break box office records, there's at least one *Mars Needs Moms* or *Treasure Planet*—movies that just plain bomb. Now, of course Disney would prefer that every Disney film perform at the level of *Toy Story 3*. But even when they don't, Disney still makes some money. How? Thanks to integration, Disney can run *Mars Needs Moms* on its cable channel and sell commercials to run during the show. It can distribute the film on DVD and reach an audience that maybe couldn't be bothered to go out to the movies. It can sell the soundtrack through its record company. Maybe it can even turn the story into a children's book published by Disney Publishing. Spreading the same content across a variety of Disney's media products and distribution channels means the risk of taking a loss on a bad movie is pretty small.

Not bad. Not bad at all. At least if you're Disney. There's a potential down-side to consider, though. That's where the responsiveness part comes in. If there's little to no risk involved in producing certain kinds of movies, then chances are you'll want to make lots and lots of those kinds of movies, right? What happens, though, when someone comes to you with an idea for a movie that hasn't really been done before or might appeal to a smaller audi-ence only? Your incentive to take the risk of trying something new and un-tested (people might hate it) or responding to the needs or desires of a less mass-sized audience (you might not be able to spread the content across all your different platforms and properties) would be pretty low indeed. That's one reason why, for all the volume of content pouring forth from the mass media faucet, there isn't as much variety as there could be. Not everyone gets what they want; not everyone's voice gets heard. That's a bit of a wrinkle in the law of supply and demand.

Now let's take this out of the entertainment context and back into journal-ism again. The same economic forces that encourage, if not compel, corpo-rations to create certain kinds of entertainment fare also encourage, if not compel, those same corporations to focus on certain types of news content.

FIGURE 4.2
Business concerns—from how much newsgathering equipment costs to how much money is in the travel budget—can have an impact on the practice of journalism.

Picsfive/ Shutterstock

What is tried and true? What is cheap to produce? What appeals to the widest possible audience, even if a somewhat smaller audience could benefit greatly from something else? Even if you are not particularly concerned about how those economic forces shape the variety of movies available at your local theater, you would be rightly concerned about the limitations they pose on your ability to get quality journalism from your local newspaper or television station.

To summarize, mass media owners are most responsive to the needs of the bottom line. They have to be. After all, they've got lots of shareholders who expect—demand—a return on their investment. This is one reason why we said at the beginning of this chapter that the government isn't the only, or even the most important, entity that can get in the way of journalism doing what it's supposed to do in a democracy. The commercial nature of the mass media industry can also get in the way.

This is not to say that profit and public service are mutually exclusive. Indeed, research shows that quality journalism sells just as well if not better than junky journalism. It's just that the pressure to do more with less, to cut corners to make shareholders happy, to focus on cheaper and lighter news rather than expensive and serious reporting, is always there. It's worth noting that in the beginning of days of television in the United States, the news was something networks offered to meet their public interest obligations. It wasn't expected to make a profit. When the news magazine program "60 Minutes" came along and demonstrated that news *could* make money, well, then, the news was *expected* to make money. It had to stand on its own without whatever cash the commercials from the entertainment shows might bring in. Once that happened, entertainment values began seeping more and more into the news, not just in television, but in print media too. Trouble is, it's often hard (or even just wrong) to make serious news, like war in Afghanistan or a tornado in Joplin, Missouri, entertaining.

There is yet another twist to this story of how the commercial media system encourages certain kinds of responsiveness—to shareholders, to the mass audience—over others. So far we've been talking about media "products" being sold to media "consumers." Turns out, even those terms take on different shapes and meanings in a commercial media system, with more implications for how journalism is practiced.

▶ THE DUAL-PRODUCT MODEL

Imagine you own a restaurant; let's say a seafood place. To operate such a restaurant, you need to develop a menu, design a nice dining room, equip a kitchen, purchase lots of fish and ingredients for tartar sauce, and hire chefs, servers, busboys and maybe a bartender or hostess. People come to your restaurant, order something delicious off your menu, receive excellent service, pay the bill—maybe even leave a hefty tip!—and go on their way. Who is who in this scenario is pretty clear: You are the merchant selling seafood and the experience of eating a nice meal in a restaurant. Your customers are the people who bought and ate the food and enjoyed that experience. With any luck, what the customers pay covers your costs to provide all that tartar sauce and service, plus leave a bit of profit for you.

Now think about the news business. If you own a cable channel, let's say CNN, you also have some designing and planning to do, equipment to buy and people to hire. You need people who can create video packages from anywhere in the world, who can do research, interview guests and deliver the news on the air clearly, and handle all the behind-the-scenes technology of sending content to and from satellites. You need cameras and computers—lots of them. You might even need body armor for the journalists reporting from war zones. At first glance, you might think that who is who in this scenario is just as clear as it was with the seafood restaurant. You are, in some sense, a merchant who sells the news and other interesting content via your channel. Your customers are the people who watch that programming. But where's the transaction, the exchange of money between merchant and customer? The person who orders a lobster dinner at your restaurant pays for the lobster dinner, right? But the people who watch your shows on CNN pay only indirectly, if at all—and what they pay doesn't begin to cover the costs for all that body armor, set design and editing software CNN needs to produce those shows.

So who pays? Well, advertisers do. Toyota and Walmart and Applebee's. Geico and Gatorade. They and a host of other companies pay loads of money to CNN to run commercials during all that programming. In the days when people watched only over-the-air broadcasting, commercial advertising made TV essentially "free" to viewers. All you needed was a television set (and an antenna!). With cable and satellite, people do pay for television—they pay for access to certain channels or packages of channels. Depending

FIGURE 4.3 Times Square is an icon of New York City and of bold and flashy advertising. Photo taken in September, 2009.

Luciano Mortula/ Shutterstock

on the channel, those payments mostly go to the cable and satellite companies, not the networks or channels producing the programs. So advertisers are still paying your television bill for you. Isn't that nice? Well, sure. We like free stuff as much as the next guy. But this model of media funding—the advertiser-supported model—has some trade-offs and downsides too.

Why does a company like McDonald's advertise? Lots of reasons. To tell customers and potential customers about new or seasonal menu items— is it McRib time yet?—and special promotions. To tell you why it thinks its combo meal is superior to a competitor's combo meal. To plant a seed in your mind about McDonald's so that the next time you're looking for a quick, hot breakfast on the road, you think of them first.

The bottom line, so to speak, is that McDonald's (and every other company that advertises) wants your attention. And they're willing to pay big money

4.1 THE VIEW FROM THE PROS: PUBLIC SERVICE NEWS

As traditional newsrooms have shrunk in recent years, non-profit news organizations such as the *St. Louis Beacon* have grown. Most are founded by journalists dedicated to public service over profit. But, as the saying goes: No margin, no mission. High quality reporting costs money. Creating sound business models and healthy revenue streams are among our most urgent challenges.

While building the financial engine to sustain our work, we must build in ethical principles to sustain its quality and credibility. Protecting the integrity of the reporting is paramount. "Always be drastically independent," Joseph Pulitzer said years ago, and he's still right.

But the bright lines that used to demarcate acceptable practices must be redrawn to fit new circumstances. Non-profit news organizations have different sources of funding than traditional media, different ways of engaging readers and different attitudes about partnering with outside organizations.

Take funding. Non-profits typically get most of it from individual donors, sponsors and foundations rather than advertisers. An ad rep's conversation with a prospect focuses on capacity to deliver eyeballs. Our conversations with funders focus on capacity to report news that matters and on why this is essential for creating a better St. Louis. Funders give because they support that mission. But most of them also have other personal, professional, financial or civic interests—interests that could raise questions about undue influence on the news coverage.

In the *Beacon*'s ethics policy and in conversations with funders, we emphasize that our most precious asset is the integrity of our reporting. It's the foundation that supports public trust. Our news coverage is not for sale, and that's what makes it valuable to support. To further allay suspicion, we disclose donors' names on our website, identify them in stories where they play a major role and take other steps to limit the potential for problems.

Take engagement. In the digital world, it's important to listen as well as talk. We welcome discussion of our news coverage and solicit advice about how to make it more compelling. We converse with readers not only through our website, but also on social media, through the Public Insight Network and in person at *Beacon* events.

But we draw a line between acceptable advice and unacceptable interference. Clearly, it would be unethical to promise favorable coverage—or any coverage, for that matter—to individuals or organizations that do not otherwise merit attention. Taking money to fund such coverage would be even worse, as would special attention to donors, board members and others with close ties. While welcoming discussion, we need to make news judgments independently.

Take partnerships. Competition still has its place, but in the new media ecosystem, collaboration with other organizations is often the best way to increase the reach and impact of our work. The *Beacon* has collaborated not only with other media organizations but also with civic-minded institutions such as the Missouri History Museum. We welcome the opportunity to learn from and work with others, but always maintain control over our work.

Based on experience with funders, engagement and partnerships, we've begun to redraw the bright lines that clarify ethical practices for a new era. Here are some key points:

- News judgments should be based on merit, not connections or finances.
- Funding should be transparent.
- Multiple revenue streams enhance independence.
- A broad spectrum of donors protects against undue influence by any particular interest.
- Funding for general operations and broad coverage topics raises fewer conflicts than funding for specific articles or projects.

Guidelines like these help journalists know what's right in a new age. Doing what's right still requires what it always did—fortitude and courage.

LEARN MORE: Visit the site of the *St. Louis Beacon*. Note the page that lists all current donors (www.stlbeacon.org/#!/page/current_donors) and the ethics policy (www.stlbeacon.org/#!/page/about_ethics). How else is the site different than one produced by a metropolitan daily? (You can compare the site with www.stltoday.com, the website of the *St. Louis Post-Dispatch*).

Margaret Wolf Freivogel is the editor of the *St. Louis Beacon.*

DISCUSSION QUESTIONS

How do you react to advertising on websites you visit? Do you find it an annoyance? Would you rather pay directly for the content or endure increasingly intrusive online advertising? Will the advertising model work to support media companies as they scale back their legacy products (newsprint, broadcasting)?

to try to get it. Did you catch that? Advertisers are paying for your attention. That means you—your eyeballs watching CNN—are a product too. That is the essence of the dual-product model. Media companies, like CNN, are really selling two products. The first is the programming, which is "sold" to viewers. The second is the viewers' attention, which is sold to advertisers. But in that model, only the advertisers really pay the bills.

▶ **DUAL-PRODUCT MODEL:** Media companies sell two products, not just one. The first product is the content, whether it's news, entertainment or whatever. It is sold to consumers. The second product is the attention of the audience reading, viewing or otherwise interacting with that content. This is the product sold to advertisers. Given that most of the money is made off the second product, the needs of advertisers can sometimes override the needs of consumers.

This model doesn't apply just to television. Consider the newspaper (the printed kind). Newspaper owners spend money to gather and distribute news, paying for reporters, computers, wire services, paper, delivery drivers, etc. But the amount of money people pay in subscriptions or at the newsstand doesn't even come close to covering all those production costs. Advertisers pay the lion's share. And they do it because they need to get their message out to customers. They need your attention.

Indeed, pretty much every kind of media in the United States follows this model. Sure, there are a few magazines, such as *Consumer Reports* and *Cook's Illustrated*, and a few public radio and television stations that don't run commercial advertising. But on the whole, the dual-product model reigns supreme.

Welcome to your life as a product. (And here you thought you were just a mere consumer and citizen . . .)

So, are both products in the dual-product model created equal? Not really. Given that viewers don't really pay CNN every time they tune in to watch, which product do you think is most important? The one that really pays the bills. This brings us back to the responsiveness issue we mentioned earlier. Because owners are inclined to be most responsive to the demands of shareholders, they also are inclined to be most responsive to the advertisers who help them meet those demands. That means the advertisers have quite a lot of say in the kinds of eyeballs they want to buy, which, in turn, influences the content produced to attract those eyeballs. This all sounds disgusting. How about a non-eyeball-related story?

This might just be urban legend, but the CEO of Bloomingdale's department store was once rumored to have told Rupert Murdoch, owner of the *New York Post*, a tabloid newspaper: "Your readers are our shoplifters."

Yes, that was intended as an insult. It was the CEO's way of saying that Bloomingdale's had no interest in advertising in the *Post* because no one Bloomingdale's wanted to reach was a reader of the *Post*. Those readers were, instead, the kind of people Bloomingdale's would be happy to keep far, far away from their stores.

Even if untrue, it's kind of a fun story and a useful way of explaining how the dual-product model might encourage news media organizations to cover certain kinds of news over others. Want to get the Bloomingdale's account? How about some nice stories on luxury vacations and the stock market? The Bloomingdale's demographic might not be as interested in a story about public housing. If that kind of thinking really takes hold—and we're exaggerating a little here to make the point—then some of the basic functions and obligations of journalism begin to erode. If there are problems in public housing, then the public probably needs to know about them, even if they'd rather read about Acapulco and the increase in Google's stock price.

> **DISCUSSION QUESTIONS**
>
> In a digital delivery environment, executives can easily track where audiences go for information and how long they stay there. Is this good or bad for the media business? For journalism? Can it be good for both?

▶ **CONCLUSION**

So now you know where Sam Zell was coming from when he made the claim that giving people what they want comes first and giving them what they need comes second. He was speaking as a businessman, not a public servant. He was taking the market approach to media. And you also know why at least one journalist, Sara Fajardo, was a little concerned to hear him say so. She was thinking about the content people need as more important than the entertaining stuff they often want. That's the public sphere approach.

When we talked about the debate over regulating radio earlier in this chapter, we also used those labels—"market" and "public sphere"—to refer to the different perspectives about whether the radio industry should be under private or public ownership. Indeed, those labels are a convenient way to compare and contrast two ways of thinking about media's purpose and the implications of taking one perspective or the other.

A similar debate arose in 2011, as one of the worst recessions in U.S. history and growing concerns about the budget deficit led to a number of proposals for spending cuts. Even though it represents just a tiny fraction of the federal budget, funding for public broadcasting (the Corporation for Public Broadcasting and National Public Radio) was at the top of some people's lists to be cut. Why? Because some people believe the government has no business paying for something that, they argue, the market can provide more efficiently. Those defending public media from cuts, though, argued that leaving all media to the whim of the market virtually ensures that certain kinds of important programming will disappear. Profits, they argue, aren't the only or best way to measure the success of media. The quality of the content and how well it serves the overall public interest is. As we write this book, no final funding decision has been made. And in some sense, this is exactly the kind of battle that will arise again and again, as the United States continually tries to square its democratic needs with its commercial media system.

Chapter Four Review

Chapter Summary

Suggested Activities

Read More

▶ **CHAPTER SUMMARY**

The economic structure of mass media can and does shape how journalism is practiced. While a commercial media, such as that in the United States, enjoys freedom from government control, it faces other pressures on its performance from the requirement to make profits and satisfy (sometimes numerous and fickle) owners. How the Internet is presenting some challenges to traditional economic formulas, but also might make worse some of the constraints on media's ability to produce quality news, is the subject of the next chapter.

▶ **SUGGESTED ACTIVITIES**

1. Pick two or three local news outlets in your region (a newspaper, a television station, a radio outlet). Find information about the ownership.

Are the outlets owned by families, chains, a non-profit group? What other entities does the company own? How easy is it for you (and the wider public) to find this information? How transparent is ownership? Can you find evidence of cross-promotion and content sharing across entities? The findings can be shared amongst the whole class or written up as a short report.

2. Read Ken Doctor's 2011 Neiman Journalism Lab blog post about media concentration (www.niemanlab.org/2011/07/the-newsonomics-of-u-s-media-concentration/). After reading this chapter, research if these trends have continued in recent years. Are we seeing "smart, digital-first roll-ups align with massive consolidation"? What evidence can you find as to whether Doctor's 2011 prediction was right or wrong? Share your findings in a class discussion or brief papers.

3. Invite the publisher of your local newspaper or the general manager of a local broadcast outlet to class to discuss issues raised in this chapter. What pressures does he or she feel from above to maximize profits? How do you balance that with the need to do quality journalism? Are there parts of the newsroom that are more profitable than others (for example, sports)? What are the implications in a digital delivery era when we can easily track which stories attract audiences? How do you balance what people need vs. what people want?

4. An alternative if you cannot connect with a local media executive is a video on the same issues. In 2005, the University of California, Santa Barbara, invited three of the nation's top editors to discuss current issues on a panel titled "Media Ownership, Media Bias: A Crisis in the Newsroom." C-Span recorded the two-hour session (www.c-spanvideo. org/program/MediaBias&showFullAbstract=1). Start about eight minutes into that video. Watch eight minutes (to about minute 16), where the editors comment on profits vs. public responsibility. Discuss the issues raised in this clip with the rest of your class—and how they complement the material presented in the chapter. For fun, watch the classic 2.5-minute clip on how to run a newspaper from Citizen Kane www. youtube.com/watch?v=tzhb3U2cONs).

5. Visit the interactive Stanford University history project on the spread of American newspapers throughout the United States (www.stanford.

edu/group/ruralwest/cgi-bin/drupal/visualizations/us_newspapers).
The site is fun to play with and to visualize the spread of newspapers
west as the country grew. Most pertinent to the issues in this chapter,
however, are the changes documented in the past 75 years. Draw up a
timeline starting in 1945 and then hit the next entry to read about these
developments. Pay close attention to the visuals. What can you learn?
What will the visual look like in 10 years? 20 years? Write a 350–500
word post on the class discussion board on this topic.

▶ **READ MORE**

Suzanne Kirchhoff, "The Newspaper Industry in Transition," Congressional Research Service, September 9, 2010, accessed June 21, 2012. www.fas.org/sgp/
crs/misc/R40700.pdf.

"Members Only: Two Cheers for High-Cost Subscription Journalism," *Columbia
Journalism Review*, March/April 2011, accessed June 21, 2012. www.cjr.org/
editorial/members_only_marchapril11.php.

Steve Waldman, "Information Needs of Communities: The Changing Media Landscape in a Broadband Age," Federal Communications Commission, July 2011,
accessed June 21, 2012. www.fcc.gov/info-needs-communities#read.

"Who Owns What," *Columbia Journalism Review*, accessed June 21, 2012. www.cjr.
org/resources/.

5

New Voices, New Models

Brent Gardner-Smith never meant to be a media owner. It's just worked out that way.

In fact, all Gardner-Smith ever wanted was to be an investigative reporter, and once he was, his goal was to keep that title. But a six-week furlough at his beloved *Aspen Times* brought the economic tsunami sweeping journalism right into his own backyard and began to focus his attention on how he might ensure that a local, independent source of watchdog reporting remained in Pitkin County and the communities of Aspen and Snowmass Village.

So, in 2010, Gardner-Smith managed to land an internship at ProPublica—the gold standard of non-profit journalism—through his master's program at the University of Missouri.

ProPublica captured headlines when it was established in 2007 with a $30 million initial commitment primarily from billion-aire banker Herb Sandler and his wife Marion. The ProPublica budget was structured at about $10 million a year over three years. Their goal: fill

DISCUSSION QUESTIONS

What are the risks to the role journalism plays in democracy when news organizations eliminate reporters devoted to investigative journalism? Can this role truly be filled by other journalists as they cover their beats or by non-profits working with the outlets to fill the gaps? Do shrinking numbers of investigative journalists make the press more susceptible to well-funded advocacy groups providing their own data as they make claims? Are media owners making a mistake when they choose to cut these jobs?

in some of the gaps left by the erosion of investigative journalism in daily newspapers by creating an institution freed from the profit pressures of corporate ownership.

That's Gardner-Smith's goal, too. But is such a large grant in a small, yet deep-pocketed town like Aspen a possibility? Would a local philanthropist give $3 million to hire 10 journalists for three years?

He's off to a strong start. Just four months after he returned to Aspen, Aspen Journalism secured a one-year, $50,000 start-up grant from a local community foundation. Gardner-Smith has formed a non-profit corporation, populated a board, applied for non-profit status, opened a bank account, secured an Internet connection in a small office near downtown, bought libel insurance, and leaned on his talented 20-something son to set up a WordPress.

"So now, pinch me, I'm the editor, executive director and sole employee of Aspen Journalism, which seeks to produce investigative journalism in the local public interest," he said.

Similar stories are unfolding across the country, as journalists determined to keep telling stories create new platforms for distributing news. Some follow the non-profit model, others are based on what is being called "hyperlocal" and still others are straight-ahead for-profit plays. The economic struggles of the traditional press are engendering more experimentation and innovation than ever before.

Four key trends in developing the "new news" seem to be gaining attention:

- ▶ payment for Web access to news;
- ▶ new funding models for journalism;
- ▶ responding to Web search trends to develop news content;
- ▶ new approaches to local news development.

From start-ups such as Voice of San Diego in 2005 and MinnPost in 2007 and the nationally ambitious rollout of ProPublica with a $10 million annual pledge from its creator, the billionaire banker Howard Sandler, to more recent additions such as *California Watch*, the *Texas Tribune* and the *St. Louis Beacon*, these new models are fostering a rebirth in local news coverage with an emphasis on engagement through the online channel.

While the so-called "legacy media" struggle to re-engineer themselves in the digital age, these models are worth examining. It's also worth taking a close look at one old-school media company, the Journal Register Co., which has embraced the revolution like no other media company, and has literally saved itself in the process.

To set the tone, look at what online journalism sage Clay Shirky said in a 2009 essay entitled "Newspapers and Thinking the Unthinkable":

> So who covers all that news if some significant fraction of the currently employed newspaper people lose their jobs?
>
> I don't know. Nobody knows. We're collectively living through 1500 (*a reference to the revolutionary period following Gutenberg's printing press*), when it's easier to see what's broken than what will replace it. The Internet turns forty this fall. Access by the general public is less than half that age. Web use, as a normal part of life for a majority of the developed world, is less than half that age. We just got here. Even the revolutionaries can't predict what will happen.

Right. Exactly right. But we can glean a bit of insight from looking at what's working, or even at what's not. In an age of total upheaval, everything is a lesson, a step forward.

Experimentation yields failure more often than success, of course, but that's not the lesson here. The lesson is that not trying is a sure ticket to obsolescence.

Let's take a look at just a fraction of what's going on out there in the world of new models and new voices for journalism.

◄ LEGACY MEDIA: Media products predating the Internet, typified by a dependence upon heterogeneous audiences, advertising income and one-way communication from sender to receiver.

Imagine if Walter Cronkite had Twitter. @mosttrustedmaninamerica: JFK killed in Dallas, gunman sought.

Or when the Berlin Wall fell.

@breakingnews: Berlin Wall falls; thousands dance in the streets.

There's still breaking news, all right. It just breaks quicker. Or at least it seems to from my perch as executive producer at WCNC NewsChannel 36 in Charlotte, NC.

The viewer used to have to wait until the 6 o'clock news to get what's happening. Their first exposure to news each day was in the morning reading the paper and then on the radio on the way to work. It was at the end of the day before our audience was sitting down in front of the television.

Today, most folks live in a three-screen environment— the television, the computer, and their mobile device—and not necessarily in that order.

You don't wait anymore. You can't. Because you will get beat. Big stories are broken on your station's website far before the newscast. The question of the day is asked on Facebook and the hot entertainment story hits your station's Twitter followers. The late breaking news is sent to your viewers through a text or e-mail alert. All of this happens hours before your normally scheduled newscasts.

And news does not just come from the reporters to the anchor desk. In fact, most of the time, that's the last stop.

The last 10–12 years, especially the last five, has seen an enormous transformation of not only how news is presented, but also how it gets to the viewer in the first place. Breaking news doesn't just come from the police scanner. Viewers call and e-mail it in. The first crew on the scene snaps a picture with their smartphone and e-mails it back to the station. That gets posted to the website, and a breaking news alert is e-mailed out to the viewers. It takes just seconds—and you have a long way to go until 6 o'clock.

The viewer will not wait until the evening news anymore. In a society where everything is "now" or "instant" and when the world is changing sometimes second by second, the information has to get out there right now. People are news hounds and they want the latest and most up-to-the-second facts immediately.

Tools such as Facebook, Twitter and Skype has made not only the news delivering process easier, but also has changed the newsgathering process as well.

It's an easy way to localize a national or international story. While working as the 10 p.m. producer at KTRK-TV in Houston during the 2010 earthquake in Haiti, we reached out to the community on Facebook and Twitter to tell us their stories. Sometimes, it's as easy as writing "do you know anyone affected by this event" and the responses flood in. Years ago, about the only hope you had to localize the story is to head to a restaurant from that culture or head to a neighborhood. Now, sometimes, the news simply comes to you. If there's breaking news, get on your station's Facebook page and write "have you heard about the explosion at First Street and First Avenue? Snap a picture and send it to us." So as your crews are going to the scene, you have "citizen journalists" who can help you report the news as well. I've found if you ask the viewer for help, they'll get it to you. This is the case, especially in severe weather situations. If you have 10,000 Facebook fans, then you essentially have thousands of crews in the field. We use it to our advantage.

Viewers want their voices heard. They want to speak out. If you ask their opinion, they'll get it to you. Facebook is the best resource available for immediate interaction and feedback both to and from the viewer. More people are on it than any other social media site around the world. It's very easy for someone who watches your station to see it, click it and send it. So you're ahead of the game.

Even though Twitter is seen by far fewer pairs of eyes than Facebook, it is still a valuable tool in the newsgathering process. It is a way to get quick information out instantly. It is often incredible to see all of the news coming in from around the world second by second. It is often a play-by-play of a situation or breaking news event and with various hashtags and retweeting, you can turn that into a good way to get the news from the field to the viewer.

Skype can get you to places where you don't need a massive satellite or live truck. You just need your laptop. In this "now" culture of information, facts and pictures, the viewer will forgive you if the picture isn't crystal clear, if your hair is messed up a little bit, or if you take a moment to say "as my photographer pans over." Most television viewers just want the news and if your sleeves are rolled up and you get a little dirty in the process, that's fine.

Some television news stories you learn about on Facebook, tweet about it while you're headed there and then Skype at the scene. Call that the social media trifecta.

I am sure you would never have heard Walter Cronkite say "if you have any images of what's happening, send us a Facebook message." The reality of television today, you have to be quick. But you have to be right. You have to double check all of the facts and information you receive from viewers, just like you would a source. Receiving news and tips immediately isn't a substitute for being accurate, complete and correct. If your viewer is helping you out, you owe that to them.

Adam Darsky is a nationally recognized, award-winning journalist who currently serves as an executive producer at WABC-TV in New York City. It's the most recent stop in his 15-plus year television career. Prior to that, he was the executive producer of newscasts at WCNC-TV in Charlotte, NC and the 10 p.m. news producer at powerhouse ABC affiliate KTRK-TV in his hometown of Houston, Texas. Adam has produced news at television stations in Tucson, Arizona, Savannah, Georgia and Sherman, Texas.

Adam received a First Place National Headliner Award in 2011 for best newscast. In 2009, Adam was awarded with an Emmy for News Producer of the Year in Texas.

▶ NEW FUNDING MODELS: NON-PROFIT JOURNALISM?

Gardner-Smith's Aspen Journalism finds itself one of many non-profit journalism shops that emerged in the aftermath of years of shrinking newsroom budgets, staff layoffs and outright closures.

Literally dozens of non-profit or break-even propositions have been launched in recent years, recession or not. They range from ProPublica, the Pulitzer Prize-winning non-profit with 34 reporters bankrolled by a multi-year, $10 million annual gift by a wealthy retired banker, to the *New Haven Independent*, a scrappy non-profit start-up launched by a 30-year news veteran with an annual budget of $575,000 and an editorial staff of nine and a keen eye on local news.

Across the country, the realization that many traditional news organizations today view investigative journalism as a luxury that can be put aside in tough economic times, and the vacuum created in communities large and small as newsrooms shrink, has ushered in a wave of non-profit news shops. In some markets, the non-profits are filling a critical gap in investigative reporting, which has grown even more intense since a 2005 survey by Arizona State University of the 100 largest U.S. daily newspapers showed that 37 percent had no full-time investigative reporters, a majority had two or fewer such reporters, and only 10 percent had four or more. Television networks and national magazines have similarly been shedding or shrinking investigative units. Moreover, at many media institutions, time and budget constraints are curbing the once significant ability of journalists not specifically designated "investigative" to do this kind of reporting in addition to handling their regular beats.

Non-profits have for the most part featured news being ignored by struggling metro media outlets. At the *New Haven Independent*, the journalism is intensely local. A "Cop of the Week" feature highlighting great police work is a staple and one of the most popular features on the site, and a typical day's coverage is the stuff of local journalism: local political races, crime coverage much more granular than its mainstream competition, and a host of interactive features aimed at engaging a lively, well-educated community.

ProPublica is the exception to the rule, really: an incredibly deep-pocketed organization with ample reporting staff and a national footprint.

Jennifer LaFleur, an experienced computer-assisted reporter with stints at newspapers—*The Dallas Morning News* and the *St. Louis Post-Dispatch* to name but a couple—went to work for ProPublica because she felt so strongly about filling the void in investigative reporting.

"ProPublica was founded to fill the gap in investigative reporting created as so many news organizations have cut as newsrooms have downsized," she says. "Investigative reporting is time-consuming and expensive and many organizations don't have the resources for it. We fill that gap, not only by doing our own stories, but by making our stories, data and other tools available to journalists around the country—for free."

LaFleur says that she has not once been told she does not have the resources to do a story. And she revels in the freedom to move quickly without a lot of red tape in her way.

"Because we're a smaller operation, we are more nimble," she said. "At some newspapers, getting a database online takes the approval of many and much more time. At ProPublica, I don't have to go through the layers of bureaucracy to get something done."

ProPublica is a start-up—an organic media organization formed in the digital age. So-called legacy media companies have had to do a lot more work to transform themselves—some have tried and failed, others moved too slowly and succumbed to economic reality. Others have found their footing, and not a moment too soon.

▶ JOURNAL REGISTER CO.: AN OLD MEDIA COMPANY PIVOTS

When, in 2009, the Journal Register Co. filed for Chapter 11 bankruptcy, it seemed like the latest tough luck story in U.S. media circles. And the company certainly seemed to fit the Internet-devours-legacy-media script: Journal Register, based in Yardley, PA, publishes 18 dailies and more than 350 multi-platform products, ranging from non-dailies to weeklies to magazines in six states, mostly in the East, including such venerable titles as the *New Haven Register* in Connecticut and the *Oakland Press* in Michigan. The linchpin of its digital strategy, *The Register Citizen*, is a small community daily dating back to 1874. Its print circulation had fallen from 21,000 in the late 1980s to 8,000 in 2010, making it an unlikely home for a digital renaissance.

> ### DISCUSSION QUESTIONS
>
> In recent years, we've been exposed to news reports of publications cutting back circulation and production days, journalists being laid off and sharp cuts in media operations. Why might news about shifts in the news industry be covered differently than these same shifts in other industries? Can journalists be objective in reporting this news? Do these stories take on more importance because journalists are covering their own industry?

When the company exited bankruptcy protection six months later, with owners that included banking giants JPMorgan Chase and Wells Fargo, it began a transformation that offers insight into the way forward for traditional media companies.

February 1, 2010, was CEO John Paton's first day on the job, a day that Jon Cooper, the vice president in charge of content, remembers very well.

"John came in, and he immediately went digital-first," he said. "Now, the allocation of resources will be about providing news and information on the platform of the audience's choosing. This was a signal change in the business."

Part of the transformation, Cooper said, was about the redistribution of staff. In Connecticut, all of the company's titles now report up to one editor.

"We took the old manufacturing model, in which everything went from a printing and distribution standpoint, and instead we take all the reporting

◀ **DIGITAL-FIRST:** An editorial strategy of serving their audience as quickly and as locally as possible, meaning that legacy media organizations reorder their publishing priorities to break news over digital media first.

resources from an entire region's assets and array them across media forms," Cooper said. "Our business has been defined as what we can deliver by truck—and that has dominated our thinking—but now we can use social networks to take a much deeper dive into what our audience is thinking about."

So, when *The Register Citizen* moved into a renovated factory space replete with glistening high-tech finery, it signaled a sea change in an unlikely place. The new space has a cafe, a public lounge and free Wi-Fi—all designed to let the public see *The Register Citizen* as its own property.

All printing and traditional non-news operations like circulation are being outsourced. *The Register Citizen* holds open newsroom meetings each weekday afternoon and streams them live on its website as reporters share their stories, followed by a live chat to viewers who ask questions and feed information to reporters. The company has held more than 3,200 training sessions to create the sort of cross-trained, digitally agile journalists such a workplace demands.

The early results have been promising: *The Register Citizen's* Web traffic is six times its print circulation, and the company's digital ad growth is twice as large as the industry's, as digital revenue has grown from almost zero to 11 percent of ad revenue in less than a year.

5.2 THE VIEW FROM THE PROS: DIGITAL FIRST

Many newspapers struggle with giving their websites as much attention as they give their print editions. Most papers' newsrooms still pulse to the rhythms of print production—writing and reporting during the day, editing at night—even though their websites demand 24/7 attention and are an increasingly important part of their businesses. One community newspaper, the *Columbia Missourian* in Columbia, MO, decided to try something different to break old habits. The fact that the *Missourian* is run by the Missouri School of Journalism and staffed by its students, working with professional editors, makes it an even more interesting place to experiment.

Like many newspapers, we've called ourselves "Web first" for a long time, but we knew we weren't, really, when it came to editing. The *Missourian's* production rolled along the factory assembling line from mid-afternoon to midnight. Meanwhile, the website came together sort of automagically, requiring minimal effort on the part of copy editors to select a fresh set of stories to highlight on the home page periodically. We were "Web first" in name only, and yet we saw the changes underway in the business of news and knew we had to evolve to become a digital newsroom.

We decided we needed a radical change.

First, we segregated all print production processes from the day-to-day operations of the newsroom. We set the print edition of the newspaper aside, and made it the vehicle for copy that had already been broken online. This changed our orientation entirely from one where the daily newspaper product ruled the discussion and the day's workflow to one in which the news—broken right then and there, digitally—dominated the day's work.

Most of our copy editors, most of the time, would have no involvement with the print product.

Instead, they'd become "interactive copy editors." They would focus on getting stories to our website quickly and accurately, on finding ways to increase reader engagement with our work online, and on making sure the website is always putting its best possible foot forward. The work of a copy editor would be just beginning when an article published. Interactive copy editors might work with Twitter or Facebook, link Google maps, do simple surveys, add text links and optimize headlines in addition to editing.

Interactive copy editors would also remake the home page and re-rank stories, have comment duties and correct errors. The *Missourian* also started an initiative called "Show Me the Errors" that allows readers to report errors in stories through a link that appears with each story on the Web.

A small team of editors and designers, working separately, would manage all the details of the print edition, from story selection to final proofing, piggybacking as much as possible on the work of the interactive copy desk. They—not the managing editor, metro editor or senior news editor—would effectively "own" the print edition.

Today, the *Missourian* has an interactive copy desk for the Web and a smaller print copy desk. The newsroom really is driven by the interactive side of the operation.

We even rearranged the furniture to make the interactive copy desk the focal point of the room and to push the print desk into an area by itself. That change created a center feature called "The ICE Box" (for Interactive Copy Editor), which sits next to "The Hub," where many of the newsroom decision makers sit.

We also rearranged the work schedules to distribute more copy editors throughout the day, with particular emphasis on early morning. The interactive desk is almost continuously staffed now throughout the day.

It has gone surprisingly well. We succeeded in resetting the rhythm of the whole newsroom.

We're no longer focused on the paper tomorrow—the print team worries about that for all of us. Instead we're occupying news editors and copy editors with the work of producing the website 18 hours a day every weekday.

Interactive copy editors are in charge of our social networks. They regularly promote our work on Twitter and Facebook, and respond to readers' feedback there.

Interactive copy editors also monitor the comment boards at the end of every article. They take down comments that violate our policies, and they jump in when the conversation demands a *Missourian* response. Copy editors even mediate conflicts among commenters and solicit comments on stories that ought to be sparking them but aren't.

Our website has improved tremendously and, with our interactively focused copy desk, we see room for much more improvement as we do more to leverage our connections with readers on social networks and find new ways to make stories more interactive online. Meanwhile, our designated print team has done a great job maintaining the print edition, and their exclusive focus on print has even improved the product in some ways. Like the interactive copy editors, the print editors' focus is no longer divided between two products, and they can give the print edition the full attention it deserves.

LEARN MORE: For another perspective on changes to copy editing for newsrooms, read this blog entry from Steve Buttry, director of community engagement and social media for the Journal Register Co. (http://stevebuttry.wordpress.com/2012/05/25/copy-editing-its-taught-me-a-lot-but-it-has-to-change/).

Nick Jungman is managing editor of the *Wichita Business Journal*. He spent two years as a visiting editor in the *Columbia Missourian* newsroom and as a visiting assistant professor in the Missouri School of Journalism. Before that, he was a reporter and editor for *The Wichita Eagle*, Kansas' largest newspaper, and its website, Kansas.com.

Under its post-bankruptcy CEO Paton, Journal Register has become a forward-thinking, innovative organization with a digital-enterprise management style. Paton and other company executives are the first to describe the community newsroom as a work in progress, and they promise many more tweaks in the years to come, but the results speak for themselves.

Much of these early efforts are organized around the company's Ben Franklin Project—an effort to put publishing back in the hands of the people by publishing a daily newspaper only using free, open source tools available on the Internet.

The other component of the Ben Franklin project is to involve audiences in story selection and in the content itself. People in Journal Register communities are encouraged to comment on news topics, to send in videos and links, and to interact with journalists as they develop editorial content. The goal? Turning local news coverage into facilitated community conversations.

The Journal Register Co., which in 2011 was purchased by a hedge fund and spun off into a new company, Digital First Media, that manages the news operations of Journal Register and Media General, has come full circle, from a failing legacy media company to a nimble digital player looking to emerge from a second bankruptcy on firm footing for the future.

▶ PAYWALLS: THE ANSWER? AN ANSWER?

▶ PAYWALL: A system that prevents Internet users from accessing webpage content without a paid subscription. "Hard" paywalls allow minimal to no access to content without subscription, while "soft" paywalls allow more flexibility in what users can view without subscribing.

The story is timeworn by now: Media companies came late to the Internet party, and its most enthusiastic early adopters kicked off the online journalism business model by giving away content even as Craigslist, Google and AutoTrader.com, to name but a few, cannibalized the classified business and placement ads that long had served as a financial rock for the news business. TV followed print media's lead, all with the unrealized promise that with traffic would come lucrative advertising dollars.

For a variety of reasons, that never quite worked out. The metrics for click-through ads never reached the predicted heights, and while media brands became a trusted source for online news, the market for online journalism has suffered mightily in the free content ecosystem.

Whether 2011 will be seen as the watershed year—the year that news sites began seriously experimenting with paid content online—remains to be seen. News sites launched a variety of different online paywall models in 2011, some with more success than others.

A host of media companies, including Dow Jones Local Media, the *Augusta* (GA) *Chronicle*, the *Concord Monitor*, and most famously, the New York Times Co., erected paywalls in some form of fashion in 2011.

Some of the earliest paywalls in the business offer a predictable tale: steep drops in traffic but unforeseen benefits, as discourse improves and a smaller base of paid online circulation replaces a much larger but unprofitable readership. At *Variety*, which put up a paywall in 2009, traffic on the magazine's site fell from 3.2 million impressions in December 2009 to 1.9 million in March 2010.

> ## DISCUSSION QUESTIONS
>
> What do you do when you encounter a paywall (or even a registration requirement) when you click into a site you've been referred to on Facebook, Twitter, Pinterest or e-mail to read a story? Will you register? Will you pay? Think about the types of content you would consider paying for online (typically entertainment content like music, movies, games and books). What would digital news have to offer you for you to make that leap to beyond the paywall?

Variety weathered the decline, and its numbers have stabilized. *Variety* President Neil Stiles told the eMedia Vitals blog:

> The number of unique visitors to *Variety* will decline, but the people who remain on the site are our core audience. These are ultimately the people we want to reach.
>
> (O'Regan, 2010)

So the theory of free content is yielding to the theory that a higher-quality audience will lead to higher engagement, and better response to online ads.

And despite the general assumption that charging for digital content will inevitably result in a drop in traffic, that's not always true—at least when news outlets adopt a more measured approach to their paywalls. The earliest paywalls—like *Newsday*'s way back in 2009—resulted in dramatic drops in traffic and, along with them, drops in digital advertising. *Newsday* saw traffic drop by more than half in the year after it launched its paywall.

It was more a moat than a paywall, however: For a while, the company was charging an eye-popping $260 annually for access unless you subscribed to its parent company Cablevision's high-speed Internet access, in which case you got to read *Newsday* for free (this plan has since been abandoned).

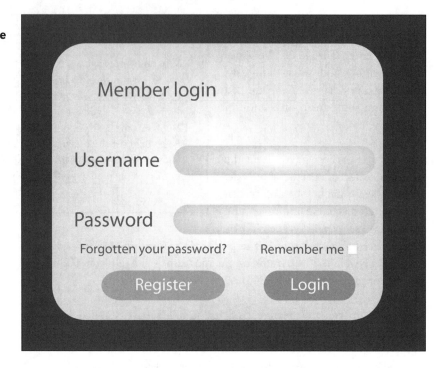

The moat gave way to a more charitable approach: the metered model approach, or "freemium" strategy, in which visitors can view the majority of website content for free, while unlimited access requires a weekly or monthly subscription. Metered paywalls are catching on—a critical access point for news widely available on the Web while producing at least some revenue. In fact, metered paywalls at the *Augusta* (GA) *Chronicle* and *Lubbock* (Texas) *Avalanche-Journal* both have seen traffic and page views increase, and other news outlets report similar good news.

Augusta's paywall is fairly typical: The newspaper charges $6.95 a month for a Web-only subscription, $2.95 a month for print subscribers to read online (in addition to the $16 per month cost of a seven-day subscription), and the first 10 articles are free each month.

The *New York Times'* website—which allows visitors 20 daily free visits before asking them to obtain a digital subscription—ensures that users that don't want to pay can return the following month, or even the next day, for more stories. This is essential to growing readership, as casual users continue to come back to the site.

It's a particularly low paywall, but that's a design feature, not a flaw. In other words, the *New York Times* thinks (and there is evidence to support this) that sharing content pretty freely brings them new readers who then will pay for digital content, not so much because they are forced to, but because they are encouraged to.

The *Times* allows anybody, anywhere, to read any article they like. If you follow a link to the *Times* from a blog or an aggregator, you'll never hit the paywall. It's an open-door, grown-up way of dealing with content and with payment, and it is built on the assumption that, as a Wired blogger so eloquently put it, "Paying for something you value, even when you don't need to, is a mark of a civilized society."

And it is working.

In the summer of 2011, the *Times* announced that its metered paywall ended the second quarter with more than one million digital subscribers. To be fair, most of those—about 750,000—are print subscribers who have taken advantage of the digital access offer. But that still means that the *Times* added a quarter of a million new, paid readers in a quarter!

Small potatoes, really, but the potential is exciting. And that's because the *Times*, and other news companies, now realize that the real currency of online news is engagement and sharing—the realm where the news meets the social network.

Then there's ProPublica, which we discussed earlier in the chapter. As a non-profit, they have taken the softest paid content approach, using a six-visit meter to ask for a donation. Different approaches to the same age-old problem of how to pay for journalism.

▶ HYPERLOCAL: COMING FULL CIRCLE

In the end, journalism online is witnessing a return to the small-town, local news flavor that many veterans remember as the origin of their career in the news business. Having lost the franchise on international and national news to the largest players, and having watched as news staffs shrank in the face of the economic recession and an eroding print business model, an increasing number of journalists are turning to so-called **hyperlocal** news—hyperlocal meaning it is intensely focused on a defined geographic niche, be it a neighborhood, a zip code or, in some cases, a city. Hyperlocal news most often is generated by a resident of that geographic area, and often is distributed through blogs and citizen-generated content is welcome.

▶ **HYPERLOCAL:**
A form of journalism marked by its intense focus on locality, community news defined by geography, often with a single-issue lens.

Some hyperlocal sites offer general interest community news; others are tightly focused on a single issue such as public schools, the environment or the police. Many are one-person operations, fueled by the passion of a single person, but a host of for-profit hyperlocal sites have emerged as well, with decidedly mixed early results.

In the Washington, DC, market, TBD.com earned early praise for its social media savvy and hyperlocal coverage, but its owner, Allbritton Communications—which has enjoyed much more success with its Politico newspaper and website—trimmed the site's staff after a six-month run. TBD.com now is a much smaller, stand-alone website focused on local entertainment and lifestyle features—a far cry from its origins as a full-scale hyperlocal site.

It's a cautionary tale about the difficulty of turning hyperlocal news into a sustainable advertising market: by getting so intensely local, it's hard to reach beyond local mom-and-pop advertisers to the larger retailers and car dealers that can pay the bills. Still, local online advertising—gift shops, plumbers, regional hospitals, car dealers—is expected to reach $15.9 billion this year, according to Borrell Associates, a market research firm, so it's a puzzle well worth solving.

The 400-pound gorilla in the hyperlocal market is Patch.com, a much more massive hyperlocal experiment with much deeper pockets. Internet giant AOL acquired Patch in 2009 and immediately announced plans to invest $50 million in constructing a national network of "Patchers," one-person bureaus dedicated to hyperlocal coverage in a network of affluent metro suburbs all over the country.

Patch has already set up sites in nearly 800 towns. By the end of 2011, it expected to be operating 1,000 Patch sites—each one with an editor and a team of freelance writers.

The good news? Patch has employed hundreds of journalists, each equipped with a laptop computer, digital camera, cellphone and police scanner. The journalists, which AOL calls local editors, generally earn $38,000 to $45,000 annually, and work from home. They are expected to publish up to five items daily—short articles, slide shows or video—in addition to overseeing freelance writers.

The coverage is uneven, but improving as Patch hones its editorial functions. Its sites are filled with the stuff of local journalism—police calls, fires, local governance, and a healthy dose of festival news, arts and entertainment and local schools coverage. Patchers are a snapshot of the do-it-all converged journalist: they are expected to write, shoot and edit, capture video and closely monitor analytics to look for editorial formulas that work.

5.3 THE VIEW FROM THE PROS: NICHE CONTENT

When Pete Scantlebury left his Atlanta home for journalism school, he certainly didn't think he'd be covering sports for a website for a living five years later.

Then again, he didn't really care who he was covering sports for—so long as he was covering sports. Scantlebury works for PowerMizzou.com—the online passion pit for diehard Missouri Tigers fans. PowerMizzou.com is a member of the Rivals Network, a collection of college sports sites from all over the country.

In many ways, Scantlebury's work life resembles that of the sports beat writer—he interviews players and coaches, covers practices and games, files feature stories on off days and is always, always looking for the next story.

The depth with which PowerMizzou.com covers the Tigers, though, means that Scantlebury spends far more time on any given subject that a beat writer would, most notably the recruiting of new talent to the Tiger football team.

"I'm on the phone just about all day, every day during December and January," he said, talking to high school coaches and college-bound seniors, trying to divine whether they'll attend one school or another.

This is red meat for PowerMizzou's slavishly devoted readers, who hang on every word as signing day approaches.

Unlike the beat writer, Scantlebury posts information as he gets it nailed down—sometimes three or four stories a day, with a minimum of two daily stories—as well as a number of replies to existing posts. His stories are self-edited—"that took some getting used to," he says—but the reader base lets him know if there are errors or holes pretty quickly.

That's another new reality of online journalism: Scantlebury spends the first part of every day "babysitting the board," as he calls it, checking on the discussion board and moderating comments that cross the line in terms of good taste or unfounded allegations.

Then he spends a few minutes every morning touching base with the audience and responding to some posts, something he says is critical to feeding the base and creating online community.

"These people know me, and in online terms, I know them," he said. "In terms of the audience, we are much more in touch and receptive to their ideas and suggestions."

When Scantlebury began in journalism school, his job didn't even exist. Today, he says it is an ideal fit for him.

"It's much more freedom than I would have envisioned coming out of school," Scantlebury said. "I'm originating the stories and writing them, and I'm ultimately responsible.

As far as the journalism is concerned, I am not doing one thing differently as far as the principles are concerned. I still have to stand behind every word."

THINK ABOUT IT: What is your dream job? Don't be limited by what exists now, as the example above shows us. Are the skills you are learning in college transferable to that job? What new skills might you need to hone? Are all of those learned in a classroom?

Peter Scantlebury is a college sports writer for PowerMizzou, a member of the Rivals.com network, where he serves as college football recruiting editor and assists in beat coverage of the University of Missouri football and men's basketball teams. Scantlebury graduated from the University of Missouri School of Journalism in 2008.

Patch is joined by a host of hyperlocal players, some large commercial players, others one-person start-ups. Together, they form a chaotic, disparate but fascinating area rife with experimentation and innovation.

For example, Internet innovator David Cohn's Spot.Us allows communities to pick and choose which stories to cover—and the community funds the work of the journalists.

Cohn founded Spot.Us in the fall of 2008 in San Francisco to test his business model, and formally launched the site in Los Angeles and Seattle in 2009 and 2010, respectively. The Spot.Us model is unique among the hyperlocal models because it allows users to donate money to fund specific stories through its website.

On Spot.Us, reporters pitch local and regional story ideas on topics such as problems with local transit systems, the local effects of the Mexican drug wars and gang issues in the Bay Area, to name but a few of the dozens of stories seeking funding at any given moment.

Once a story idea has met a predetermined funding goal through individual donations, a reporter researches, reports and then publishes the story on Spot.Us. Final news stories appear as print packages, video clips, audio

FIGURE 5.2 Widely available technologies like cellphones and smartphones **put the power of newsgathering in everyone's hands.** Here, a protestor at the G20 Summit in Toronto gathers images of riot police. Photo taken in June, 2010.

Arindambanerjee/ Shutterstock

pieces or a convergence of media. In some cases, a reporter may have partnered with a public media outlet, which will publish the story as well.

Instead of typical banner advertising seen on websites, Spot.Us allows companies to buy community-focused sponsorships, which allows them to conduct market research surveys of Spot.Us users. Users who complete surveys are rewarded with donation credits to put toward the story of their choice.

Spot.Us is breaking new ground in donor choice as well as donor transparency, as supporters can follow a story from its inception to publication. That deep engagement with community members on stories and issues they care about is where the real potential lies.

Part news organization, part distribution platform, Spot.Us ultimately fills a gap between journalists and funders, emerging as a viable source of crowd-funded reporting projects.

Note that all of these efforts seem to be changing what's valuable, and thus valued, in terms of media performance. In yesterday's world, news audiences were aggregated and sold to advertisers—we were essentially selling attention—literally, numbers of eyeballs on a single title—to advertisers.

Early online business models were all about "traffic"—clicks were the coin of the realm. Impressions are just another way of counting those eyeballs, though; the goal still was to create the largest, heterogeneous audience you could build for your site.

The fragmentation of the Internet, and the rise of social networks, gives the news media a new metric: engagement. As Alan D. Mutter said in a blogpost on the wildly entertaining Reflections of a Newsosaur: "large and undifferentiated audiences don't matter in the digital realm as much as ones that are homogeneous, engaged and readily targetable for advertisers."

He continued:

> In each of the last nine months through June 2011, the Newspaper Association of America has reported that the average visitor spends about 3.5 minutes per session on the industry's websites. By contrast, the average visit at Facebook in June, 2011, was 11.1 minutes, up 33.7% from 8.3 minutes in same month in the prior year, according to ComScore, which tracks statistics for both NAA and Facebook.

> Engagement is rising at Facebook because it has created a compelling place for people to get and give information about everything from what's in the news and what's on sale to the hottest new music and where the gang will meet for drinks after work.

> While newspapers can't possibly compete head-on with Facebook, they can play to the passions of their readers—and those they would hope o attract—by creating optimized online, mobile and social products across a wide variety of topics ranging from gardening to small business.
>
> (Mutter, 2011)

So we've moved from a goal of a mass audience to a goal of a carefully selected, highly engaged audience. No longer can we sell a huge market we know little about to advertisers merely craving eyeballs. That fundamental difference in terms of the goal of on-line journalism—from audience attraction to audience engagement—is more than just economic, however. It promises to reinvigorate the relationship between journalists and audience, a relationship that grew far too distant in the era of mass audience.

> ## DISCUSSION QUESTIONS
>
> In what ways might general news organizations, which have been aiming to serve large audiences for many years, work to build smaller but more deeply engaged audiences? Should core products be divided and given their own identity?

In *The Story So Far: What We Know About the Business of Digital Journalism,* the Tow Center for Digital Journalism at Columbia University offers a rich look at why big audiences are no longer the ultimate goal of journalism.

In a chapter entitled "Traffic Patterns: Why Big Audiences Aren't Always Profitable," the researchers break down the problem:

> At its most basic level, advertising is a numbers game. A news organization needs a certain number of readers or viewers, and the more it gets, the more ads it can sell and the more it can charge those advertisers. Users also spend varying amounts of time with the magazine, newspaper or broadcast, and the more time they spend, the more an advertiser values the audience.
>
> (Grueskin, Seave and Graves, p. 22)

So we can boil it all down to numbers—(1) numbers in terms of eyeballs and (2) numbers in terms of engagement, or time spent with the media product.

Digital platforms are great at the first part of the numbers game. New sites pull in millions of online readers, every day. The problem is, chasing eyeballs is an outdated way of thinking about audience.

Where we once thought of the product itself as the basis of revenue—that big stack of magazines waiting to be mailed, or that truckload of newspapers—in the digital world, consumption of media is the basis for revenue. Engagement itself has become the measuring stick for assigning value to content.

By chasing after large audiences rather than deeply engaged ones, news organizations are sacrificing advertising revenue. Publishers who have a

◀ **ENGAGEMENT:** The depth of the involvement that a news customer has with a media product. Engagement can be measured empirically or through anecdotal evidence.

"direct relationship with fans can push better contextual advertising"—that is, ads that relate directly to a user's habits and interests.

▶ **MONETIZATION:**
The process of converting something that once was free into a product that is sold.

It's an eye-opening study, a hopeful look at an industry comprised of a wild mix of start-ups and so-called legacy media, all attempting to figure out how to monetize digital content. The result of all of this activity is an emerging media ecosystem in which legacy media compete with an ever-evolving array of hybrids—some more distribution platform, others more content engine.

For ease of thinking, let's organize them into loose, fluid categories, subject to change daily:

1. *Aggregators and Curators (Platforms):* Think Flipboard, Pulse, Spot.Us, or even Facebook. Then there's Storify and TechMeme and Summify—curated aggregation platforms that allow you to summarize the entirety of a story in the social networks.
2. *Personality-fueled Blogs/Single-Issue Deep Dives*: (DeadSpin, Tech-Crunch, GigaOm, Talking Points Memo, BusinessInsider). These are brands that began with a borderline-obsessive dive into a single topic that then morphed outward.
3. *Disruptors:* Some of these are start-ups that were purchased by legacy media, such as Everyblock, Zite and @BreakingNews, but each began as an organic news company bent on delivering content in new ways—ways that changed the marketplace. Disruptors go about things in completely new ways, altering the landscape.

These new types of media companies are redefining what it means to be in the journalism business. In his book *Here Comes Everybody* (2009), Shirky offers three requirements for social action sites:

1. *Is there a plausible promise?* Why would anyone want to join? Is it a promise that will draw the crowd?
2. *Are the tools effective?* Do the site's tools facilitate collaboration and allow the community to easily come together? The tools must be easy enough for users of all technological levels to use the site in its intended purpose.
3. *Is there an acceptable bargain with the users?* What is expected of the user and are the returns to the user enough to make the user want to participate?

The emerging media platforms are working to address these three critical requirements, with varying levels of success. Some, like Spot.Us, are valuable not only for what they are accomplishing immediately, but also because they generate secondary levels of innovation and collaboration.

Cohn put it this way in a blog post:

> What we need right now is 10,000 journalism startups. Of these 9,000 will fail, 1,000 will find ways to sustain themselves for a brief period of time, 98 will find mediocre success and financial security and two will come out as new media equivalents to the *New York Times* . . . I don't know what that organization will look like or who it will be—but that's what we need and we face some serious challenges along the way.
> (Cohn, 2008)

The wide range of experimentation in this space offers tremendous hope for journalism's future. The stakes couldn't possibly be higher.

One last word from Shirky:

> Society doesn't need newspapers. What we need is journalism. For a century, the imperatives to strengthen journalism and to strengthen newspapers have been so tightly wound as to be indistinguishable. That's been a fine accident to have, but when that accident stops, as

FIGURE 5.3 The "Afghan Explorer," the semi-autonomous mobile robot being developed at the Massachusetts Institure of Technology's Media Lab in Cambridge, MA, can practice elements of journalistic reporting in hostile or off-limits environments. Enabled by global wireless technology, solar power and sophisticated computing, the Explorer is able to navigate both urban and rural terrains. Its unique combination of hardware and software allow it to gather video, image, sound, conduct two-way interviews, and interact with local populations, even in areas deemed off-limits by local and U.S. military authorities.

MIT Media Lab/Getty Images

it is stopping before our eyes, we're going to need lots of other ways to strengthen journalism instead.

When we shift our attention from "save newspapers" to "save society," the imperative changes from "preserve the current institutions" to "do whatever works." And what works today isn't the same as what used to work . . . Any experiment, though, designed to provide new models for journalism is going to be an improvement over hiding from the real, especially in a year when, for many papers, the unthinkable future is already in the past.

(Shirky, March 2009)

It's that critical.

Chapter Five Review

Chapter Summary

Suggested Activities

Read More

▶ CHAPTER SUMMARY

The field of journalism is experiencing transformative change ushered in by the digital age—change that offers both promise and peril for news organizations. The Internet has been an incredibly disruptive technology, but has also yielded an incredible array of innovative new models for doing journalism. Everything we thought we knew about the way journalism is created, distributed and paid for is being challenged, if not replaced, by other technologies that shrink time, space and speed to market. While the legacy media continue to struggle with the pace of change, hopeful signs emerge daily. It's an exciting if terrifying time to enter the business.

► **SUGGESTED ACTIVITIES**

1. If there is one thing the modern media economy has given us, it's a never-ending supply of brand-new media companies. Research and find a list of interesting media start-ups. Use the list to contact someone—an entrepreneur at the heart of one of the start-ups—and arrange an on-line chat or e-mail Q&A. Basic questions might include: What sparked the entrepreneur's idea? What have been the biggest challenges in getting that idea off the ground? What's the company's business model?

2. Spend about 10 minutes in class looking at job listings for journalists (a good site is www.journalismjobs.com). What jobs can you find that might not have existed 10 years ago? Are jobs out there that could have been filled by someone graduating in 1990? Discuss your findings with the class. What do the job listings tell us about changes in the industry?

3. Watch this clip from The Colbert Report about CNN's layoff of editors and photojournalists: www.colbertnation.com/the-colbert-report-videos/403149/november-28–2011/stephen-colbert-s-me-reporters. Discuss the points Colbert was trying to make by poking fun at CNN's "iReport" social network newsgathering concept. What are the risks of relying too heavily on the public to produce content?

4. Go to the website of *The Register Citizen*, one of the Register Journal Co. papers mentioned in this chapter (www.registercitizen.com/). Find some features not common on other community newspapers. Review the features that are similar to those in other papers. In what ways is this company promoting innovation? In what ways could it go further?

5. Spend one week reading ProPublica (www.propublica.org/; or if you have a local non-profit news site, use that). Keep a diary of each day's experience. Was there new content daily on the site? What sorts of stories were broken? Did the stories appear to be written by journalists or citizens? Was there a mix of news and entertainment features? Write a brief summary of what you saw and reflect about how what you read differed from a traditional news site (for example the site of your local newspaper). Post a 500-word entry to the class discussion thread set up for this topic.

▶ READ MORE

Mark Briggs, *Journalism Next: A Practical Guide to Digital Reporting and Publishing*, Washington, DC: CQ Press, 2010.

David Cohn, "Why We Should Feel Bullish for the Future of Journalism," November 14, 2008, http://blog.digidave.org/author/david-cohn/page/37.

Dan Gillmor, *We the Media: Grassroots Journalism by the People, for the People*, North Sebastapol, CA: O'Reilly Books, 2006.

Bill Grueskin, Ana Seave and Lucas Graves, "The Story So Far: What We Know About the Business of Digital Journalism," Tow Center for Digital Journalism, Columbia Journalism School. http://www.cjr.org/the_business_of_digital_jour nalism/the_story_so_far_what_we_know.php

Jeff Kaye and Stephen Quinn, *Funding Journalism in the Digital Age*, New York: Peter Lang Publishing, 2010.

Alan Mutter, "Reflections of a Newsosaur." http://newsosaur.blogspot.com/2011/10/ engagement-new-digital-metric.html.

Rob O'Regan, "Measuring the Audience Impact of Paywalls: Quality over Quantity," April 28, 2010, http://www.emediavitals.com/blog/17/measuring-audience-impact-paywalls-quality-over-quantity.

Clay Shirky, *Here Comes Everybody: The Power of Organizing without Organizations*, New York: Penguin, 2009.

Clay Shirky, "Newspapers and Thinking the Unthinkable," March 2009, www.shirky. com/weblog/2009/03/newspapers-and-thinking-the-unthinkable/

6

What do Journalists Owe Us?

Having your byline appear on the front page of the *New York Times* would be the culmination of a dream for many a young journalist. Just don't use Jayson Blair as an example of how to get there.

Here's the beginning of a story occupying coveted front-page space on May 11, 2003:

> A staff reporter for *The New York Times* committed frequent acts of journalistic fraud while covering significant news events in recent months, an investigation by *Times* journalists has found. The widespread fabrication and plagiarism represent a profound betrayal of trust and a low point in the 152-year history of the newspaper.

> The reporter, Jayson Blair, 27, misled readers and *Times* colleagues with dispatches that purported to be from Maryland, Texas and other states, when often he was far away, in New York. He fabricated comments. He concocted scenes. He lifted material from other newspapers and wire services. He selected details from

photographs to create the impression he had been somewhere or seen someone, when he had not.

And he used these techniques to write falsely about emotionally charged moments in recent history, from the deadly sniper attacks in suburban Washington to the anguish of families grieving for loved ones killed in Iraq.

(Barry et al., 2003)

Wow, talk about harsh! The message here is: Plagiarists, liars and other assorted cheaters, beware! You won't get away with it forever, and when you're caught . . . well, let's just say it won't be pretty.

Indeed the *Times* devoted a lot of resources to investigating and exposing all of Blair's misdeeds. The story, which five reporters and three editors spent a week reporting and writing, catalogued Blair's journalistic crimes and the multiple failures at many levels of the *Times*' management to notice and stop him sooner. The tale took 150 interviews to uncover and 14,000 words and more than four newspaper pages to tell. Why all this effort? Think back to your earlier reading about the kind of verification that's so central to journalism. That's true even if the story is, uncomfortably, at your own doorstep. In the end, "disgraced reporter" became Jayson Blair's unofficial title.

There's a chance—a chance that causes us pain, but a chance nevertheless—that some of you reading this might be wondering just what the big deal is. So Blair copied some things here and there and wasn't always where he said he was.

▶ **PLAGIARISM:** A kind of intellectual theft, in which one passes off someone else's work and ideas as his own.

That has to be pretty common, right? And who does it really hurt, anyway? Why all the drama? Well, the answers are "no," "lots of people," and "because the Times takes its responsibilities seriously."

But wait—the *Times* story says it better:

Every newspaper, like every bank and every police department, trusts its employees to uphold central principles, and the inquiry found that Mr. Blair repeatedly violated the cardinal tenet of journalism, which is simply truth.

The *Times* is saying that, in toying with the truth, Blair undermined the integrity of the paper, potentially damaging its relationship with the readers who depend on it and with the news sources and subjects it covers. To call the truth the "cardinal tenet" of journalism is to say that the truth is the key standard by which it is judged. Without truth, journalism isn't really journalism.

But of course you know that already from Chapter 2, where you discovered that journalism, even though it resists easy definition, is *aimed at gathering, verifying and reporting truthful information of consequence to citizens in a democracy*. Furthermore, you learned that to "do" journalism—to meet the requirements of the definition—is to think about the audience as citizens first, to practice a rigorous verification process and to act independently. One way to think about journalism ethics—the subject of this chapter—is that it involves the kinds of situations in which something or someone gets in the way of a journalist being able to meet the letter and the spirit of that definition.

DISCUSSION QUESTIONS

Why did the *New York Times* take such effort, give so much space in its paper and give so much attention to unraveling the lies and plagiarism committed by Jayson Blair? Think about the public perception of journalists, which surely is shaped by Hollywood portrayals of unethical journalistic behavior. What role should reputable journalistic organizations take in educating the public about ethical practices when scandals like those involving the *News of the World* erupt?

▶ BLACK, WHITE AND GRAY

For all the handwringing in the journalistic community over the lack of ethics Blair demonstrated—and trust us, there was a lot of handwringing—the episode actually isn't very interesting as an ethics case study. (We do consider it to be a fascinating case study in newsroom management, however.) That is, all the things that Blair did wrong are *obviously* wrong, and he knew it. They violate the truth, the "cardinal tenet of journalism." There's no gray area when it comes to the kind of outright fiction Blair was producing. If a story says you were in Portland, Oregon, then you had better have been in Portland, Oregon. If a story indicates you interviewed someone, then you had better have interviewed that person. To do otherwise is to lie to the readers and to steal from the other journalists whose work you copied. Really. It's just that simple. Blair wasn't faced with any tricky ethical dilemma. He made stuff up because he wanted to look like a better journalist than he was. That huge front-page investigation into the mess made it crystal clear that Blair's actions were completely contrary to the *Times'* understanding of its ethical obligations.

The now-defunct London tabloid, the *News of the World*, could not make that kind of crystal clear distinction. The paper is now defunct because of a scandal that began coming to light in 2009. Journalists at the *News of the World* hacked into the voicemail accounts of everyone from Prince Harry to actor Jude Law to the families of soldiers killed in Iraq. Why? To get a scoop. To be first with a juicy detail or two. It's unethical behavior, of course. The episode also has spawned a criminal inquiry—indeed, a particularly troublesome aspect of the scandal is evidence that the police routinely aided *News of the World* reporters in their misdeeds. In one case, the hacking even misled the family of a missing girl into thinking she was still alive and checking her own voicemail.

Like Blair, these journalists assaulted the integrity of the news organization and its relationship with readers. And, also like Blair, the lengths to which the reporters, photographers and editors all the way up the chain of command went to cover their tracks indicates they knew just how indefensible their actions were. But that's where an important difference between Blair and the *News of the World* emerges. Rather than the case of a single, "rogue" reporter, the *News of the World* case is one that suggests an entire news organization had lost its sense of public purpose and ethical principles, however flimsy those principles might have been in the first place. (If you know anything about the London tabloids like the *News of the World*, you know they are infamously trashy, with lots of gossip and sensationalism, but hard news, too.) It is extremely difficult for individuals to practice ethical journalism when the culture of a news organization does not encourage, or even actively discourages, ethical practice.

As the evidence about the *News of the World's* actions mounted and public outrage grew, the British government launched a formal inquiry into the practices and ethics of the press, calling a wide range of people who had been hurt by the tactics of the *News of the World* and other tabloid newspapers to testify. Witnesses have offered many tales of privacy invasion and relentless press harassment that are a useful, if grim, reminder about why ethics in journalism matters. An article in the *Guardian* summarizing some of the lessons of the Leveson Inquiry noted:

FIGURE 6.1
LONDON—JULY 10: Last day of the famous tabloid *News of the World* website after the scandal of phone hacking by the newspaper, on July 10, 2011 in London. The *News of the World* had been on sale since 1843.

Dutourdumonde/ Shutterstock

Irresponsible reporting can have tragic consequences. Witnesses have claimed press coverage of their private lives contributed to the death of those close to them. Former footballer Garry Flitcroft claimed coverage of his extramarital affair contributed to the eventual suicide of his father, who suffered from depression. Margaret Watson, whose teenage daughter Diane was murdered by a classmate in 1991, told Leveson her son Alan was found dead with copies of two articles misrepresenting the circumstances leading up to his older sister's death in his hands. Charlotte Church also claimed the *News of the World* had written a story about her stepfather's affair despite the fact her mother had recently attempted suicide.

(Robinson, 2011)

The press is powerful. It ought to exercise its power responsibly. (Spider-man fans will recognize this as Uncle Ben's wise words to Peter Parker: "With great power comes great responsibility." The philosopher Voltaire, though, probably gets first credit for it.) To act responsibly often means going beyond what the law requires. Jayson Blair's fabrications and even most of the *News of the World's* actions weren't illegal. But they were entirely contrary to their obligations as journalists. Being a journalist is voluntary. So is being a doctor or a lawyer—you decide that's what you want to do, and you go do it. Doctors and lawyers get licenses and take oaths. Journalists in the United States don't do either of those things because, as we have seen, they are considered contrary to free press principles. Nevertheless, in taking on the role of journalist, you are—voluntarily—taking on a set of responsibilities related to that role. Doctors and lawyers make commitments to serve their patients' and clients' interests. Journalists make commitments to the public. The voluntary nature of all this means that journalists are self-policing. One of the things this chapter addresses is how to think about what the rules are and how to "police" them, even if only for yourself.

So what Blair did was obviously wrong, and what the *News of the World* did was both obviously wrong and illegal. We should tell you right now, though, that neither scandal, thankfully, represents a common ethical issue in journalism. They are dramatic, interesting cases that have received tons of attention, and rightly so. But the vast majority of ethical questions journalists face aren't about whether or not it's OK to make stuff up or commit a crime. Let's look at one more example to get a sense of the kinds of ethical situations journalists face more routinely.

Here's the first paragraph of an Associated Press story from the summer of 2011:

> BENTON, N.Y. (AP)—A car trying to pass a farm tractor on a curve sideswiped an approaching van carrying 13 Amish farmers through the rural Finger Lakes region of New York on Tuesday, sending the van under the tractor, killing 5 passengers and injuring 10 other people, police said.

It's the kind of terrible event photojournalists cover all the time. The *New York Times* carried the AP article and photograph, which shows rescue workers at the scene of the crash, along with many other people holding up sheets and blankets, presumably to block the view of the dead. The *Times* also ran a separate story, "Amish, Quiet Presence in New York, Gain Attention in Tragedy," describing the community's response to the incident. Accompanying that article was a photograph of a group of Amish mourners with a buggy in the foreground.

Those sound like pretty routine news photographs, right? It's easy to imagine coverage of similar accidents that would include a photo of the scene and of the people affected by the tragedy. Many news organizations avoid showing particularly gory photographs of accidents, and most avoid photographs of dead bodies altogether. Neither of these photographs was that kind of image. So what, if anything, raises an ethical caution flag here? The reluctance of the Amish to be photographed at all, much less to having their faces shown in a photograph. Photojournalists working on stories involving the Amish are caught between informing the public about an event and potentially harming those involved in the event. Now *that* is much closer to a true ethical dilemma—a conflict between two legitimate interests—than anything in the Blair or *News of the World* cases. How can a photojournalist do her job without causing undue harm? What's the ethical path to take?

You're probably beginning to realize this ethics business might look easy on the surface but can get pretty complicated, pretty quickly. What does it mean to say that an action is "unethical"? What kinds of difficult choices do journalists routinely face, and how do they decide what to do? To answer those questions, we'll first need to lay some groundwork in ethics and then build from that groundwork to the specific case of journalism, using some of the insights you gained about the norms and expectations of journalism in previous chapters. By now you have a pretty good idea of what journalism is supposed to do in a democracy and all of the factors (economic, technological, etc.) that can help or hinder journalism's ability to do its job. With ethics, we enter murkier territory, where doing one's job as a journalist has the potential to cause harm to others, where journalists are often required to balance the interests of the public against other equally important interests. Murky indeed. Let's get started.

▶ ETHICS IS . . . NOT WHAT YOU THINK

Our first task is to define "ethics" so we can go about our business of applying ethics to journalism. Philosopher Peter Singer notes that "ethics" is derived from the Greek word, "ethos," and "morality" comes from the Latin word, "mores"—and the meaning of both "ethos" and "mores" is "customs." So ethics and morality refer in some way to the customs of a group of people. No wonder the terms are often used interchangeably—they essentially come from the same word! But "customs" represents just the starting point. When we talk about ethics, we aren't describing how it is customary among the Amish to wear certain kinds of clothes or how tipping waiters is customary in the United States but not in many European countries. Rather, ethics goes beyond matters of taste or tradition to matters of right and wrong.

Scholars at the Markkula Center for Applied Ethics say people often (mistakenly) equate ethics with their personal feelings, religion, the law, or societal standards. While ethics might be connected to each of these, none defines ethics on its own. After all, one's personal feelings, a society's standards and even the law can often deviate sharply from what is right. As the Markkula Center scholars note, Nazi Germany was morally corrupt, and laws permitting slavery violated fundamental notions of ethics. And even though most religions have high ethical standards, to equate ethics with religion would mean that ethics would apply only to religious people. Certainly an ethics that applies to everyone would be preferred.

If ethics isn't the same thing as personal feelings, religion, law or societal standards, what is it?

> ▶ MORALITY: A code of conduct. As the *Stanford Encyclopedia of Philosophy* notes, this term can refer either to a description of how a group or society actually behaves (what norms and standards it follows), or to a more universal code of conduct that everyone should endorse.

> Ethics is two things. First, ethics refers to well-founded standards of right and wrong that prescribe what humans ought to do, usually in terms of rights, obligations, benefits to society, fairness, or specific virtues . . . Secondly, ethics refers to the study and development of one's ethical standards. As mentioned above, feelings, laws, and social norms can deviate from what is ethical. So it is necessary to constantly examine one's standards to ensure that they are reasonable and well-founded.
>
> ("What is Ethics?" Markkula Center for Applied Ethics)

We will spend most of our time dissecting the first "thing" in that definition, though in doing so we are suggesting just how important the second "thing" is too. The more you learn about and develop your own ethical standards, the more you can contribute to the maintenance of high ethical standards in journalism overall.

So, first things first. What are those standards, rights, obligations, and so forth mentioned in the first part of that definition, and where do they come from? Thousands of years of philosophy have offered many different answers. Because we are not philosophers and, more important, because knowing the source of those obligations is less important for our purposes here than simply learning what the obligations are and how to act on them, we will not attempt to recap all of moral philosophy. (We strongly encourage you to take an actual philosophy course to explore this incredibly interesting stuff in depth.) Rather, we are going to present just one approach, an approach that has the benefit of being pretty straightforward and practical as well as including insights from major strands of philosophical thought.

DISCUSSION QUESTIONS

How are ethical challenges journalists face in their daily work similar to those faced by average citizens in daily life? How are they different? Couldn't journalists use their innate sense of right and wrong to guide them through most challenges they will face on the job. Why do we need special codes?

▶ **MEET W.D. ROSS, INTUITIONIST**

Ethics helps us figure out what we, as moral beings in the world, ought to do. As the definition above suggests, knowing what we ought to do involves knowing what our duties are. W.D. Ross, an influential British philosopher of the 20th Century, developed a moral framework based on the idea that our intuition can tell us what those duties—what he called *"prima facie"* duties—are. Some journalism ethics scholars, notably Thomas Bivins and Christopher Meyers, have discussed ways to incorporate Ross's insights into journalistic practice. We will use Meyers's recent work to help us understand where Ross is coming from. To say these duties are *"prima facie"* is to say they are self-evident, obvious, universal, intuitively knowable. If that sounds a little magical or weird, Meyers says, consider that recent advances in biology, neurology and psychology suggest human beings might be "hard wired" for ethics. But even without that scientific support, Ross's argument makes some, well, intuitive sense. For example, think about the duties you have just by being a person in the world. What do you owe other people? It's hard to disagree with the idea that if you make a promise, you should keep it—that you have an obligation to the person to whom you made the promise. Likewise, it's tough to argue against the notion that avoiding harm to others is an obligation everyone has. These ideas seem obvious and universal, don't they? Of course you ought to keep promises and avoid causing harm; to act otherwise is to call into question your ability to live in society with others. There's a word for that: psychopath.

So the basic idea in Ross's theory is this: There are several *prima facie*, or common sense, duties that—all other things being equal—you are obligated to act on. The "all other things being equal" part is important, as you'll see when we apply Ross's theory to actual decision-making. But let's have a look at all the duties first, again with Meyers's help. The list below divides

6.1 THE VIEW FROM THE PROS: HOW GOOD JOURNALISM CAN HARM

Two years later, I still wonder what happened to the four Ethiopian farmers whose names I used. In the months leading up to Ethiopia's May 2010 elections, reports emerged that the ruling party's campaign message in some parts of the East African country were as simple as this: vote for us or starve. Poor families in the Ethiopian countryside who did not support the ruling party were being denied access to the food aid supplied by the United States and other Western countries that supports more than six million people in the country.

Reporting this story as a foreign correspondent was not easy. Prime Minister Meles Zenawi's government has been intolerant of critical reporting since taking power in 1991. Foreign correspondents are sometimes detained or expelled for reporting on human rights abuses or humanitarian issues such as malnutrition that make the country look impoverished and the government appear inept—and local journalists are regularly jailed on trumped up charges or flee into exile.

In addition, those affected by the politicization of food aid were mainly in the countryside—often hundreds of miles from the capital. In December of 2009, seven farmers from northern Ethiopia who traveled to the capital Addis Ababa to meet with rights groups and foreign diplomats to talk about the problem were arrested, jailed and interrogated by security personnel. They were later escorted back to their villages, and a British researcher for Human Rights Watch who had planned to meet with them was expelled. A week later, when a translator and I traveled to the north to try to track the men down and interview them, we were captured by the intelligence service, held for two days and taken back to the capital where I was threatened with expulsion.

I spent weeks cooling my heels in Addis Ababa trying to figure out how to report the story without getting ejected from the country where I'd lived for three years. The foreign aid agencies were of little help—while many aid workers privately acknowledged the problem, the agencies themselves

did not want to risk having their programs shut down by facilitating such a story. And as I had learned, a foreigner traveling in the affected areas asking questions drew near-instant attention from plain-clothes security personnel.

Eventually I decided to send a brave Ethiopian journalist named Eskinder Nega to the countryside by himself to try to quietly meet with farmers willing to talk to a foreign reporter. Eskinder, who had already been jailed six times by the government, would then send the men to the capital one by one by bus so as not to attract attention, and I would interview them individually there.

As my plan moved forward, my ethical dilemma was this: Should I use the names of the farmers? On the one hand, planning and enacting the scheme was a big task. It involved multiple two- and three-day trips to the countryside by Eskinder, paying for the farmers to travel up to two days each way to and from Addis Ababa and arranging for them to be discreetly housed and fed without attracting the attention of watchful eyes. As such, I wanted a story that would be as bulletproof as possible when I presented it to my editors, who I thought would require strong evidence to publish such articles because they implied complicity by U.S. and other Western aid agencies in the abuses. Additionally, each of those interviewed had given permission for their names and hometowns to be used in any story.

On the other hand I knew the government could be ruthless with those who criticized it or made it look bad, no matter how vulnerable they were. Most memorably, in 2008 the government had closed two feeding centers for severely malnourished children in the midst of a drought, sending all the patients home to their villages to fend for themselves. The reason? The foreign nuns who ran the feeding centers had allowed television crews from the BBC and al Jazeera to film on their grounds and conduct interviews. As for food aid politicization, the only other organization that had done similar research—Human Rights Watch—had published a lengthy report but withheld the names of the farmers it interviewed.

In the end I decided that for the credibility of the story, I would use the real names of the farmers, though I described only the general part of the country where they came from in the hope that this would provide them with some measure of protection. The stories they told me had been universally sad: One man reported losing a three-year-old daughter after his family had been kicked out of an aid program because of his support for a small opposition party. A second opposition supporter reported that his wife had divorced him so that she would be allowed back in to the food aid program in their district. A third was beaten so badly by ruling party officials that his finger had to be amputated.

After they went back to their villages, the *New York Times*, *Newsweek* and *IRIN*, a humanitarian news service operated by the United Nations, carried bits of what they had told me. I left Ethiopia soon afterwards, and the ruling party won 99.6 percent of the seats in parliament that year. To this day I don't know what became of any of them—save Eskinder the journalist, who was back in jail as of June 2012. Given how little impact any of the articles had in affecting the policies of the Ethiopian government or the Western countries that fund its aid programs, I worry the decision I made to name them may have been the wrong one.

THINK ABOUT IT: Would you have used the farmers' names? Would the credibility of the story have been harmed with partial names or pseudonyms? If the farmers willingly gave permission to use their names, was the journalist right to respect these wishes? Is it the duty of the journalists to protect sources who speak openly and know the risks they are taking?

Jason McLure was an Africa correspondent for Bloomberg News from 2007 to 2011. He now writes for Reuters, *CQ Researcher* and other publications from Littleton, New Hampshire.

the duties into "perfect" and "imperfect" ones and includes very brief descriptions of what the duties mean. Perfect duties are those that are strictly binding—you must do them—while the imperfect ones are strongly encouraged—you really, really should do them if you can. This distinction, too, will be important when it comes to decision-making.

Perfect Duties

1. Fidelity (Keep your promises.)

2. Nonmaleficence (Avoid causing harm.)

3. Reparation (Make up for harm you've caused others. Meyers notes this is a perfect duty only if the harm was intentional or the result of gross negligence; otherwise it's an imperfect duty.)

4. Respect for persons, including oneself (Treat every person as a being whose autonomy—for example, their ability to make choices—must be honored.)

5. Formal justice (Give people what they've legitimately earned and treat people equally.)

Imperfect Duties

1. Beneficence (Do what you can to improve the lives of others.)

2. Gratitude (Show appreciation for what others have done for you.)

3. Distributive justice (Distribute social goods in a way that benefits the least advantaged people and protects liberty.)

4. Honesty (Avoid misleading people into believing what is false. Note that Meyers includes this as an imperfect duty, not because truth isn't impor-tant—it's essential!—but because some forms of deception are meant to actually help prevent harm.)

5. Self-improvement (Work to develop your moral, intellectual and physical qualities.)

Being able to recognize which obligations are most at stake in any given situation and to weigh them against one another is the essence of ethical decision-making based on Ross's framework. Even though these duties aren't really ranked, nonmaleficence usually overrides all the other duties, and per-fect duties generally come before the imperfect ones. The imperfect duties are "imperfect" because you won't always be in a position to act on them. It wouldn't be fair to hold you strictly accountable for beneficence—improving others' lives—for example, if the choice you are facing involves picking the lesser of two evils and not choosing between something that will improve others' lives and something that won't. On the other hand, the "perfect" duty of nonmaleficence—to avoid causing harm—always holds. You can be held accountable if you don't choose the least harmful course of action.

How would this work in real life? Let's take the Amish example from a few pages ago. Which of these duties were most relevant for the photojournal-ists covering the traffic accident? Certainly avoiding harm was important, as the Amish consider photographs depicting them to violate their religious beliefs. What about respect for persons? In this particular case, respect could refer both to the autonomy of the Amish people to consent (or not) to being photographed and to the autonomy of the public, which is enhanced by having access to the kind of information about public events the photo-journalists provide. Avoiding harm and respect for persons are both perfect duties, so the photojournalists were facing a difficult decision. Were any im-perfect duties relevant here? Maybe honesty, if you wanted to argue that not

FIGURE 6.2 Part of practicing journalism ethically is being sensitive to whether and how people from different religions and cultures, such as the Amish, want to be portrayed in news.

Kathmanduphotog/ Shutterstock

showing images of the Amish would be somehow misleading to the wider audience. After considering these duties, you might decide that avoiding harm to the Amish and respect for the autonomy of the Amish outweighed the photojournalists' obligations toward the public in this situation. And having reached that conclusion, you would be on your way to making ethical decisions about how to cover the accident. Notice we said *"on your way"* to making ethical decisions. Thinking about the duties is a big part of the decision-making strategy, but it's not everything, as you'll see below.

One last general note about Ross before we turn our attention entirely to journalism. In focusing on duties, what is Ross NOT focusing on? Consequences. Two of the main categories of ethical theory are consequentialism and deontology. In very rough terms, consequentialism, as the word implies, argue that one may judge the rightness or wrongness of an action according to the consequences it produces. If the action produces a good outcome, then the action is itself a good one. Utilitarianism, which you may

DISCUSSION QUESTIONS

How much of a role should potential consequences play in your final decision-making? Immanuel Kant would argue they should play no role at all. Utilitarian thinking would suggest they should be at the center of all action. In what cases can journalists truly see the consequences of their actions before they formally act?

have heard of, is a consequentialist theory. A criticism of consequentialism is that it requires one to be able to accurately predict outcomes and who will benefit the most from them. Deontological theories do not judge an action by its consequences, but by . . . well, what? Whether and how well the action conforms to the rules—or, as we have been discussing in this chapter, duties. Philosopher Immanuel Kant was a strict deontologist. W.D. Ross, not so strict. Perhaps too simply put, Ross offers rules, or duties, but also flexibility in applying them according to the needs of a specific set of circumstances. And while he does not ignore consequences—indeed, carefully considering how acting on any of the duties might affect the people involved is key to this framework—outcomes alone cannot determine what's right. Philosopher Anthony Skelton says Ross "outlines a view that attempts to avoid the alleged deficiencies of utilitarianism without embracing the alleged excesses of Kantianism." There's also a bit of Aristotelian virtue theory, another category of ethical theory, in Ross's approach, most obviously in his identification of self-improvement as a *prima facie* duty. Virtue ethics doesn't contradict consequentialism or deontology, but is more concerned with the development of moral character. Pursuing virtue is what makes one a moral person.

▶ **ETHICAL THEORY:** Generally speaking, there are three categories or approaches to ethics: Deontology focuses on duties or rules, Teleology focuses on consequences, and Virtue Ethics focuses on development of moral character.

Enough philosophical background, at least for now. The bottom line is this: Ross's common sense, practical view incorporating insights from these three different strands of philosophical thinking offers a useful way to approach ethical issues in journalism. The question is how do we move from these general, common sense duties to understanding what our actual duties in a specific situation might be? How do these duties help us decide what to do?

▶ HOW JOURNALISTS SEE THEIR DUTIES

In thinking about ethics, what we are attempting to do is translate the broader principles of journalism into specific actions by real people. It's one thing to say that journalists ought to treat people as citizens first and act independently, but quite another to say exactly how that plays out as a journalist covers a story. Journalists have responded to this need for more specific guidelines for ethical behavior by creating what are called codes of ethics. One of the oldest codes is The Journalist's Creed, written around 1906 by Walter Williams, the founding dean of the University of Missouri School of Journalism (see box below). It says, in part, that "the supreme test of good journalism is the measure of its public service" and cites accuracy, truthfulness, fairness and independence among the key attributes of good journalism. But you knew that already, right? Even though it offers a few specifics—about avoiding all kinds of bribery, for example—The Journalist's Creed is more of a mission statement for journalism than a decision-making strategy for the working journalist.

THE JOURNALIST'S CREED

The Journalist's Creed was written by the first dean of the Missouri School of Journalism, Walter Williams. One century later, his declaration remains one of the clearest statements of the principles, values and standards of journalists throughout the world. The plaque bearing the creed is located on the main stairway to the second floor of Neff Hall.

I believe in the profession of journalism.

I believe that the public journal is a public trust; that all connected with it are, to the full measure of their responsibility, trustees for the public; that acceptance of a lesser service than the public service is betrayal of this trust.

I believe that clear thinking and clear statement, accuracy and fairness are fundamental to good journalism.

I believe that a journalist should write only what he holds in his heart to be true.

I believe that suppression of the news, for any consideration other than the welfare of society, is indefensible.

I believe that no one should write as a journalist what he would not say as a gentleman; that bribery by one's own pocketbook is as much to be avoided as bribery by the pocketbook of another; that individual responsibility may not be escaped by pleading another's instructions or another's dividends.

I believe that advertising, news and editorial columns should alike serve the best interests of readers; that a single standard of helpful truth and cleanness should prevail for all; that the supreme test of good journalism is the measure of its public service.

I believe that the journalism which succeeds best—and best deserves success—fears God and honors Man; is stoutly independent, unmoved by pride of opinion or greed of power, constructive, tolerant but never careless, self-controlled, patient, always respectful of its readers but always unafraid, is quickly indignant at injustice; is unswayed by the appeal of privilege or the clamor of the mob; seeks to give every man a chance and, as far as law and honest wage and recognition of human brotherhood can make it so, an equal chance; is profoundly patriotic while sincerely promoting international good will and cementing world-comradeship; is a journalism of humanity, of and for today's world.

Source: http://journalism.missouri.edu/jschool/#creed.

Professional organizations such as the Radio Television Digital News Association (RTDNA), Society of Professional Journalists, and National Press Photographers Association have developed codes for their members that get a bit closer to how-to-make-an-ethical-decision territory. Let's see how they do that.

The RTDNA code states, "Professional electronic journalists should operate as trustees of the public, seek the truth, report it fairly and with integrity and independence, and stand accountable for their actions." Sounds like The Journalist's Creed. But for each element of that general statement—public trustees, truth, fairness, integrity, independence and accountability—the code offers much more specific instructions. For example, under the heading "Integrity," the code says journalists should:

▶ *Identify sources whenever possible. Confidential sources should be used only when it is clearly in the public interest to gather or convey important information or when a person providing information might be harmed. Journalists should keep all commitments to protect a confidential source.*

▶ *Clearly label opinion and commentary.*

▶ *Guard against extended coverage of events or individuals that fails to significantly advance a story, place the event in context, or add to the public knowledge.*

▶ *Refrain from contacting participants in violent situations while the situation is in progress.*

▶ *Use technological tools with skill and thoughtfulness, avoiding techniques that skew facts, distort reality, or sensationalize events.*

▶ *Use surreptitious newsgathering techniques, including hidden cameras or microphones, only if there is no other way to obtain stories of significant public importance and only if the technique is explained to the audience.*

▶ *Disseminate the private transmissions of other news organizations only with permission.*

Now that's a pretty detailed list! And notice how many of the instructions on that list fit with Ross's common sense duties. For example, "clearly label opinion and commentary" sounds an awful lot like something related to the duty of respect for persons as well as the duty of honesty. And "refrain from contacting participants in violent situations while the situation is in progress" would appear to relate to the duty to avoid causing harm, wouldn't it? How about the rule that begins, "Guard against extended coverage . . . "? What duty might that speak to? The RTDNA is essentially admonishing journalists to avoid sensationalizing a story or giving an event too much coverage. If you were thinking that sounds connected to some kind of justice—formal or distributive—you'd be on the right track. The duty to avoid causing harm is connected as well.

The main sections in the Society of Professional Journalists code are "seek truth and report it," "minimize harm," "act independently," and "be accountable." And, like the RTDNA code, more specific guidelines are offered for each section. (Notice, too, how similar the SPJ code and Kovach and Rosenstiel's elements of journalism from Chapter 2 are.) The "seek truth and report it" section has the longest list—17 items—including these related to duties of respect for persons, justice, beneficence and self-improvement:

▶ Diligently seek out subjects of news stories to give them the opportunity to respond to allegations of wrongdoing.

▶ Tell the story of the diversity and magnitude of the human experience boldly, even when it is unpopular to do so.

▶ Examine their own cultural values and avoid imposing those values on others.

▶ Avoid stereotyping by race, gender, age, religion, ethnicity, geography, sexual orientation, disability, physical appearance or social status.

▶ Support the open exchange of views, even views they find repugnant.

▶ Give voice to the voiceless; official and unofficial sources of information can be equally valid.

These codes of ethics show how the journalism profession has translated general ethical duties into the sphere of journalism practice. So far, so good. But even specifics like these can only get you so far. Where in the code does it say what to do if you uncover evidence that a candidate for public office cheated on his fiancée (now wife) 20 years ago? You could think back to what you've learned about perfect duties and remember you're supposed to avoid harm. OK, you might think, "I'll drop the story because it will harm the candidate." But if you also consulted, say, the RTDNA code to get a better idea of how duties play out in the professional arena, you would discover you're supposed to "provide a full range of information to enable the public to make enlightened decisions." Hmm. There's so much more you need to know and so much more to think about, you realize. Is a candidate's personal life important for citizens to know about? Has the candidate stressed his character as an important reason to vote for him? Does it matter how long ago the cheating happened? Does his wife know about the cheating, or will your story be the first time she's heard about it? Does that matter?

So many questions. And it almost seems like the more you ponder the duties and whatever a code of ethics has to say, the more questions you have. Congratulations! You have officially entered the murky world of ethics. Trust us—that's a good thing. Understanding your duties and how the profession puts them into practice can help you recognize an ethically problematic situation when it arises and sensitize you to the issues and factors you'll need to consider in making a decision—a good decision—about what to do. But there's always the chance, indeed the near certainty, that the situation will involve two or more potentially conflicting duties or that the code of ethics will be silent on the

DISCUSSION QUESTIONS

Doing good journalistic work often means that a journalist contributes to causing some sort of harm. Many cases involve weighing competing harms. Does that mean journalism is an inherently unethical profession? Why or why not?

FIGURE 6.3 BELLEFONTE, PA—JUNE 21: Former Penn State assistant football coach Jerry Sandusky arrives at his child sex abuse trial at the Centre County Courthouse on June 21, 2012 in Bellefonte, Pennsylvania. Sandusky was ultimately convicted of 45 criminal counts of sexual abuse on 10 boys over a 15-year period and is serving a 30- to 60-year sentence.

Mark Willson/Getty Images

specific situation you are facing. The world rarely offers up problems with simple, black or white solutions, so you need to be able to navigate the gray area a little bit. You just need a way to bring order to your thinking.

▶ A PROCESS FOR ETHICAL DECISION-MAKING

Chances are you consider yourself to be a pretty good person, capable of making sound ethical decisions. We're not disputing that. By offering up a process for making decisions, we are simply trying to engage your ethical reasoning abilities in an organized way. And we are trying to help you avoid

6.2 THE VIEW FROM THE PROS: ETHICAL ISSUES IN NEWS AGGREGATION

I am managing editor of a weekly business newspaper that is part of a chain of similar papers. In addition to our weekly paper, we maintain an electronic version of the paper that is continually updated with current news.

Over the past couple of years, several of our sister publications began publishing morning blog posts and e-mails that summarized and linked to content originally created by other news sources. The benefits of this were evident: These markets experienced a dramatic rise in morning traffic to their websites as they gave readers more information early in the day that could help them do their jobs better.

The apparent success of news aggregation caused us to seriously consider adopting it for our publication. We were concerned, however, about assuring the accuracy of third-party content and avoiding plagiarism. We did not want to steal the work of others. So what seemed at first glance a practical or technical issue was actually an ethical issue too.

Our editorial team, including our publisher, editor, Web producer and myself, began discussing implementation of a morning edition blog and e-mail during the summer of 2011. Our goal was to decide whether to implement it and, if so, to develop a written implementation plan and staff guidelines.

One of the first things we discussed was whether to include news aggregation within the blog posts. Ultimately, we decided the benefits to our subscribers and the practicality of needing a way to get six to eight blog posts up by 7:30 a.m. justified doing news aggregation.

The next question was how to do it the right way. There were no established guidelines. I spoke with journalists in several other markets to get a sense of the system they used, and we were able to develop a plan from there. The principal issues we addressed were:

- Ensuring that the content is accurate. One of our first rules for the Morning Edition writers was to make sure that they always pull from reliable news sources, not from individual blog posts or opinion pages. We also try to verify the news with more than one online source. Finally, the stories have to pass our own believability test—do we really believe it happened as reported? If the answer is no, further reporting is needed. If the issue is one that could be potentially contentious, further reporting is completed before we post it online.
- Avoiding plagiarism. There is a gray area between adding a link to another news source and copying all of the source's content and reusing it. To address this, we do not copy and paste any of the text from the aggregated stories. Everything is rewritten. Writers are required to cite the source and include a link to the original story and highlight the original source by using a phrase such as "The Philadelphia Inquirer weighs in on the issue again today . . ."

We also decided that whenever possible, we would add our own original content to the post. For example, if we had past stories about the issue, we might include links to our own past stories. This way, we are giving readers additional information on top of what the other news source had.

After we launched "Morning Edition" late last year, we noticed that the posts seemed to blend in on our homepage with our other daily updates, which have original reporting. To address this issue, we created a "Morning Edition" image that we attach to each of the posts. We found that this alerted readers to the fact that the story is a Morning Edition story, and it distinguished them from our regular Web stories. Although this is not a perfect solution, it does provide a way for readers to distinguish between the two types of posts.

Morning Edition has been a big hit with readers. Web traffic rose. The guidelines have proven to be useful in writing the posts. And our extensive discussions about not only whether to aggregate, but how to avoid the potential ethical pitfalls of aggregation, was worth the effort.

LEARN MORE: A group of writers and editors in 2012 was seeking to form the Council on Ethical Blogging and Aggregation (read the nytimes.com story here: www.nytimes.com/2012/03/12/business/media/guidelines-proposed-for-content-aggregation-online.html?pagewanted=all). As you work through this chapter of the book, check online to see if the group has made progress and whether uniform standards for content shared through aggregation have been established.

Jennifer Curry is managing editor of the *Pittsburgh Business Times*.

an all-too-common trap: Going on gut instinct alone. What your gut tells you is important "data"—it's especially good at alerting you to situations that involve a potential ethical issue—but ethical decisions need to involve your mind too. Even if you reach the same conclusion at the end of the ethical decision-making process that your gut told you was the right decision upfront, philosopher Deni Elliott points out that going through the process offers important benefits. First, you will know you considered all the important factors surrounding the situation that needed to be considered, which means that, second, you will be better able to defend your decision to people who might disagree with you.

Yes, people will probably disagree with you. That's the nature of the beast when you're dealing with potential harms, conflicting duties and the like. But we're willing to bet that if you go through this process and can communicate about what you weighed and considered at each step, even those who disagree with your conclusion will agree that your process was sound. That's more than half the battle. Also, keep in mind that journalism is a distinctly public enterprise—you provide information about the public, to the public. Of course your ethical reasoning should be open to public view as well.

Meyers proposed a framework based on Ross that we have adapted for your use. There are nine steps:

1. Start with an open mind.
2. Get all the facts you can.
3. Listen to what your gut is saying.
4. Identify which duties are at stake.
5. Figure out what kind of conflict you're facing.
6. Brainstorm and analyze.
7. Reach a conclusion—and try to reach consensus with co-workers too.
8. Try to minimize whatever harm your decision might cause.
9. Look toward the future.

Now let's go step by step, using the cheating candidate example from a few pages ago. As you will recall, our hypothetical candidate for public office—let's say he's running for governor of your state—cheated on his fiancée 20 years ago. That former fiancée is now his wife. You are wondering whether you ought to report this information about him. You are hesitating, because your gut tells you this kind of information could cause harm to the candidate, to his wife, or someone else, but that it might also be the kind of information that it is your job, as a journalist, to report.

Step One: You might have opinions about adultery or politics or this candidate or his wife that could blind you to important details or otherwise skew your decision-making process. Try to clean the slate. One way to do that is to engage in ethical decision-making with others, so you'll have multiple perspectives on the issue. If you work in a traditional newsroom, you'll have an editor or producer or news director with whom to talk things over. If you're working more independently, perhaps blogging for your own site, you'll want to find a trusted friend to fill this role.

Step Two: Time to do some reporting! All those questions we raised about this case earlier—for example, has the candidate used his personal character as a campaign issue, does his wife already know—are essentially factual questions. Here are some different kinds of facts that might be relevant to the case at hand:

Journalistic facts: These are the kinds of things you would need to do a real story, but with a particular focus: figuring out who has the most at stake—who will be most affected—in this situation. Let's say you learned about the affair from the woman with whom the candidate cheated, who said, "People ought to know what a terrible person Mr. X is." Let's also say the candidate has not made personal character an important part of his campaign, his wife (as far as you know) is unaware of the cheating, the election is just two weeks away, and the candidate's opponent trails the candidate by just three points in the latest opinion poll. All of these facts suggest that the revelation of the cheating could affect the outcome of the election and harm the candidate and his wife personally. As you think about who would be affected by this story and how, you might uncover even more questions that require more fact-finding. Keep going until you think you've got everything relevant to the situation.

Professional facts: This is where you get to put those fundamental principles of journalism into action and make use of a code of ethics and any kind of policy your workplace might have. In this case, we know that the basic job of journalism is to gather, verify and report *truthful information of consequence to citizens in a democracy*. Most codes of ethics include similar language about journalism's purpose. So you're right to be thinking that this affair might be something you should report, as it provides voters with additional information about the candidate. But it also means that, even if you decide to report it, you might still have some work to do to get the information up to the standard of "verified." What do professional codes or norms tell you about basing a story entirely on one person's statement, especially if that person seems to have some sort of grudge?

Legal facts: Are there any laws or rules that might affect what you would cover in your story or how? This case doesn't seem to offer any particular legal issues, but consider how important these kinds of facts might be if the candidate were accused of cheating on his taxes, not his fiancée, or if the information about the candidate came to you via illegal means, perhaps sealed court documents.

Social/political facts: What political party does the candidate belong to? Is your state socially conservative or socially liberal? These are facts about the context in which you would be reporting this information. You might also include under this heading any background about the woman who tipped you off. She says she wants people to know the candidate is a terrible person—is that a personal motive, or does she have a particular political agenda? Why are you learning this information now, just two weeks before Election Day? Can you verify the information?

Big picture facts: These facts are sort of like social and political facts, but on a much bigger scale. Sure your story is just one story, but it is happening in the larger context of an increasing polarization in American politics. Partisanship is stronger than it has been in decades. That's one "big picture" factor that influences how people would understand your story. Another factor might be changing norms and expectations about personal relationships. Is cheating on a fiancée as big a deal as cheating on a spouse? If you decide to do the story, would you characterize what the candidate did as "cheating"?

Just two steps into this process, and you already have gathered tons of information. Time to pause and reflect on whether you still have an ethical conflict on your hands. Yep—you might be done! Listen to what Meyers says:

> More often than not, when step two has been properly completed, the conflict disappears. That is, the clear majority of ethics conflicts are really about confused facts . . . or about different stakeholders believing different facts. When these are corrected, agreement routinely follows over the value questions, and the problem resolves.
>
> (Meyers, 2011, p. 326)

Starting with an open mind and getting lots of facts will let you know pretty darn quickly whether the problem is one of conflicting facts or conflicting duties. If the woman's claim about the cheating turns out to be false—well, that's easy. No story. Or if we uncover the additional fact that the woman was paid by the opponent to tell her story, that's easy too—but a very different story. Nothing we've uncovered so far, however, suggests that this is a simple case of confused facts. So let's proceed with the rest of the steps. The next one makes a lot more sense now that we've taken this pause.

Step Three: Gut check. We weren't kidding when we said your gut can provide valuable information in ethical decision-making. Here's where that happens, but with a bunch more facts on the table, your gut can make a more informed choice. Also, this is a good opportunity to compare what your gut is telling you with what other folks' guts—your editor, best pal or whoever—are telling them. Does everyone seem to be leaning toward doing the cheating story? Why? Perhaps you all agree that this is exactly the kind of story journalism is supposed to do—inform the public so it can make good choices—and that nothing you've been able to find suggests that the story is untrue. Maybe you're heading toward a consensus that the question isn't so much whether to do the story, but how best to do it. That's fine, but you've got to keep going.

Step Four: Go back to the list of perfect and imperfect duties and think about which ones are particularly relevant to this case and how. You'll want to go beyond just listing the duties to thinking about which ones are most strongly at issue and to whom you owe the duty. For example, you might think differently about a perfect duty owed to the person likely to suffer the most harm and an imperfect duty owed to the person likely to be harmed least. At least two perfect duties—nonmaleficence and respect for persons—seem to be involved in our candidate cheating case. Both are owed to the candidate, his wife, and the woman who brought the information to you. A duty to avoid causing harm is also owed to the public. What about the duty of fidelity? The relationship between journalism and the public implies a certain kind of promise about telling the truth. As the SPJ code of ethics says, truth-telling isn't just about not lying, it's about being forthcoming with information too. Perhaps that applies here.

Are there any imperfect duties that seem especially relevant? Could you make an argument for the duty of beneficence? Do you believe that giving voters information about the candidates constitutes a way of helping them improve their lives or at least avoid some kind of future harm? It's something to consider, but also something difficult to pin down.

Step Five: So, what type of conflict is this? By "type," we mean is this really an ethical dilemma or, rather, something that causes ethical distress but is not, technically, a dilemma? A dilemma, Meyers tells us, exists when two legitimate, but competing, duties are at stake so that any decision you make will produce a moral harm of some kind. Ethical distress occurs when even though you might agree on what the ethically best course of action is, something prevents you from acting on it. That something might be institutional pressures or legal constraints. Why is this distinction important? Because it can have a bearing on how you decide to try to resolve the issue. A dilemma means, whatever you choose, harm is likely to occur. So you'll want to figure out how to minimize it. If there's distress but no dilemma, you might focus your efforts on overcoming whatever barrier to ethical action you face.

As we determined in Step Four, we have at least two perfect duties at stake in our candidate scenario. That sounds like an ethical dilemma. Whatever we decide to do about the story, then, we will also have to come up with ways to minimize the harm we cause. More on that in Step Eight.

Step Six: Think. And think some more. You've come into this process with an open mind, assembled lots of facts, checked your gut, determined which duties are most at stake, and figured out you're facing an ethical dilemma. Now is the time to mull all of that over. Think through several different scenarios. As Meyers points out, this is the easiest step to describe, but probably the most difficult one to do. One trap to avoid: Framing your decision as either/or. Whichever route you choose, there are more and less ethically defensible ways to travel it.

Step Seven: With any luck, you've been conducting all or part of this decision-making process in the company of others who share your desire to make an ethically sound choice. Step Seven is when you try to reach agreement with one another about that choice. Consensus isn't always possible, but try to come to agreement on as many things as you can. Then, well, someone has to make a decision.

Step Eight: Try to minimize the harm that will accompany your decision. In Step Five, you identified which people have the most at stake and are, therefore, the most likely to suffer harm. Knowing what kind of duty you owe them might help you figure out how to minimize that harm. The various scenarios you considered in Step Six will be helpful here as well.

Let's say you decide to produce some kind of story about the 20-year-old cheating incident. Often, as is arguably the case here, providing as much context as possible will be important, including the facts that this happened a long time ago when the candidate was not yet married. You'll want to offer the candidate and his wife the opportunity to respond to the cheating claims. You'll want to be as clear as you can about the woman's motives for bringing the information forward so close to Election Day. This is just for starters. Also think about things like how big a headline the story should get or whether it would appear at the beginning of the newscast too.

Step Nine: Looking toward the future means considering ways you can avoid facing this kind of ethical dilemma again. Would it be helpful to develop some new policies or offer additional interpretation of the ethics code? It's entirely possible that this is the kind of ethical dilemma that is almost unavoidable in journalism. If so, your focus would be on developing policies to minimize harm, not avoiding the dilemma altogether.

▶ WANT TO KNOW WHAT WE WOULD DO?

So would we! Seriously, there are too many unknowns in this hypothetical scenario to render a verdict now. But we *are* pretty suspicious about the timing of this revelation, so close to Election Day. Our decision would focus on what we could determine about the source's motives. Sketchy motives and this "story" might not be a story at all, or a very different kind of story about campaign politics. Our gut feeling—and that's all we've got now, with all those unanswered questions—is that there's a story of some kind here, but maybe not the story the source is trying to tell.

If making your way through the case of the cheating candidate made your brain hurt a little, take comfort in knowing that going through the steps of this process gets easier the more you do it. With practice and experience, you will get better at thinking about duties and what is at stake for the people involved. Use the resources listed at the end of the chapter to find other cases to practice on.

Chapter Six Review

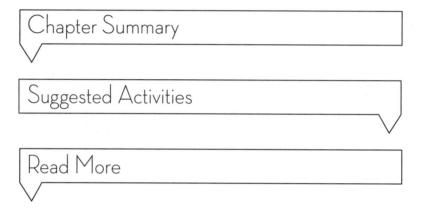

Chapter Summary

Suggested Activities

Read More

► CHAPTER SUMMARY

Journalism ethics involves figuring out how to align our job duties with the duties we have to people. There's no getting around the fact that harm to someone is a frequent byproduct of journalism—even, and sometimes especially, the journalism most closely aimed at helping citizens be self-governing. Good journalism involves uncovering things people would prefer remain hidden or pointing a finger at a problem for which no one seems to want to take responsibility. Ethical journalists try to fulfill their duties to citizens and the subjects of news, while also trying to avoid or minimize harm to them and even, where possible, working to prevent it. Philosopher W.D. Ross helps us understand the nature of our "common sense" duties, perfect and imperfect, so we can weigh them in all kinds of situations. But harm is likely to be a routine part of your life as a journalist. Being able to thoughtfully consider and defend your actions using the kind of ethical decision-making framework we introduce in this chapter will help ease that burden.

▶ SUGGESTED ACTIVITIES

1. Meeting your ethical responsibilities as a journalist involves having a good sense of what your general responsibilities are. Think about the type of job you'd like to have after graduation (TV producer, sports editor, multimedia reporter or even a job outside of journalism). Next, break into small groups (find one or two classmates who have similar aspirations to you) to make a list of what job responsibilities you would have ("interview people," "create slideshows," etc.). Then, in a second column next to that list, write down how those tasks relate to an ethical obligation discussed in this chapter. The idea is to connect job duties with ethical duties.

2. Discuss with the class how you use journalism in your daily lives. Should standards be different for journalists? Read this post from Poynter.org on how to use Facebook ethically: www.poynter.org/how-tos/digital-strategies/176649/7-ways-journalists-can-make-better-ethical-decisions-when-using-facebook/. Write down how you might change your Facebook profile or alter your activities after reading this (and after the class discussion).

3. Watch the last 10 minutes of Jayson Blair's address to students at Washington and Lee University, found online at www.youtube.com/watch?v=kFePfsBlocA&feature=related. (The best information starts at about 14 minutes into the clip.) Should a journalism program have invited Blair to give lessons on ethics? Can we learn the most from the worst practices? How do you feel about Blair after watching this presentation?

4. Watch some excerpts from recent movies or television shows about journalists. (One good one is "State of Play," starring Russell Crowe. Or see other suggestions at: http://teachj.wordpress.com/2007/05/28/10-great-journalism-movies-for-summer/). Where do the Hollywood version of journalistic ethics and what this book tells us about ethics diverge? What rings true for how ethical journalists behave? What impact do movies like this have on public perceptions of the profession?

5. Pick one case from the Indiana University page listing a variety of journalistic ethical scenarios (found at http://journalism.indiana.edu/resources/ethics/). Each member of your class should choose a different case. On a discussion thread set up for the class post brief details about your case, and then work through the ethical decision-making process outlined in this chapter. Post a 300-word reaction to the board to go with your summary. Which steps were most difficult to address? What decision did you reach? Did your conclusion surprise you? Comment on at least one other post on the board.

▶ READ MORE

"5 Amish Farmers Are Killed in Crash Upstate," AP, *New York Times*, July 19, 2011. www.nytimes.com/2011/07/20/nyregion/amish-farmers-killed-and-9-others-injured-in-crash-upstate.html?ref=nyregion.

Dan Barry, David Barstow, Jonathan D. Glater, Adam Liptak and Jacques Steinberg, with research support provided by Alain Delaquérière and Carolyn Wilder, "CORRECTING THE RECORD; Times Reporter Who Resigned Leaves Long Trail of Deception," *New York Times*, May 11, 2003. www.nytimes.com/2003/05/11/us/correcting-the-record-times-reporter-who-resigned-leaves-long-trail-of-deception.html?pagewanted=all&src=pm.

Thomas H. Bivins, *Mixed Media: Moral Distinctions in Advertising, Public Relations, and Journalism*, New York: Routledge, 2009.

Cara Buckley and Peter Applebome, "Amish, Quiet Presence in New York, Gain Attention in Tragedy," *New York Times*, July 20, 2011. www.nytimes.com/2011/07/21/nyregion/driver-of-passing-car-charged-in-deaths-of-5-amish-farmers.html.

Leveson Inquiry: Culture, Practice and Ethics of the Press. www.levesoninquiry.org.uk/.

Christopher Meyers, "Appreciating W.D. Ross: On Duties and Consequences," *Journal of Mass Media Ethics* 18 (2003): 81–97.

Christopher Meyers, "Reappreciating W.D. Ross: Naturalizing Prima Facie Duties and a Proposed Method," *Journal of Mass Media Ethics* 26 (2011): 316–331.

James Robinson, "The Leveson Inquiry: What We've Learned so Far," *Guardian*, November 30, 2011. www.guardian.co.uk/media/2011/nov/30/leveson-inquiry-learned-so-far.

Peter Singer (Ed.), *Ethics*, Oxford: Oxford University Press, 1994.

Anthony Skelton, "William David Ross," *The Stanford Encyclopedia of Philosophy (Fall 2010 Edition)*, ed. Edward N. Zalta. http://plato.stanford.edu/archives/fall2010/entries/william-david-ross/.

"What is Ethics?" Developed by Manuel Velasquez, Claire Andre, Thomas Shanks, S.J., and Michael J. Meyer, Markkula Center for Applied Ethics. www.scu.edu/ethics/practicing/decision/whatisethics.html.

To see some examples of codes of ethics, please turn to the Appendix.

7

The Foundations of Free Expression

June 27, 2011 was a banner day for fans of Grand Theft Auto, Mortal Kombat, Postal 2 and any number of other violent video games played by millions of hardcore gamers.

On that day, the United States Supreme Court handed down its ruling in *Brown v. Entertainment Merchants Association*, striking down as unconstitutional a California law banning the sale of such games to minors.

Concerned with the level of graphic violence in video games, California enacted a law prohibiting the sale or rental of violent video games to minors. The law addressed video games that allow the player to "kill, maim, dismember or sexually assault an image of a human being."

Writing for a 7–2 majority, Justice Antonin Scalia said the country has no tradition of restricting depictions of violence for children. He said California's law did not meet the high legal bar set by prior First Amendment cases to infringe on the First Amendment or the rights of parents to determine what's best for their children.

LEARNING OBJECTIVES

▼
Understand the reasons for, and the limits of, First Amendment protections.

▼
Grasp the critical importance of free expression in democracies.

▼
Understand the broad history of free speech in the United States.

▼
Understand several key First Amendment principles and the cases that gave rise to them.

FIGURE 7.1 The government generally cannot punish what you say, but can often regulate where and when you can say it.
Laurin Rinder/Shutterstock

"No doubt a state possesses legitimate power to protect children from harm," Scalia wrote in the majority opinion. "But that does not include a free-floating power to restrict the ideas to which children may be exposed" (p. 2735).

Although regulating children's access to depictions of sex has long been established, Scalia said there was no such tradition in the United States in relation to violence. He pointed to violence in the original depiction of many popular children's fairy tales like *Hansel and Gretel*, *Cinderella* and *Snow White*.

"Certainly the books we give children to read—or read to them when they are younger—contain no shortage of gore," Scalia added (p. 2736).

No matter that video games don't fit anyone's standard definition of free speech—like books, plays and movies, video games communicate ideas, and that was good enough for the Court to protect them. It's one case in a long line of decisions empowering speakers and stymying attempts by governments large and small to restrict disfavored forms of expression.

▶ THE POWER OF FREE EXPRESSION

The freedoms afforded speech, and yes, even violent video games, in the United States truly are breathtaking. The First Amendment, enshrined in the Bill of Rights, remains deceptively straightforward:

Congress shall make no law respecting an establishment of religion, or prohibiting the free exercise thereof; or abridging the freedom of speech, or of the press; or the right of the people peaceably to assemble, and to petition the Government for a redress of grievances.

Have any 45 words generated more controversy, engendered greater debate and resulted in more titanic legal clashes in our nation's history?

Think, for a moment, about those words, and their central meaning. We can see, in these 45 words, the intent of the Founding Fathers to create an institution—the press—free to say what it wants, freed from government efforts to censor or punish that viewpoint.

It's also quite clear that the First Amendment is about telling the government what it *can not* do—"Congress shall make no law . . ."—rather than telling people what they *can* do. That's an important distinction, known as the difference between "positive liberty," in which governments grant rights to people, and "negative liberty," in which the people tell their government what it can and cannot do.

We could also logically conclude that should government seek to punish the press after the fact, for what it has said, it will face an uphill fight: The First Amendment, if it means anything, means that you should be free to say or publish what you like. The colonists suffered under the British system of prior restraint, meaning that the Crown could stop a publication before it even hit the presses. Stopping speech before it happens is the ultimate form of repression, and became a major point of contention in the pre-revolutionary United States.

◀ **PRIOR RESTRAINT:** Government prohibition of speech in advance of publication.

It's easy to assume that the American patriots, who used the colonial press to foment popular discontent into full-blown revolution, wished to completely reject the British system of media controls. The reality is much more complex.

That's not to say that the colonists appreciated the British law of the

DISCUSSION QUESTIONS

What impact do you think the context in which the American press operated under British rule had on those drafting the First Amendment? Some have argued that the authors put this amendment first in the Bill of Rights for a reason. Do you agree?

7.1 THE VIEW FROM THE PROS: A FREE PRESS FOR STUDENT JOURNALISTS?

If you think press freedom is all a big history lesson, take a second to reflect on what happened to journalist Chase Snider.

The setting was Springfield, MO, in the fall of 2010, and a public gathering was quickly getting out of hand. A young woman was trampled and had to be taken away by ambulance. Another suffered an allergic reaction as partiers began flinging food at each other, prompting a second emergency response.

Snider was there covering the event as editor of a local news website, taking photos and working with his staff to write a story about what happened.

None of that coverage, however, would ever see the light of day.

Officials ordered Snider to turn over copies of his photographs and then delete them. The story was not to run. As far as the readers were concerned, it never happened.

While it all sounds like something from a third-world dictatorship, it's just one of the many blatant acts of censorship that happen every year in this country.

Snider was a high school senior covering that campus event as editor of the student newspaper. That fact forces him and thousands of his colleagues across the country to live in a different First Amendment universe.

Since the Supreme Court's 1988 *Hazelwood* decision, school officials have had vast (though not unlimited) power to control the content of student publications. The theory among the justices back then was that schools should have reasonable control over what happens in the classroom—a fine idea, assuming you trust administrators to act reasonably.

The reality in many schools has been a concerted effort to squelch anything that might create controversy, embarrass the school, or cause discomfort. For journalism—a discipline that prides itself on holding the powerful accountable and creating dialogue—that environment is intolerable.

Since we opened our doors more than 35 years ago, the staff of the Student Press Law Center—a DC-area non-profit that provides free legal support to student journalists—have had our work cut out for us. Each year we take about 2,500 calls from high school and college students, along with their advisers, with questions about the law. That number doesn't include the countless schools where censorship has become so routine that no one thinks to question it.

Unfortunately, it's no longer a safe assumption that you're free and clear when you get to college, either. While it was unthinkable at one time, some courts have begun applying the *Hazelwood* standard to public colleges and universities. And dozens of schools have tried doing an end-run around the First Amendment by firing journalism advisers or pulling funding when the coverage gets too hot.

Fortunately, there's reason for optimism. Seven states have passed laws nullifying *Hazelwood* for high school students. An eighth, Illinois, has done so only for college students. Some school districts and colleges have declared their student publications to be "public forums," and recognized the importance of uncensored journalism. Volunteer attorneys like those from the SPLC are standing up for students in court.

A free press is a fragile concept. That's why the founders protected it in the constitution, so it wouldn't be up for repeal with every new controversy. America's students, however, don't have the luxury of taking the First Amendment for granted.

The good news is that where student press freedom does exist, students are empowered to tackle the important issues we expect of journalists. They have a voice and a means to use it responsibly. They learn by doing.

As for Chase Snider, he and censorship would go on a second date. A few weeks after the "mosh" event, he tried to cover a minor car accident in the school's parking lot. Officials threatened to suspend him if he didn't stop taking photos. And after he posted a written account to the newspaper's website, the story was quickly pulled offline. Snider was suspended as editor.

He didn't learn about the promise of a free press from a history book. He learned about it through the reality of a tumultuous and intimidating senior year. He learned that, at least within the schoolhouse gates, the promise can ring pretty hollow.

LEARN MORE: Visit the Student Press Law Center online at www.splc.org/. Read about recent cases. A good FAQ on First Amendment rights for college journalists is found on the "Know Your Rights" page.

Brian Schraum is publications fellow at the Student Press Law Center in Arlington, VA. He received his master's degree from the Missouri School of Journalism in 2010.

press. The British recognized the disruptive power of the press in the early 16th Century and began devising numerous schemes to restrict publication. The Crown for many years used an elaborate system of patents and monopolies to control printing in England. Licensing or prior censorship was also common. Criticism of the government, called seditious libel, was outlawed. Not only was truth not a defense against government punishment for seditious libel; the maxim of the day was "the greater the truth, the greater the libel."

Freedom of the press today is recognized as a uniquely robust element of the American legal tradition, but it is important to note that it is a right that has been won only through many hard-fought battles.

▶ NO LAW?

And as for that clear-as-a-bell "Congress shall make no law . . ."? Well, that lasted for less than a decade after the nation was founded.

In 1798, Congress enacted the Alien and Sedition Acts, as repressive an assault on free speech as we've ever seen. Dozens of political editors and politicians were prosecuted under the laws, which made it a crime to criticize both the president and the national government. Several justices of the Supreme Court presided at sedition act trials and refused to sustain a constitutional objection to the laws.

When John Adams was voted out of office in 1800, his political rival, Thomas Jefferson, brought this embarrassing chapter to a close—for 117 years, anyway.

◀ **SEDITION:** Sedition is the crime of revolting or inciting revolt against government. Under First Amendment doctrine it is quite rare, but sedition remains in the United States Criminal Code.

In World War I and again in the 1940s, Congress enacted new sedition laws aimed at a wide variety of opposition speakers, as war protesters, socialists, anarchists and other political dissidents became the target of government repression.

Even as the legislative branch was largely ignoring the First Amendment, something remarkable was taking place in the judicial branch. The United States Supreme Court, in a series of decisions ranging from 1919 to 1957,

**FIGURE 7.2
NEW YORK—
SEPTEMBER 30:
Unidentified
demonstrators
with "Occupy Wall
Street" march
in Downtown
Manhattan on
September 30,
2011 in New York.
*Lev Radin/
Shutterstock***

slowly but steadily began to raise the bar when it came to punishing so-called "dangerous speech."

What changed? Well, a lot of things. In a series of rulings stemming from the World War I sedition cases, the Supreme Court created the "clear and present danger test."

Justice Oliver Wendell Holmes put it this way:

> The question in every case is whether the words used are used in such circumstances and are of such a nature as to create a clear and present danger that they will bring about the substantive evils that the United States Congress has a right to prevent . . . When a nation is at war, many things that might be said in time of peace are such a hindrance to its effort that their utterance will not be endured so long as men fight, and that no Court could regard them as protected by any constitutional right.
>
> (*Schenck v. United States*, 1919, p. 52)

It's a paranoid test reflective of a paranoid era, a period in which a fragile federal government embroiled in an unpopular foreign war saw threats, some real, some imagined, and responded by stifling speech. The problem with the "clear and present danger" test, as Holmes began to realize almost immediately, is that it equates speech with action—a huge logical leap, and one that placed the Court in the unenviable position of determining the tendency of speech.

Then in *Gitlow v. New York* in 1925, the Court ruled that the guarantees of freedom of speech apply to actions taken by all governments. Free speech became a fundamental liberty, opening the door to a much broader protection of freedom of expression in the nation.

Meanwhile, the American mass media was taking shape and, along with it, new First Amendment challenges. The Red Scare of the 1940s and 1950s ushered in a new round of sedition laws aimed at suppressing suspected Communist sympathizers—but by then, the courts had grown more resistant to government punishment of mere speech, absent any sort of action.

Finally, in 1957, the Supreme Court ruled in *Yates v. U.S.* that to sustain a conviction, the government would have to be able to prove that the defendants advocated specific violent or forcible action toward the overthrow of the government.

It was a signal moment: from that day forward, the government found it impossible to prove such intent, and the laws that made the Red Scare possible crumbled.

In 1969, the Supreme Court raised the bar even higher, ruling in *Brandenburg v. Ohio* that advocacy of unlawful conduct is protected by the Constitution unless it is directed toward inciting or producing "imminent lawless action and is likely to incite or produce such action."

DISCUSSION QUESTIONS

Think about criticisms leveled against President Barack Obama (or earlier, against President George W. Bush) on social networks, blogs, talk shows and other platforms. Think of the worst of these that you can recall. Now, view those through the context of U.S. First Amendment policy and law starting in 1798 and going through 1969. In which eras might these statements have landed the authors in jail? How did the thinking of lawmakers and judges change over this time period?

In the course of 50 years, the Supreme Court had moved from the near-total deference of the "clear and present danger" test to requiring the government to demonstrate that speech is so closely tied to action that the danger is imminent. It's a remarkable journey, one that reflects a nation increasingly confident in letting its speakers speak freely.

▶ THE LIMITS OF FREEDOM

The same process of judicial expansion of protection for speech has taken place in the law of defamation.

▶ **DEFAMATION:** Any intentional false communication, either written or spoken, that harms a person's reputation; decreases the respect, regard or confidence in which a person is held; or induces disparaging, hostile or disagreeable opinions or feelings against a person.

Libel occurs when a false and defamatory statement about an identifiable person is published to a third party, causing injury to the subject's reputation. A libelous statement can be the basis of a civil lawsuit brought by the person or group allegedly defamed or, in rare cases, a criminal prosecution.

There is no uniform law for libel. Each state decides what the plaintiff in a civil libel suit must prove and what defenses are available for the media. Prior to 1964, libel law in the United States represented a modest improvement over the British law of colonial times, but truth as a defense still barely registered in state libel laws. Then a case emerged that gave the Supreme Court an ideal vehicle for bringing libel law under the protections of the First Amendment.

New York Times v. Sullivan remains one of the Court's most majestic opinions, a watershed moment for free speech. It was as much a civil rights case as a libel case.

▶ **LIBEL:** Written or broadcast defamation. A false statement that damages a person's reputation.

In *Sullivan*, the Court again demonstrated its growing commitment to free speech—and its clear relationship to democracy—by striking down Alabama's libel law.

The case arose from an ad that appeared in the *New York Times*—a newspaper reviled by segregationists in the South for what they saw as its meddling coverage of the civil rights movement. The ad was placed by the Committee to Defend Martin Luther King and the Struggle for Freedom in the South, and called attention to what the committee described as a system of repression:

In Montgomery, Alabama, after students sang "My Country, Tis of
Thee" on the State Capitol steps, their leaders were expelled from
school, and truckloads of police armed with shotguns and tear-
gas ringed the Alabama State College Campus. When the entire
student body protested to state authorities by refusing to register,
their dining hall was padlocked in an attempt to starve them into
submission.

("Heed Their Rising Voices," 1960)

L.B. Sullivan, a commissioner of public affairs for Montgomery, sued the
New York Times Co. for libel. His argument was that the assertions in many
places were factually incorrect. And he was quite right: in several places,
errors of fact were made. The students sang "The Star Spangled Banner."
The police didn't exactly make a ring around the campus; they merely in-
undated the campus. Though unmentioned in the advertisement, Sullivan
nonetheless claimed that the charges of police mistreatment implied his
involvement.

On the basis of such minor, and arguably unimportant, errors, Alabama juries handed down $3 million in damages. The first case, a $500,000 judgment, was upheld on appeal by the Alabama Supreme Court. The Alabama
Court's opinion consisted of a single sentence: "The First Amendment of the
U.S. Constitution does not protect libelous publications."

And so far as any court up to that moment had ruled, they were quite right.
The U.S. Supreme Court was about to change all of that.

In a ringing endorsement of the importance of free speech in a democracy,
the Court struck down the Alabama verdict and rewrote the law of libel in
a single day.

Justice William Brennan Jr. wrote for a unanimous Court, with Justices
Hugo Black and Arthur Goldberg writing concurring opinions.

This was the first time that the Court invoked the First Amendment to prevent libel actions. Such actions, wrote Brennan, could no longer claim "tal-
ismanic immunity from constitutional limitations." The Court also likened
the Alabama libel law to the old threat of seditious libel—of liability based
on criticism of public officials.

In language that has become the most famous line in First Amendment history, Justice Brennan declared:

> [W]e consider this case against the background of a profound national commitment to the principle that debate on public issues should be uninhibited, robust, and wide-open, and that it may well include vehement, caustic, and sometimes unpleasantly sharp attacks on government and public officials.
>
> (*New York Times Co. v. Sullivan*, 1964, p. 270)

This time there were 44 words. And with those words, the First Amendment sprang to life. Brennan captured the essence of freedom of expression, a principle born out of centuries of struggle.

7.2 THE VIEW FROM THE PROS: LIBEL LAW'S EVOLUTION DURING THE CIVIL RIGHTS MOVEMENT

The law of libel changed drastically in the 1960s with a lawsuit arising from an advertisement in the *New York Times* which asked for money and support for Martin Luther King Jr. and "the struggle for freedom in the South" during the civil rights movement.[1] The ad had charged police brutality against civil rights protestors in Montgomery, Alabama, but it had a handful of inconsequential errors. Those minor mistakes would have typically meant a win for the plaintiff in a libel suit in 1960. What you may not realize is that the case might have signaled the death knell for the *New York Times*, which faced several large libel suits filed by Southern public officials who were angry about coverage of civil rights issues. Southern leaders had begun using existing libel laws to craft what amounted to a sedition law to stop the press from covering the civil rights struggle in an attempt to maintain the racial status quo.[2]

However, the U.S. Supreme Court revolutionized libel law in *New York Times v. Sullivan*.[3] Shattering precedent, the nation's high court created a new standard that required public officials to prove actual malice and insured that citizens were free to exercise their First Amendment right to criticize the government.

Had the Supreme Court failed to overturn *Sullivan* and create the actual malice doctrine, the case's impact on the civil rights movement would have been staggering.[4] Without the world looking at the South through the lens of the national press, Southern officials and other segregationists would have been free to continue to squelch activism in their own way.[5] "The last desperate reaction of a clinging

---

1. "Heed Their Rising Voices," *New York Times*, March 29, 1960, 25.

2. Kermit L. Hall and Melvin I. Urofsky, *New York Times v. Sullivan: Civil Rights, Libel Law, and the Free Press* (Lawrence: University Press of Kansas, 2011).

3. 376 U.S. 254 (1964).

4. Anthony Lewis, *Make No Law, The Sullivan Case and the First Amendment* (New York: Random House, 1991). Lewis,

a Pulitzer Prize winning reporter, covered the Supreme Court for the *Times* when this case was argued.

5. For a more complete analysis of civil rights-related libel cases, see Aimee Edmondson, "In Sullivan's Shadow: The Use and Abuse of Libel Law During the Civil Rights Movement" PhD diss., University of Missouri, 2008. See also, Aimee Edmondson, "In Sullivan's Shadow: The Use and Abuse of Libel Law Arising from the Civil Rights Movement, 1960–1989," *Journalism History* 37:1 (April 2011): 27–38.

regime was to try to suppress the message itself," wrote legal scholar Rodney A. Smolla in 1986. "If one could not stop the marches, one might at least keep the marches off television and out of the newspapers."[6]

In the *Sullivan* opinion, the Supreme Court turned away from the common law tradition handed down from English courts to extend a right unique to the United States: constitutional protections of speech critical of the government, even speech that is false. By 1964, when the case was overturned, southern officials had filed at least $388 million in libel actions against newspapers, news magazines, television networks and civil rights leaders.[7] *Sullivan* and its companion cases accounted for $5.6 million, a huge sum at the time and one that threatened the financial solvency of the *Times*.[8] But it was not just the *Times* that felt the pain of the adverse libel judgment. Editors from other publications could not send a reporter or photographer into the South to cover civil rights demonstrations without fear of being sued.[9] The Supreme Court's unexpected decision thus widened the doors for the national press to cover civil rights demonstrations and activities in the South.

Northern journalists had begun swooping into the region in the 1950s to write about race, telling the story of the civil rights movement as it unfolded and telling the story from the largely unheard black point of view.[10] Plaintiffs such as Sullivan and other police officers had heavy stakes in shutting down the protests. Sullivan and Birmingham police commissioner Bull Connor gave mobs of Ku Klux Klansmen time to waylay Freedom Riders at the Montgomery and Birmingham bus stations before calling in their officers to haul the wounded demonstrators off to jail.[11] It was Connor who made an international spectacle out of Birmingham with his lunging police dogs and skin-shredding fire hoses that washed young protesters down the street and into newspapers and broadcasts around the world.[12] He filed several libel suits worth millions in response to civil rights coverage in the *Times* and on CBS News, suits that were strikingly similar to *Sullivan*.

Before *Sullivan* was overturned, similar libel suits arose out of the Ole Miss riots in 1962 as Air Force veteran James Meredith sought to desegregate the university. Mississippi police were angered by coverage of their handling of the riots as reported in the *Saturday Evening Post*.[13] A similar libel suit also arose out of coverage of the 1963 March on Washington, when yet another southern lawman, the sheriff of Etowah County, Alabama, disputed a flashback scene of his brutality of civil rights protestors in an article for *Ladies Home Journal* written by the famous playwright Lillian Hellman.[14] Still more southern police officers and public officials filed libel suits for coverage of the Freedom Summer murders of three civil rights workers in Philadelphia, Mississippi, in 1964.[15]

Scholars and other media experts agree the *Sullivan* case stopped what surely would have been an even greater onslaught of libel suits for civil rights coverage. What might be the last case came in 1988, when the film *Mississippi Burning* appeared in theaters across the nation and told a fictionalized story of the three murdered civil rights workers in Neshoba County, Mississippi. The same litigious former

6. Rodney A. Smolla, *Suing the Press* (New York: Oxford University Press, 1986), 43.

7. John Herbers, "Libel Actions Ask Millions in South," *New York Times*, April 4, 1964.

8. Lewis, *Make No Law*, 151.

9. Harrison E. Salisbury, *Without Fear or Favor* (New York: Times Books, 1982), 384.

10. Gene Roberts & Hank Klibanoff, *The Race Beat, the Press, the Civil Rights Struggle, and the Awakening of a Nation* (New York: Knopf, 2006). Also see David Halberstam, *The Children* (New York: Fawcett Books, 1998), 293. Freedom Riders like John Lewis began counting on the national media to tell their stories, for example.

11. This point has been widely established in the literature. See, for example, Howard K. Smith, *Events Leading Up to My Death: The Life of a Twentieth-Century Reporter* (New York: St. Martin's Press, 1996); See also J. Mills Thornton III, *Dividing Lines, Municipal Politics and the Struggle for Civil Rights in Montgomery, Birmingham and Selma* (Tuscaloosa: The University of Alabama Press, 1991).

12. William A. Nunnelley, *Bull Connor* (Tuscaloosa: The University of Alabama Press, 1991).

13. *Curtis v. Birdsong*, 360 F. 2d 344.

14. *New York Times*, "Curtis Publishing Is Named in a $3 Million Libel Suit," February 27, 1964.

15. For example, *Rainey v. CBS*, Neshoba County Circuit Court, Case No. E78–0121 (1978).

sheriff Lawrence Rainey sued Orion Pictures for libel, but he quickly dropped the case when lawyers for the film company said they would prove truth, the ultimate defense in a libel suit, that Rainey was responsible for the deaths of the three civil rights workers whose bodies had been found in an earthen dam in rural Mississippi. Twenty-six years had passed since the *Sullivan* decision. Members of the media, exercising their First Amendment right and responsibility to report on events about public officials and on events of public interest, had spent millions trying to defend that right.

THINK ABOUT IT: Read the original advertisement from *The New York Times v. Sullivan* case, found at in the National Archives at www.archives.gov/exhibits/documented-rights/

exhibit/section4/detail/heed-rising-voices.html (note: the text is easier to read in the Transcript version of the exhibit). Does it surprise you that this case stemmed from ad copy produced by an advocacy organization and not from information gathered by a journalist working for the newspaper? Should publishers and media executives be held responsible for all content, even advertising? Why might the Supreme Court not have made a distinction between paid content and work produced by journalists?

Aimee Edmondson is an assistant professor at Ohio University. A newspaper reporter for a dozen years, she earned a doctorate in journalism from the University of Missouri in 2008.

Having set the stage for a broad interpretation of speech rights, Justice Brennan found that though some of the statements in the *Times* advertisement were false, that could not be the end of the matter, because "erroneous statement is inevitable in free debate."

Given that, even certain false statements "must be protected if the freedoms of expression are to have the 'breathing space' that they 'need . . . to survive'" (pp. 271–272).

DISCUSSION QUESTIONS

About half of those responding to a First Amendment Center/American Journalism Review survey said the First Amendment goes too far in the rights it guarantees. Do you agree? Why do you think so many people believe the First Amendment should be curtailed? What can and should journalists do to help audiences understand the need for a strong First Amendment?

And then, in a sweeping exercise of judicial power, Justice Brennan crafted a new rule to better protect freedom of speech and press without granting a free pass for intentional falsehoods: Public officials now would be unable to recover damages for a defamatory falsehood relating to official conduct unless the official can prove that the statement was made with "actual malice"—that is, with knowledge that it was false or with reckless disregard of whether it was false or not.

▶ DRAWING LINES

It's hard to overstate the importance of the Court's ruling in *New York Times v. Sullivan*. In a single day, laws that had been used to silence and intimidate speakers were swept aside, replaced with a new standard that better protected speech, as the nation careened toward the late 1960s, the culmination of the civil rights movement, the anti-war movement and Vietnam. The stage was set for the greatest expansion of First Amendment rights in the nation's history, and the societal turmoil bubbling up ensured that the courts had plenty of cases pitting the rights of speakers and the authorities trying to keep a grip on things.

In 1971, in the famous case of *New York Times Co. v. United States*, the Court ruled that a court order instituting a "prior restraint" on news stories based on the Pentagon Papers—a top-secret history of U.S. involvement in Vietnam—was unconstitutional. In its opinion, the Court said that "Any system of prior restraints comes to this Court bearing a heavy presumption against its constitutional validity" (p. 714).

So we can see that some regulatory methods, like prior restraint, are all but forbidden by the First Amendment. To what extent can the government regulate speech and expression?

As the sheer number and variety of speech and expression cases began to grow, governments at all levels began to enact a variety of laws aimed at controlling the means of protest. Some of these laws seemed reasonable enough on their face, while others clearly were designed to inhibit speech. Lines needed to be drawn for lower courts to be able to make sense of it all. The result of all of this judicial activity was a pair of tests for determining whether laws interfere with free expression in ways that violate the First Amendment.

Start with this general rule of thumb: Normally, the government may punish people for causing various harms, directly or indirectly. But it generally may not punish speakers when the harms are caused by what the speaker said— by the content, in other words (unless, of course, the speech falls within one of the First Amendment exceptions, such as incitement, false statements of fact, threats, obscenity or fighting words).

In order to focus on whether or not the content of the speech is what is being regulated, judges employing First Amendment analysis also focus on the form of the regulation.

The United States Supreme Court created a test for doing just that in a 1968 case, *United States v. O'Brien*. David O'Brien was a Vietnam War protester who was convicted under a federal law that made it a crime to destroy a draft card. O'Brien set fire to his card at a protest.

The law, on its face, was pretty clear: it required all males above the age of 18 to obtain and carry a draft card, in order for the military draft to run smoothly (remember, these are in the days before the personal computer, when a paper card really was that critical to something like the draft . . .).

The Court rejected O'Brien's arguments that the law was unconstitutional because it infringed his right to free speech. Instead, the Court looked at the purpose of the law itself and at Congressional intent, and found the sole motivation to be orderly administration of the draft.

O'Brien had plenty of ways to express himself. He just couldn't burn a draft card, because the government had a strong interest in making sure people had their draft cards on their persons.

So, having found the statute content-neutral, the Court created a new test to judge the constitutionality of such laws, ruling that the law will be upheld if: (1) it furthers an important or substantial government purpose, (2) the government purpose is unrelated to the suppression of expression and (3) the restriction is narrowly tailored to accomplish the substantial purpose.

The Court uses the *O'Brien* test to analyze regulations the government argues are not about content, but about regulating the "time, place or manner" of speech. There are lots of these laws that pass First Amendment scrutiny, such as noise ordinances regulating how loud music can be played at 2 a.m., or law regulating the size and density of billboards on the side of highways.

What if the law is about regulating content?

Then the test gets a lot stiffer.

It can be tough to see the difference, at least at first blush. One way to think about time, place, manner restrictions is by using the "5 Ws and a H" of journalism. If a law is aimed solely at how, when or to some extent where speech is conducted, the law more likely than not has no effect on the content of speech.

On the other hand, if the law is aimed at the "why," the "who" or the "what" of speech, the law may not be content-neutral, and in fact, may be content-based.

Content-based statutes face the toughest test of them all: so-called "strict scrutiny" review. Courts almost always strike down content-based laws under First Amendment challenge unless they (1) use the least restrictive means possible to (2) advance a compelling government interest.

7.3 THE VIEW FROM THE PROS: WIKILEAKS AND THE FIRST AMENDMENT

WikiLeaks is a website that publishes political and government documents, many of them classified at one level or the other. The idea behind the site is that secrecy and democracy are incompatible. Although that's hardly radical, WikiLeaks and its founder, Julian Assange, have embedded that idea in a framework somewhat at odds with the institutional ethics of journalism. Consider the backstory.

In April 2010, WikiLeaks released a classified video of a U.S. Army helicopter in Baghdad opening fire on a group of people that included a Reuters photographer. From the P.O.V. of the helicopter's gun-sight, the video clearly shows the killings. Assange titled the video "Collateral Murder," and later, as a guest on Stephen Colbert's show, Assange said he wanted the title to "create maximum possible political impact."

In July 2010, WikiLeaks published more than 75,000 classified U.S. documents about the war in Afghanistan—publishing them in cooperation with the *New York Times*, the *Guardian* and *Der Spiegel*. The documents consisted of field reports prepared by troops on the ground, giving day-to-day accounts of the war. The Pentagon condemned WikiLeaks and demanded that the website return the leaked documents. Assange refused, but by then Bradley Manning,

a 20-something U.S. intelligence analyst, was sitting in a military prison, suspected of providing the classified material to WikiLeaks.

In October 2010, WikiLeaks published nearly 400,000 classified U.S. documents about the war in Iraq—again publishing them in cooperation with major newspapers around the world. Although the U.S. government accused WikiLeaks of endangering national security, one month later WikiLeaks began publishing U.S. diplomatic cables. The first batch totaled about 220, and since then WikiLeaks has published more than 2,500. They provide a he-said-she-said account of contemporary diplomacy. The *New York Times* reported that the cables give you a "look at bargaining by embassies, candid views of foreign leaders, and assessments of threats."

In response, Secretary of State Hillary Clinton said the release of the cables was "not just an attack on America's foreign policy interests; it [was] an attack on the international community." Director of National Intelligence James Clapper said the "actions taken by WikiLeaks are not only deplorable, irresponsible, and reprehensible—they could have major impacts on our national security." And Attorney General Eric Holder announced that the Justice Department and the Pentagon were investigating the leaks to determine if criminal charges would be filed. As of this writing, a federal grand jury is meeting in Virginia to weigh the government's evidence against WikiLeaks and Assange.

The possibility of prosecution brings into question the proper balance between free speech and national security. There's no one law that makes it a crime to publish classified information—no catchall that says, "Thou shalt not disclose." Instead, there's a patchwork of laws serving that function, each applying in different circumstances. Take, for example, the Espionage Act of 1917, which might be used to prosecute WikiLeaks for communicating or transmitting defense information. Such a prosecution would trigger First Amendment challenges.

The first is called "strict scrutiny," and the second is called the "clear and present danger" test. They both require the government to meet a high burden before punishing someone for publishing. It's unclear how those challenges would play out, because the government hasn't released factual findings from its investigation. One thing, however, is clear: It doesn't matter in this context whether WikiLeaks is part of the press. The First Amendment doesn't belong to the press. It protects the rights of all speakers, sometimes on the basis of the Speech Clause and other times on the basis of the Press Clause. Remember, the First Amendment says, "Congress shall make no law abridging the freedom of speech, or of the press."

To argue that the First Amendment would protect WikiLeaks and Assange, as publishers, only if they're part of the press is to assume (1) that the Speech Clause wouldn't protect them, and (2) that there's a major difference between the Speech and Press Clauses. In reality, most of the freedoms that the press gets from the First Amendment are no different from the freedoms that everyone gets from the Speech Clause. This is true even for the core freedoms essential to the press. The few times the Supreme Court has decided cases using the Press Clause alone, the same results could have been reached using the Speech Clause. As a result, one commentator said not long ago that "the Press Clause today is an invisible force in the law."

So what does this mean for WikiLeaks? On the one hand, it could be a good thing for WikiLeaks and Assange. If the Justice Department prosecuted them for publishing, they wouldn't have to argue that they do journalism or deserve to be protected as members of the press. They could just call on the Speech Clause, which would trigger strict scrutiny or the clear-and-present danger test.

On the other hand, it could be a bad thing for the legacy press. Bill Keller, former executive editor of the *New York Times*, summed up the problem in February 2010. He said, "It's very hard to conceive of a prosecution of Julian Assange that wouldn't stretch the law in a way that would be applicable to us. American journalists . . . should feel a sense of alarm at any legal action that tends to punish Assange for doing essentially what journalists do. That is to say, any use of the law to criminalize the publication of secrets."

Putting Keller's remarks in legal terms, unless the Supreme Court all of a sudden decided to interpret the Press Clause differently from the Speech Clause, any prosecution of WikiLeaks for publishing secrets would affect the legacy press and their rights to do the same. That would be significant because in the last 40 years, with the exception of cases targeting government employees, the Supreme Court has never upheld a prosecution for the publication of truthful information about the government.

THINK ABOUT IT: What are the downsides of separating the speech and press clauses in the First Amendment? What upsides might exist? How does this issue relate to the definition of journalism (and who is a journalist) as discussed in Chapter 2?

Jonathan Peters is a media lawyer and doctoral student at the Missouri School of Journalism. He blogs about free expression for the *Harvard Law & Policy Review*, and he has written on legal issues for *The Atlantic, Slate, The Nation, Wired* and PBS.

It's tough to find a compelling interest at stake where speech is concerned, at least most of the time. That's why flag-burning laws, for all the emotion invested in them, will never survive constitutional scrutiny.

Take the leading case in the area, *Texas v. Johnson*. Gregory Lee Johnson was convicted and sentenced to a year in prison and a $1,000 fine for burning an American flag during a protest at the 1984 Republican National Convention in Dallas under a Texas statute that made it a crime to "desecrate" the flag.

Johnson appealed his conviction all the way to the United States Supreme Court, which in a 5–4 decision said that the state of Texas had found no compelling interest. The state's argument that preserving the sanctity of the flag was such an interest actually constituted government picking and choosing viewpoints.

"If there is a bedrock principle underlying the First Amendment," Justice William Brennan wrote for the Court, "it is that the government may not prohibit the expression of an idea simply because society finds the idea itself offensive or disagreeable" (p. 414).

That's what the Court calls "viewpoint discrimination," and it's the most basic, yet also the most powerful, rule under the First Amendment: When you get right down to it, viewpoint discrimination means that the government can't tell us what to think or say. And when it tries, through passing laws, to limit what we can write or say, it had better have a compelling reason for doing so.

Think about that a minute: This rule, which effectively removes government from the content business, establishes a system in which the fewer people agree with a speaker's point, the greater that speaker's protection. The state is so limited in what it can do to speech that speech flourishes in the absence of regulation.

Don't take our word for it: look at the just how powerful First Amendment law has become. The best evidence available might just be the Rev. Fred Phelps.

You might not recognize the name, but surely you remember the signs: "Thank God for Dead Soldiers," "Fags Doom Nations," "America is Doomed," "Priests Rape Boys," and "You're Going to Hell," among other similar messages, displayed at the funerals of American soldiers.

The reverend's attention-getting, highly offensive posters made him quite possibly the least popular speaker in the country, yet when one solder's

FIGURE 7.3 Jacob Phelps, grandson of Westboro Baptist Church pastor Fred Phelps, demonstrates outside the U.S. Supreme Court while justices heard oral arguments in *Snyder v. Phelps*, which tests the limits of the First Amendment, October 6, 2010 in Washington, DC. Albert Snyder sued the Westboro Baptist Church after his son, Marine Corps Lance Cpl. Matthew Snyder, was killed in Iraq in 2006 and members of the church held signs and demonstrated outside his funeral. The church and its members preach that U.S. deaths in Afghanistan and Iraq are punishment for Americans' immorality, including tolerance of homosexuality and abortion.

Chip Somodevilla/Getty Images

family sued him for intentional infliction of emotional distress and intrusion upon seclusion, the Court wasted little time in finding that that the First Amendment protected Reverend Fred Phelps's hateful and harmful speech.

To Chief Justice Roberts, who wrote for an 8–1 majority, the issue was rather straightforward. Phelps's speech was on matters of public import, Phelps's signs were on public land next to a public street, and Phelps and his fellow protesters stayed away from the actual funeral service.

"Snyder could see no more than the tops of the signs when driving to the funeral. And there is no indication that the picketing in any way interfered with the funeral service itself," Justice Roberts wrote (*Snyder v. Phelps*, 2011, p. 14).

He added that states could enact reasonable content-neutral time, place, and manner restrictions on speech at funerals. These lawsuits didn't fit the bill because they sought to punish Phelps specifically because of the "what" of his speech. That Phelps is, quite possibly, the least popular speaker of our generation, speaks to the underlying value at the heart of the First Amendment: tolerance.

More than anything else, free speech requires us to tolerate speech we find repulsive, shocking, offensive, or just plain wrong. The First Amendment scholar Lee Bollinger has written eloquently of the "social ethic" created by the system of free expression, in which society learns to exercise self-restraint and recognize the intolerance in each of us. In *The Tolerant Society: Free Speech and Extremist Speech in America*, Bollinger points out an uncomfortable truth: we are often eager to repress speech we disagree with, and so we have built a legal system of protection to overcome that impulse.

Rather than look at speech like Phelps's as the price we must pay for free speech, Bollinger sees it as an opportunity to prove our commitment to tolerance. "The free speech principle involves a special act of carving out one area of social interaction for extraordinary self-restraint, the purpose of which is to develop and demonstrate a social capacity to control feelings evoked by a host of social encounters"(p. 10). So it's a matter of building that tolerance, day by day, citizen by citizen. It's a massive investment, really, and one that shows just how seriously we take free speech in the United States.

That's not to say, however, that protection for speech is absolute, not by any means. No majority of the United States Supreme Court has ever interpreted the First Amendment as absolute, and while we enjoy broad freedom to speak and to write as we wish, the courts have been less expansive when it comes to the means by which news is gathered. This creates some real limits when it comes to the ways journalists can access government information, use anonymous sources or enter other people's property in the pursuit of news.

Courts generally hold that journalists have no greater rights than those of the general public—a principle known as "laws of general applicability."

One area where the laws of general applicability run headlong into the work journalists do is in the use of anonymous sources. Reporters sometimes make promises of confidentiality to sources in exchange for information, particularly in investigative reporting. Sources in such stories often fear retribution from those in power, yet in some stories dealing with fraud, abuse or corruption, a single source can make all the difference in the public airing of important stories. Or a grand jury investigating a crime may seek to force a reporter to reveal the source of a story. In other cases, journalists may be asked to testify at a criminal or civil trial. It's a fundamental conflict between the rights of journalists and the duty of every citizen to testify to help the courts determine justice.

▶ SECRETS, AND WHEN TO KEEP THEM

Because of the work they do, journalists often find themselves at the scene of events that are important and newsworthy. Anyone wanting the facts about an event can subpoena reporters to testify about all the details. Journalists almost always resist such orders.

Their argument is that they don't want to become a de facto arm of law enforcement. Even worse, if journalists can't honor their promises of confidentiality, what source would talk to them about a really sensitive subject, knowing that their identities or their information could end up being disclosed in court?

The United States Supreme Court ruled in the 1972 case of *Branzburg v. Hayes* that reporters have no First Amendment right to refuse to answer all questions before grand juries if they actually witnessed criminal activity.

Two justices in the deeply divided opinion recognized a qualified constitutional privilege, however, keeping hope alive for journalists. Justice Powell, while agreeing with the majority, wrote a concurrence arguing that reporters would still be able to contest subpoenas if they were issued in bad faith, or if there were no legitimate law enforcement need for the information.

Justice Stewart, dissenting, made a much stronger case for a robust privilege, arguing that anything less would allow officials to "annex" the news media as "an investigative arm of government." Two other justices joined Stewart. These four justices, together with Justice William O. Douglas, who dissented in a separate opinion, gave the notion of a qualified constitutional privilege a majority.

Since *Branzburg*, many federal and state courts have found some form of qualified constitutional privilege. Where the privilege is recognized, the courts generally use a three-part balancing test to assess whether the subpoenaed information is clearly relevant and material to the pending case, whether it goes to the heart of the case and whether it could be obtained from other sources besides the media.

In recent years, however, a growing number of federal courts have become reluctant to recognize a privilege under the First Amendment. In 2005, the U.S. Court of Appeals in the District of Columbia said a grand jury's need for information outweighed any reporter's privilege after *New York Times* reporter Judith Miller refused to testify about her sources for a story about CIA operative Valerie Plame. Miller and her bosses at the *Times* took the position that her promise to hold confidential her sources' names was not one she could break. The U.S. Supreme Court refused to hear her appeal. Although her imprisonment inspired bills in Congress calling for a federal shield law, Congress has not yet passed such a law. Miller spent 85 days in jail before agreeing to testify.

At the state level, legislatures picked up Justice Stewart's three-part test and passed "shield laws" providing some protection for journalists facing orders to testify or provide notes, photographs or other reporting work product. By 2012, 40 states and the District of Columbia had some form of shield laws in place.

The lack of any federal shield law protection demonstrates just how important the laws can be for journalists. In 2001–2002, Vanessa Leggett, a freelance journalist in Houston, Texas, spent a record 168 days in jail for

DISCUSSION QUESTIONS

State shield laws protect journalists. What issues arise in defining who is entitled to this protection? If you have a blog, are you a journalist? What if you routinely share information of public interest through a Twitter or Facebook page?

refusing a federal grand jury's command to hand over notes and tapes of interviews she had made while writing a book about the murder of a Houston socialite.

▶ WHEN REPORTING BECOMES PRYING, THERE ARE CONSEQUENCES

Journalists also face limits created by the law of privacy. Almost every state recognizes some right of privacy, either by statute or under common law—the traditional court-made law that U.S. courts adopted long ago from the English standards.

A right of privacy can be violated by any means of communication, including spoken words. This tort, or civil action, is usually divided into four categories: intrusion, publication of private facts, false light and misappropriation.

▶ **INTRUSION:**
Intentionally intruding, physically or otherwise, upon another person's seclusion or solitude or another person's private affairs.

The basis of privacy law is what the courts call a "reasonable expectation of privacy." In some settings—the home, for example—individuals have a right to expect some measure of privacy. That expectation is not nearly as strong in the middle of a public street.

Although private individuals usually can claim privacy rights, that right is not absolute. For example, if a person who is normally not considered a public figure is thrust into the spotlight because of her participation in a newsworthy event, her claims of a right of privacy may be limited. Courts will allow some leeway in the name of newsworthiness, in other words.

Intrusion claims against the media often center on the behavior of journalists in the newsgathering process, such as the intrusive use of recording devices, cameras or other intrusive equipment. Trespass also can be

DISCUSSION QUESTIONS

We read regularly reports of celebrities and politicians engaged in extra-marital affairs. The lines between publications like *The National Enquirer* and *The Washington Post* began to change in the 1980s and 1990s on reporting these types of stories. Think of this news in relation to the definition of "publication of private facts" included in this chapter. Are these matters of public concern? Would they be offensive to a reasonable person? Why are these reports protected under current law? Why might reputable news organizations publish this material?

a form of intrusion. Entering another person's property without permission frequently gives rise to intrusion cases.

Journalists can also find themselves in legal trouble for publishing truthful information if that information is about the private life of a person that would be both highly offensive to a reasonable person and not of legitimate public interest.

This can be a real legal wild card, because liability often is determined by a jury after examination of how the information was obtained and its newsworthiness.

Another privacy tort, false light invasion of privacy, occurs when information is published about a person that is false or places the person in a false light, is highly offensive to a reasonable person, and is published with knowledge or in reckless disregard of whether the information was false or would place the person in a false light.

False light privacy is a close cousin of defamation, but has a couple of key differences. Most importantly, the report need not be defamatory to be actionable as false light. False light can be created by embellishment (the addition of false material to a story, which places someone in a false light), distortion (the arrangement of materials or photographs to give a false impression) or fictionalization (references to real people in fictitious articles or the inclusion in works of fiction of disguised characters that represent real people).

Those in advertising and other media fields should be aware that the use of a person's name or likeness for commercial purposes without consent gives rise to a privacy tort called misappropriation. The key here is whether the use has an overriding commercial purpose. Incidental references to real people in books, films, stories or other works, generally are not misappropriations. Even the use of a photograph to illustrate a newsworthy story is not misappropriation. The use of the same photograph to sell products in an advertisement is a different matter, as that overriding commercial purpose kicks in.

Use of a celebrity's name or likeness, without consent, to sell a product is usually misappropriation. However, other unauthorized uses of celebrities'

◀ **PUBLICATION OF PRIVATE FACTS:** The publication of information about someone's personal life that has not been previously revealed to the public, is not a matter of public concern, and the publication of which would be offensive to a reasonable person.

◀ **FALSE LIGHT INVASION OF PRIVACY:** Giving publicity to a matter concerning another person that portrays that person falsely if the portrayal would be highly offensive to a reasonable person.

▶ **APPROPRIATION:**
The use of one's
name or likeness
for personal or
commercial gain
without consent
or compensation.

images may violate their publicity rights. Trading on a celebrity's fame and popularity even for noncommercial purposes, including public relations campaigns or other promotions, is an unauthorized use of the famous person's name or likeness that could violate his or her right of publicity. The bottom line: if you want to use someone's image, get permission.

▶ CONCLUSION

In the spring of 2011, the eyes of the world were affixed on the Middle East as civil unrest gave way to revolution in Egypt, Tunisia and Libya. We watched, transfixed, as monarchies staggered and fell under popular resistance fueled by a mix of smartphones, handheld video cameras and tweets. We then watched, amazed, as some of the same notions of civic participation and public unrest landed right in the United States in the form of the Occupy movement.

What did those events teach us? For starters, that the days of tidy authoritarian controls, where states can lean on journalists and silence the public through official means, are coming to an end. The repressive response to the Egyptian protests are a fine example: Given the ubiquity of smartphones, the universal use of Twitter and Facebook to pass along scenes of violence and police misconduct and military overreach, the Arab Awakening fed on itself. The government's ham-handed attempts to silence a technologically enabled populace just led to more posts, more tweets, more pictures . . . the inescapable conclusion is that it has become nearly impossible to control speech. Non-democratic governments still manage, but not without spending a lot of time and money on the effort, and even then, with uneven results (remember the Iranian protests of 2009?).

The United States still claims the most protection for speech and expression in the world. The First Amendment is just different—it protects a lot of speech that other nations ban outright. Hate speech, for example—speech that denigrates the race or religion of others—is banned in England, Canada, France, Germany and in just about every other democratic nation in the world. Rev. Phelps wouldn't make it out of his garage with those signs he carries around in any of those countries.

We deplore Rev. Phelps's speech, but the First Amendment protects it. We learn, in turn, to tolerate speech that offends us. There is a trade-off in all of this: By broadly protecting such hatred, we avoid the risks of suppressing valuable speech on the basis that someone finds it offensive. Think about it: every few weeks someone in the United States wants to ban a book, for some reason or another. By establishing such broad protections, we avoid these fights, or at least greatly reduce the odds that they will succeed. And by doing so, we make it possible to think, to write, to opinionate.

"The right to think is the beginning of freedom, and speech must be protected from the government because speech is the beginning of thought," wrote Justice Anthony Kennedy in *Ashcroft v. Free Speech Coalition* (2002, p. 253).

If the right to think is the beginning of freedom, then we risk suffering the harms of speech like Rev. Phelps's protests because that it is a better choice than offering the potential for the risk of suppressing valuable speech.

Why do we go to such lengths to protect freedom of speech? The First Amendment scholar Zechariah Chafee Jr. said the First Amendment protects two interests in free speech: the individual interest we have in expressing ourselves, and a societal interest in the attainment of truth. Both are crucial. In fact, people free to follow their political thoughts generate the societal change. That's the essential magic of the First Amendment and the role it performs in our democracy.

Chapter Seven Review

Chapter Summary

Suggested Activities

Read More

▶ CHAPTER SUMMARY

The First Amendment provides an amazing amount of protection for journalists and citizens alike to express themselves just about any way they like. While limits do exist, the courts generally protect speech against attempts by government to regulate it unless the government has extraordinarily powerful reasons to restrict it. The courts have created a number of judicial tests for evaluating First Amendment disputes, and have created a number of areas in which media practitioners face potential legal liability for harm caused by the work they do, especially in the area of libel and privacy.

▶ SUGGESTED ACTIVITIES

1. Conduct a moot court hearing in your class. The class should split up into teams (ranging from three to six members). One team will defend a First Amendment regulation, and the other team will argue against it. One that works well is local noise ordinances. Many cases involving these ordinances can be found online at the First Amendment Center at www.firstamendmentcenter.org/tag/noise-ordinance. If you have a larger class, another two groups can debate "free speech zones" on campuses. An article from the University of Alabama's *Crimson White* on this issue can be found at http://cw.ua.edu/2010/09/26/free-speech-on-campus-raises-concerns/.

2. Create a First Amendment Storify project. Select a key First Amendment case from the many discussed on the First Amendment Center's site (www.firstamendmentcenter.org/category/press), then search for and gather elements from social media about that case. Ensure you include several Facebook posts, tweets and pictures—all of the things that Storify allows you to assemble from across the Web, in one place. Add your own narrative too. (Go to Storify.com to see examples.) You can then share the project on Facebook or on a class website with the push of a button. Compare your "story" with others created by classmates. What are the similarities and differences?

3. Have a conversation with a First Amendment "user." Of course, we're all users of the First Amendment, but many of us don't come in daily contact with someone who really leans on their right to free speech. Speak to a member of a group in your community who really speaks out on issues. Examples might include a drive-time radio host, a member of your local newspaper editorial board, a representative of a local or state political party office, a leader of the ACLU or an official with the NRA. What are their views on freedom of expression? Have their rights ever been challenged? If so, how did they respond?

4. To reinforce the information in the chapter, watch a nine-minute video about the *New York Times v. Sullivan* case produced by Thinkwell Videos: www.youtube.com/watch?v=FtqQWt7aoZ0&feature=related. What new information does this video provide? Discuss the Doctrine of Incorporation in particular to explain how the First Amendment applies to state government. Review the history of U.S. press freedom, the three-part standard for libel for public officials and the concept of actual malice.

5. Visit the Student Press Law Center online at www.splc.org/. Under "Classroom Resources," locate the First Amendment quiz. The quiz has

30 questions and takes 10 minutes to complete. The last screen will report your score and tell you how you did. Take a screen capture of your result and e-mail it to your instructor with a brief note highlighting one or two things you were surprised to learn about the First Amendment.

▶ READ MORE

Ashcroft v. Free Speech Coalition 535 U.S. 234 (2002)

Lee Bollinger, *The Tolerant Society: Free Speech and Extremist Speech in America*, New York: Oxford University Press, 1986.

Brown v. Entertainment Merchants Association 131 S. Ct. 2729 (2011)

"Heed Their Rising Voices," *The New York Times*, March 29, 1960, p. 25.

Anthony Lewis, *Make No Law*, New York: Random House, 1991.

Kent R. Middleton and William Lee, *The Law of Public Communication*, 8th ed., New York: Longman, 2011.

New York Times Co. v. Sullivan 376 U.S. 254 (1964)

New York Times Co. v. United States 403 U.S. 713 (1971)

Don R. Pember and Clay Calvert, *Mass Media Law*, 16th ed., Dubuque, IA: McGraw-Hill, 2009–2010. www.firstamendmentcenter.org.

Schenck v. United States 249 U.S. 47 (1919)

Significant historical events, court cases and ideas that have shaped our current system of constitutional First Amendment jurisprudence, presented by the Freedom Forum. Also stories, commentaries and roundups of First Amendment disputes are available at www.firstamendmentcenter.org.

Snyder v. Phelps 131 S. Ct. 1207 (2011)

Texas v. Johnson 491 U.S. 397 (1989)

The Reporters Committee for Freedom of the Press maintains online "publications and topical guides on First Amendment and Freedom of Information issues." Current stories, plus archives and much more. www.rcfp.org

8

A Declaration of Journalistic Independence

In early 2010, the United States adopted a new plan for fighting the war in Afghanistan: counterinsurgency. It was a bold and controversial strategy that involved increasing the number of ground troops to try to dominate al Qaeda while simultaneously engaging in nation-building activities that are typically the domain of diplomats, not soldiers. Proponents saw it as the only way to secure something close to a victory in Afghanistan; opponents saw it as a recipe for getting U.S. troops essentially trapped in the country with no clear way out.

After months of discussion and research, President Obama decided to go the counterinsurgency route and tapped Gen. Stanley McChrystal, a no-nonsense Army Ranger and counterinsurgency expert, to lead the charge. To say that Gen. McChrystal wielded a lot of power, both on and off the battlefield, would be an understatement. To say that he would make a great subject for a personality profile would be an even greater understatement. Indeed, Robert Kaplan's "Man Versus Afghanistan" article, published in *The Atlantic* magazine in April 2010, includes the kind of solid research, telling details and great quotes—at one point McChrystal

LEARNING OBJECTIVES

▼
Understand the central importance of "independence" in journalism.

▼
Explore and critique the concept of "objectivity."

▼
Bring together concepts from this and earlier chapters to create a deeper understanding of journalism's mission.

says, "We were hitting al Qaeda in Iraq like Rocky Balboa hitting Apollo Creed in the gut"—that are the hallmarks of good profiles.

Michael Hastings, a journalist who had covered the Iraq war for *Newsweek* magazine, and then became a contributing editor for *Rolling Stone*, also was assigned to write about the counterinsurgency and the man behind it. The very month Kaplan's article appeared, Hastings was with McChrystal and his senior aides at bases and towns in Afghanistan, as well as in Paris, where the general went to speak to NATO allies and at a military academy. His article, "The Runaway General," also features lots of dialogue and details—the

FIGURE 8.1 Annie McChrystal stands with her husband Gen. Stanley McChrystal as he is awarded the Department of Defense Distinguished Service Medal by Secretary of Defense Robert M. Gates during a retirement ceremony at Fort McNair July 23, 2010 in Washington, DC. The ceremony honored Army Gen. Stanley McChrystal, who was the commander of U.S. forces in Afghanistan and has served in the military since 1976, and who is retiring after being relieved of command for comments he made to a *Rolling Stone* reporter about President Barack Obama and his administration.

Brendan Smialowski/Getty Images

kind of material a reporter can get only with good and sustained access to his subject. Hastings is there when McChrystal's senior aides have had a bit too much to drink. He's there when the general and his aides belittle the views of people with misgivings about counterinsurgency, including President Obama, Vice President Biden, and the U.S. ambassador to Afghanistan. He's there when McChrystal faces some tough questioning from his own troops who were beginning to doubt the strategy. And Hastings reported what he saw and heard.

DISCUSSION QUESTIONS

Gen. Stanley McChrystal was fired after critical remarks he made about his boss (President Barack Obama) were published in a *Rolling Stone* article. It's not news that people criticize their bosses. Why were McChrystal's statements newsworthy? Can you think of similar circumstances where a journalist might not report criticism leveled at a prominent boss? Should we always report on disagreements of this type? Does it depend on the people involved? The type of workplace (military, politics, business, sports)? The consequences? When are situations like this news?

When the story appeared in *Rolling Stone* in July 2010, McChrystal was called back to Washington for a chat with the president. And that was the end of his command.

Wow. One article can get a general fired?! Indeed. This is one more example of the kind of power journalism has, power that must be exercised responsibly, as you learned in earlier chapters. It's also an example of the kind of work journalists are supposed to do in a democracy. A story about a controversial strategy and the man who is in charge of implementing it certainly counts as information of consequence to citizens. But this story and its aftermath also highlight the importance of a key value in journalism: independence.

▶ WHEN COMPROMISE ISN'T A GOOD THING

You've read a lot in this book about what it is journalists are supposed to do and the things—economic, legal and technological—that affect whether and how they do it. You've even been introduced to a process for helping journalists make ethical decisions, when confronted with these and other kinds of barriers to doing their jobs. What we want to emphasize now is how independence sits right at the intersection of the journalist's job and the things standing in the way of doing it. Think about it. When we talk about barriers to good journalism, we are essentially talking about people, policies and institutions that compromise journalistic independence: the push for profits that can push journalists to do fewer tough and expensive stories in favor of more easy and cheap ones; competitive pressures that sacrifice a journalist's independent judgment to the judgment of the crowd; powerful sources or advertisers who seek to steer journalists toward one kind of story or away from another.

What does all of this have to do with Michael Hastings? His work relied on a strong foundation of independence. How else could he have successfully produced a story about very powerful people who wouldn't necessarily like what he reported? Independence, as you learned in Chapter 2, means journalists operate with the public foremost in their minds and avoid splitting their loyalty to the public with loyalties to other "factions." Those factions might be political parties or religions, charitable organizations or businesses—any entity that might try to get between a journalist and the public. Hastings's chief obligation wasn't to the military or the general or the president, though of course he had ethical duties to them. His obligation was to report what he thought the public ought to know.

▶ **INDEPENDENCE:**
An essential component of journalism practice in which journalists are free to pursue truth with loyalty only to citizens and not particular interests, causes or other pressures, in mind.

But before we break out the champagne to celebrate this instance of independent reporting, we need to take a look at the reaction of other journalists to the story. Many of them weren't interested in raising a toast to Hastings at all. Rather, they were actually shocked that Hastings had done a story that put McChrystal in a less-than-favorable light.

From CNN to Fox News to NPR and beyond, journalists had a hard time understanding how someone from *Rolling Stone*—which they saw as less serious than other news outlets—could gain such great access to McChrystal in the first place, and they accused Hastings of betraying McChrystal's trust by, perhaps, reporting things that the general or his staff thought were "off the record." The first criticism sounds a little like jealousy to us, and the second? Well, it's sort of hard to imagine someone like Gen. McChrystal, who was the Pentagon's press spokesman at the beginning of the Iraq war in 2003, not knowing that a reporter following you around with a tape recorder and a notebook will consider everything fair game unless there's a previous agreement otherwise.

While those criticisms are weak enough, the amazement and criticism other journalists heaped on Hastings for squandering his great access to McChrystal by reporting the story strikes us as, well, amazing for entirely other reasons. Other journalists actually seemed to be saying that Hastings had broken some sort of rule or was a kind of traitor in reporting what he did, that whatever loyalty he owed to the general was greater than the loyalty he owed the public. CBS News correspondent Lara Logan even called his patriotism into question, saying, "Michael Hastings has never served his country the way McChrystal has."

Independence, in this view, is something you compromise for the sake of being invited to the inner circle of bigwigs and elites and to maintain your membership. Violate the "rules" of the club and you're likely to get thrown out. The problem with this view is that being in the inner circle isn't worth much if it gets in the way of your basic job as a journalist: truth-telling.

Hastings, interviewed a few days after "The Runaway General" was published, put it this way:

> Look, I went into journalism to do journalism, not advertising. My views are critical but that shouldn't be mistaken for hostile—I'm just not a stenographer. There is a body of work that shows how I view these issues but that was hard-earned through experience, not something I learned going to a cocktail party on [expletive] K Street. That's what reporters are supposed to do, report the story.
>
> (Baram, 2010)

Journalism versus stenography. That's a great way to think about the contrast between what Hastings did and what many other journalists, in trying to stay close to the powerful actors in the news, end up doing. Digging for the truth and reporting sometimes uncomfortable news is a far cry from merely reporting accurately what people in power want the public to hear. Remember *The Atlantic* profile of McChrystal we mentioned, which appeared a few months before Hastings's story? We consider it an interesting and informative piece of work about counterinsurgency and the soldiers implementing it. The fact that it didn't include the kind of "insubordinate" commentary from the general and his staff that the Hastings story did is certainly not evidence that the writer, Robert Kaplan, was somehow compromised. We don't know whether Kaplan heard the kinds of things during his reporting that Hastings did, and therefore whether he even had the opportunity to write the kind of story Hastings wrote, if he'd wanted to. Even so, it's worth noting that in his follow-up book on the war in Afghanistan, Hastings reports a conversation in which McChrystal himself describes how the news media were co-opted—that is, did not act as independent truth-seekers—during the Iraq war. Kaplan, McChrystal says, was "totally co-opted by the military." That could just be boasting by the general, but it's troublesome nonetheless.

One final word: Don't go crying for Michael Hastings. For all the heat he took for this story, he ended up winning a prestigious Polk Award and getting a book contract. Indeed, it's that very push and pull, the applause set against the anger, that makes this tale useful for thinking about the crucial, but sometimes controversial, role independence plays in journalism.

▶ FACTS, VALUES AND THE OBJECTIVITY TRAP

Independence remains the core value of journalism—the value from which all of the other values that form journalism's core functions come to life.

FIGURE 8.2 USA—CIRCA 1973: A stamp printed in the United States shows the Printer and Patriots examining a Pamphlet, from the series "Rise of the Spirit of Independence," circa 1973.

AlexanderZam/Shutterstock

Without it, journalism becomes something else—advocacy, perhaps, or public relations, depending upon its goal. Why? Because journalism must retain the ability to ask difficult questions in tough circumstances to people who'd just as soon not have to answer them.

When the story is easy, its conclusions apparent, anyone can play journalist. But when the story is difficult, the sources are reluctant and maybe even deceptive, when the partisan knives are drawn and the truth is hiding behind spin and money, journalists must be able to approach the story free from the baggage of perceived conflicts. That's not to say that the critics still won't attack: in fact, it's the inevitable attempts to shoot the messenger that make independence so important. Critics have seized on charges of bias and used the objectivity trap time and time again, and no amount of journalistic excellence is going to change that.

Fortunately, journalists can best neutralize their critics by hewing to the time-honored principles that differentiate the craft from the beer-and-circus mass media. And to do so, they must begin and end with the pursuit of truth for truth's sake, a task complicated by the many things that get between journalists and the pursuit of truth these days, from the speed of the news cycle to the creep of partisan infotainment to the economic pressures of the digital era.

◄ **OBJECTIVITY:** Commonly used to describe a person's (alleged) ability to completely detach from, and have no opinion or perspective on, a given issue. Because people can't really be objective, what we advocate here is seeing objectivity as a quality of the methods journalists employ in their work, not of the journalists themselves.

The *New York Times* seems as good a place as any to highlight just how confused we all have become about the very nature of journalism. The paper's public editor, Arthur S. Brisbane, created an Internet maelstrom in 2012 with a seemingly innocent question: Should journalists challenge "facts" that are asserted by newsmakers they write about? The blog post was prompted by reader questions like this one, which Brisbane quoted:

> "My question is what role the paper's hard-news coverage should play with regard to false statements—by candidates or by others. In general, the Times sets its documentation of falsehoods in articles apart from its primary coverage. If the newspaper's overarching goal is truth, oughtn't the truth be embedded in its principal stories? In other words, if a candidate repeatedly utters an outright falsehood . . . shouldn't the Times's coverage nail it right at the point where the article quotes it?"

In other words, this reader wondered, why are demonstrably false statements not corrected, or really even addressed, in news stories that purport to offer the truth? Good question! And Brisbane answered it with more questions—"How can *The Times* do this in a way that is objective and fair? Is it possible to be objective and fair when the reporter is choosing to correct one fact over another?"—before inviting readers to share their thoughts on the subject.

And share, they certainly did. The response to Brisbane's blog post ricocheted all over the blogosphere, punctuated by an angry, snarky tone. One typical comment, from "Fed Up" in Brooklyn, summarized the debate: "The fact that this is even a question shows us how far mainstream journalism has fallen." The vast majority of the comments, excellently summarized by the Nieman Journalism Lab blog, converge on a common theme: Readers' disgust with the notion that reporting that calls out falsehoods somehow offends the unwritten rule of "objectivity."

Here lies the disconnect between what citizens expect of journalism, and what journalism, all too often, has come to be. As pre-eminent journalism observer Michael Schudson has written, the "objectivity norm guides journalists to separate facts from values, and report only the facts." As if "facts" mean much when stripped of their context. As if "facts" somehow equal "truth."

It's a trap, really. As Kovach and Rosenstiel so eloquently illustrate in *The Elements of Journalism*, the idea that a journalist can, through some purity of thought, "be" objective holds them to an unachievable standard. It substitutes the unanswerable ("Is this *individual* objective")? for the answerable ("Is this *reporting* verifiable and replicable")? and, by doing so, makes every work of journalism ultimately suspect.

Way back in Chapter 2, we offered a mini overview of the scientific method to make a point about how the kind of verification process and transparency essential to the scientific method are similarly essential to the journalistic method. Scientists have to be open about how they collect and analyze their data, so that others can assess the validity of what they did; journalists likewise have to be open about the sources they consult and the observations they make, so that the public can evaluate the credibility of their reporting. And just as scientists have to be open to the prospect of

FIGURE 8.3
Seamartini/
Shutterstock

their experiments failing, to the idea that their hypotheses were just plain wrong, so do journalists have to be open to alternative explanations and new information that might change what they thought they knew about a given story or event.

But is all this really necessary? Why aren't scientists or journalists simply trusted at their word? Why don't we just take it on faith that a scientist's conclusions are based on a rigorously designed study, or that a journalist's story is based on a discipline of verification? Because scientists and journalists are human, that's why. Because they can't help but have opinions and experiences that could affect how they approach an experiment or a news story. One of the biggest benefits of the method each kind of investigator, whether scientist or journalist, employs is that it is objective. *The method is objective, because the person cannot be.*

▶ JOURNALISM'S BUILT-IN (NOT NECESSARILY BAD) BIASES

Journalists can't "be" objective any more than anyone else can, and the critics who decry the "mainstream media" know that. It's a bludgeon—a political one, in every sense of the word—in the form of an unreachable ideal, and a frequent companion of "bias," another over- and mis-used term. One of the most frequently heard critiques of journalism is that it has a liberal bias, that it favors liberal viewpoints over conservative ones. You may have noticed that Fox News has built its whole identity (and marketing strategy) on offering an alternative to that alleged bias.

We could write a whole book on bias—indeed, many people already have—but we will spare you the gory details. We'll just say this: Political bias is probably the least useful lens through which to examine journalism. What people see as bias in the news is very much rooted in their pre-existing beliefs about the world. Research shows that people not only seek out news and viewpoints from sources that agree with them, but also that people with opposing beliefs who are shown the same news story are likely to say the story is biased in favor of the other viewpoint. One story, two opposing charges of bias. Crazy, right?

▶ **STRUCTURAL BIAS:** A type of frame or approach, inherent to journalism practice, which favors certain kinds of news topics and presentations over others. For example, visual bias in news refers to relatively greater emphasis, especially in television news, on stories that are visually interesting over those that are not.

If political bias or liberal/conservative bias doesn't explain much about the news, what does? Is there a better set of lenses through which to examine journalism, to explain why news emphasizes the things it does? The good news is yes. The even better news is that you have already established a foundation for understanding them from your reading of earlier chapters. We can elaborate on what you learned by pointing you to the work of journalism scholar Andrew Cline, who has developed a list of nine structural biases in the news. By "structural," Cline means biases that are built into journalistic practice. As structural, or inherent, biases, these are almost invisible to us. They seem to be the "natural" order of things even though there are other practices that journalism arguably *could* adopt.

The list of biases includes "temporal" and "bad news," which easily connect back to some of the news values covered in Chapter 3, such as timeliness and conflict. And the "commercial" and "expediency" biases Cline describes certainly harken back to the cheap and easy news that journalism in the

United States is under pressure to produce, as you learned in Chapter 4. Of the five remaining biases on Cline's list—visual, fairness, narrative, status quo and glory—fairness is most relevant to our concerns here. But how, exactly, can fairness, which is a *good* thing, be a bias?

When we call something a structural bias, we aren't necessarily saying it's bad. Sure, "bias" has come to have a pretty negative connotation, particularly when you put the word "political" or "liberal" in front of it as we mentioned earlier. But we (and Cline) are using it in a more neutral, descriptive way here to understand how certain practices tend to favor one kind of presentation of news over other possible kinds of presentations. Fairness bias, for example, shows up in the news in a couple of different ways. It refers to that common journalistic practice of offering one "side" a chance to comment on news generated by the other "side." Seems fair, hence the name "fairness bias." What's biased about it? Here's Cline's explanation:

> This creates the illusion that the game of politics is always contentious and never cooperative. This bias can also create situations in which one faction appears to be attacked by the press. For example, politician A announces some positive accomplishment followed by the press seeking a negative comment from politician B. The point is not to disparage politician A but to be fair to politician B. When politician A is a conservative, this practice appears to be liberal bias.

From our perch here in 2012, when the public is very politically polarized, the idea that politics isn't "always contentious and never cooperative" might be hard to imagine. Fairness bias probably makes polarization worse by setting up every issue as a battle. What's more, this impulse toward a certain kind of fairness also gives equal weight to perspectives or "sides" even when one side has a lot more evidence behind it than the other. Fairness bias is a way journalists avoid being seen as taking sides, even when the evidence indicates there's really only one side to be taken. This "on-the-other-hand-itis" is hardly helpful to journalism's truth-telling mission, because it misleads the public about the very issues on which they must make decisions or elect representatives to make them on their behalf. It also illustrates why "fairness," "balance," "neutrality" and "detachment" are no better than "objectivity" at describing the stance journalism in the public interest must take.

Which brings us back to Arthur Brisbane, the public editor of the *New York Times*, and his question about the press acting as a "truth vigilante." Brisbane was worried about fairness and objectivity—and not necessarily the kind of fairness or objectivity of method we've been promoting in this chapter. The response from readers and the wider blogosphere? Correcting errors and falsehoods *is* fair—it's fair to the truth and to *us*.

▶ "JOURNALISTS ANGRY OVER THE COMMISSION OF JOURNALISM"

If only the case of Brisbane and the truth vigilantes were an exception. The drumbeat of objectivity-as-person (and not as method) continues to have very real effects on journalism. Let's go back to a journalist who appeared way back in Chapter 1—Anderson Cooper—to see how.

Using the heading above as the title of his post, Glenn Greenwald in the online magazine *Salon* highlighted a single instance that serves as a useful example of the way the objectivity-of-person meme damages our profession by allowing its critics to dictate the rules. The topic in this instance was the uprisings in Egypt and not American politics, which helps us to see the problem at hand even more clearly.

On February 7, 2011, Cooper opened his show with the following introduction:

"A lot happening tonight," he told viewers. "We're again devoting nearly the entire hour to Egypt, the entire hour to debunking the lies the Egyptian regime continues to try to spread about what is really happening there."

A moment later he described the "Egyptian government efforts to hold on to power by lying to Egyptians and lying to the world." Later, Cooper also noted that the government "continues to distort or hide the truth about how many people have been killed or detained in the demonstrations."

The criticism of Cooper's use of words like "lie" and "distort" was fast and furious—and, like the criticism of Michael Hastings's "Runaway General" story, much of it came not from outside of the world of journalism, but from his journalism colleagues, as Greenwald pointed out.

Los Angeles Times media critic James Rainey weighed in with a column, "Egypt: CNN's Anderson Cooper on lies and the lying liars who tell them," that seemed to make light of Cooper's use of the term "lie" and concluded that his use of the term was evidence of "Cooper's pronounced shift toward more opinion-making in recent months . . . trying to adopt the more commentary-heavy approach of [CNN's] higher-rated competitors, Fox and MSNBC (in Greenwald, 2011)."

This, despite the fact that Rainey conceded that anyone watching events unfold in Egypt would agree that the regime was lying, repeatedly:

> Indeed, it's hard to find fault with what Cooper had to say, though it did begin to sound a little one-note after about the sixth or seventh "liar, liar." We got the point a few minutes into the show. And it's doubtless many in the audience didn't understand, since the evidence appeared right on our TV screens all week.

So, to Rainey, when a journalist calls a government lie a "lie," that's veering into "commentary-heavy opinion-making" rather than objective journalism. That's a classic example of objectivity-of-person operating as a trap.

On his *Reliable Sources* program, Cooper's then-CNN colleague Howard Kurtz picked up the story, and posed the following question to guest Christopher Dickey of *Newsweek*:

> Chris Dickey, Anderson Cooper repeatedly using the word lies. Now I think most journalists would agree with him, perhaps most Americans would agree with him. But should an anchor and correspondent be taking sides on this kind of story?

Here is fairness bias at work. And here, to Greenwald, is where the notion of journalistic objectivity has led us astray:

> Rainey, Kurtz and Dickey all have this exactly backwards. Identifying lies told by powerful political leaders—and describing them as such—is

DISCUSSION QUESTIONS

Did Anderson Cooper go too far in his assertion that Egyptian leaders were lying? How might he have presented the information differently? Was he acting as the host of a show or as a journalist in this instance? Should word choice (and presentation style) differ when information is presented by a reporter in a news report or a commentator or personality on a talk show?

what good journalists do, **by definition**. It's the crux of adversarial journalism, of a "watchdog" press. "Objectivity" does not require refraining from pointing out the falsity of government claims. The opposite is true; objectivity requires that a journalist do exactly that: treat factually false statements as false. "Objectivity" is breached not when a journalist calls a lie a "lie," but when they refuse to do so, when they treat lies told by powerful political officials as though they're viable, reasonable interpretations of subjective questions. The very idea that a journalist is engaged in "opinion-making" or is "taking sides" by calling a lie a "lie" is ludicrous; the only "side" such a journalist is taking is with facts, with the truth. It's when a journalist fails to identify a false statement as such that they are "taking sides"—they're siding with those in power by deceitfully depicting their demonstrably false statements as something other than lies.

▶ ENGAGEMENT OR DETACHMENT?

Media scholar Jay Rosen, relying on the work of philosopher Thomas Nagel who coined the phrase "the view from nowhere," describes this anxiety about being seen as taking sides as "a bid for trust that advertises the viewlessness of the news producer." In a polarized political world, it places the journalist in a desperate position, trying to gain the trust of the public not by truth-seeking, but by pandering to the critics that, inevitably and somewhat ironically, won't like the results of that truth-seeking anyway. It's a losing game, every time, because every piece of serious, policy-oriented journalism is bound to make some people happy and others less so. It's an age-old attempt to secure a kind of legitimacy by making everyone happy through false equivalency or "on-the-other-hand-itis."

Can the "cult of balance," as some have called it, do real damage to our collective understanding of the world? Certainly it can, and does. Let's be clear:

Viewlessness is not objectivity, and it's certainly not independence. Sure, to have no particular view might make it look like a journalist is independent from faction. But where, if one has no view, does the view of the public interest fit in? There is always one side a journalist must take, and that's the public's side. Another way of thinking about it? Truth-seeking doesn't *have* a point of view; it *is* a point of view.

DISCUSSION QUESTIONS

Watch this clip (a trailer for the HBO series "Newsroom"): www.youtube.com/watch?v=lgFZbr wmndA&feature=relmfu. The premise of the series is a retooling of a network news program into one modeled after Kovach and Rosenstiel's "engaged independence." What pressures might this type of news 2.0 program face from owners, shareholders, audiences and newsmakers?

Taking the public's side means practicing what Kovach and Rosenstiel call "engaged independence." Rather than try to play the detached, neutral observer, an engaged, independent journalist lets the facts take him where they may, demands answers to questions sources would rather not answer, and presses the powerful for the truth. We may all agree that good journalists understand that objectivity isn't about refusing to take sides—it is about reporting the facts as they are, even when that means making one side look bad. But just because many understand that, it doesn't make methods-based objectivity the norm.

That approach to reporting has taken quite a beating over the years, as a host of well-paid critics in institutions ranging from corporations to think tanks on the left and right repeatedly set the objectivity trap, and as structural biases in journalistic practice shape stories in ways that often don't serve citizens very well. To serve citizens by giving them meaningful information they need to run their lives and make democracy function, we must focus our efforts on our methods—on verification and transparency—and challenge the assertion that good journalism doesn't have a point of view.

▶ UNCHANGING PRINCIPLES FOR AN UNCHANGING WORLD

In a world awash in information, in which old business models are falling and in which new disruptive technologies emerge seemingly daily, as you learned in Chapter 5, it's easy to panic and follow the herd, substituting quantity for quality and succumbing to a mishmash of celebrity gossip and viral videos. The shackles of an artificial "view from nowhere" may contribute to the decline of the mainstream press as the public turns to other sources in the information tide who—right, wrong or otherwise—don't really worry about taking a stand.

We don't know the magic answer to saving journalism. No one does. We do believe that abandoning the values of independence, of accuracy through verification, of transparency of practice, of objectivity-as-method, is precisely the wrong way to go. The key, to us, lies in a return to the principles outlined in this book.

To preserve some segment of the broader world of mass communication dedicated to newsgathering in the independent pursuit of functional truth, is to us the most important challenge facing journalism today. To remain a viable part of a democracy, journalism must return to its past to discover its future.

That might seem a bit simplistic, but it's not. Preserving those principles requires courage too often lacking in today's corporate newsrooms. It demands no less than a sustained effort to encourage aggressive, inquisitive, watchdog journalism that marked the rise of the American press, and that will fuel its rise again. That, in turn, demands investment in reporting, in boots on the ground and eyes on City Hall. Traditional news outlets may or may not rise to the challenge, but rest assured, someone will, for society's innate need to inform itself does not depend upon any media-specific channel.

We've moved from an era of few media producers and a mass audience to an era in which anyone can be a media producer and have an audience, even if just a tiny one. This tells us that now, more than ever, journalism must return to its core mission to differentiate itself. That core mission—informing the members of a community so that they might better live their lives—has remained the beating heart of journalism, while everything else has changed.

DISCUSSION QUESTIONS

What do you think is the future of American journalism? Are you optimistic that journalism can continue to perform a vital role in U.S. democracy? What challenges do you think are ahead? What solutions will you bring to the table when you graduate—as an audience member, a voter, a policy maker or a working journalist?

Chapter Eight Review

Chapter Summary

Suggested Activities

Read More

▶ **CHAPTER SUMMARY**

Independence is a crucial element of journalism that makes the truth-seeking work of journalists possible. But it's an ongoing fight to preserve it. Many forces are arrayed against journalistic independence, from economic pressures to do or not do certain kinds of reporting to the objectivity trap used by all kinds of political actors to squelch the publication of uncomfortable information. Even within journalism, there's not always as much agreement on how to exercise independence as one would hope. Independence, combined with an approach to objectivity that focuses on sound methods such as verification and transparency, is the key to journalism's enduring mission to provide truthful information of consequence to citizens in a democracy.

▶ **SUGGESTED ACTIVITIES**

1. Journalism scholar Andrew Cline talks about nine structural biases. These, of course, are closely aligned with the news values and the way journalists do their jobs as discussed in Chapter 3. Split into small groups (two or three) and choose a bias to explore. For about five minutes look online, on your smartphones, or in a printed daily newspaper to find one or two examples of your bias. Briefly present your findings to the class.

2. How forceful are journalists and news outlets at declaring their independence? Work independently or in small groups, picking a major news outlet. Can you find statements about the organization's stance on being objective or independent? These might be on the organization's website or might be found on another source (for example, a Q&A interview with a publisher or news executive). Share your experiences with the rest of your class. How hard were these statements to find? What did they say? If you couldn't find a statement of this type, what perception might that leave in the minds of the audience?

3. Invite a reporter either via Skype or in person to discuss with the class how he or she works to be "fair" to all sides when reporting a political issue. Prepare questions based on the chapter. Questions could include: Are there times when fairness gets in the way of the "truth" and accuracy? Do stories have to always include two or more sides? What if one side is clearly dominant in the debate? How much space should be given to minority opinion, if any? What is your response when a reader or source charges you with political bias?

4. Reflect back on the criticism Anderson Cooper came under for using the word "lies" in his report on the Egyptian regime. Compare this with the commentary leveled by famed newsman Edward R. Murrow at Sen. Joseph McCarthy in the 1950s (the subject of the movie *Good Night and Good Luck*). Watch a clip of Murrow from "See It Now" March 9, 1954 found on YouTube: www.youtube.com/watch?v=anNEJJYLU8M& feature=related. History lauds Murrow for his actions in this case. How might we look back on opinionated personalities like Sean Hannity, Rush Limbaugh, Chris Matthews or even Jon Stewart in 20 years? Discuss this with your class.

5. Political bias has been debated ever since printing presses started running in the American colonies. In fact, early newspapers were based on having a political bias. While most news outlets strive to present objective versions of events, sometimes even the inclusion of one word can project subtle forms of bias. Find an example of a news report online that could be perceived as biased from someone with a firm stance on the issue. Include a link to the story on the class discussion board and detail what could be considered biased in the report. Next, address how the journalist, editor or producer might have altered the presentation to avoid this appearance.

▶ READ MORE

Marcus Baram, "Michael Hastings, Rolling Stone's McChrystal Profiler, Says Troops Are Happy That General Was Ousted," *The Huffington Post*, June 25, 2010. www.huffingtonpost.com/2010/06/25/michael-hastings-rolling_n_625261.html.

Andrew Cline, "Media/Political Bias." http://rhetorica.net/bias.htm.

Glenn Greenwald, "Journalists Angry Over the Commission of Journalism," *Salon*, February 14, 2011. www.salon.com/2011/02/14/journalism_10/singleton/.

Michael Hastings, "The Runaway General," *Rolling Stone*, July 22, 2010. www.rollingstone.com/politics/news/the-runaway-general-20100622.

Robert D. Kaplan, "Man Versus Afghanistan," *The Atlantic*, April 2010. www.theatlantic.com/magazine/archive/2010/04/man-versus-afghanistan/7983/.

Bill Kovach and Tom Rosenstiel, *The Elements of Journalism: What Newspeople Should Know and the Public Should Expect*, New York: Three Rivers Press, 2007.

Howard Kurtz, "Reliable Sources," CNN, June 27, 2010. http://transcripts.cnn.com/TRANSCRIPTS/1006/27/rs.01.html.

Jay Rosen, "The Politico Opens the Kimono. And then Pretends it Never Happened," PressThink blog, June 24, 2010. http://archive.pressthink.org/2010/06/24/an_openthekimon.html.

Appendix

Preamble   Members of the Society of Professional Journalists believe that public enlightenment is the forerunner of justice and the foundation of democracy. The duty of the journalist is to further those ends by seeking truth and providing a fair and comprehensive account of events and issues. Conscientious journalists from all media and specialties strive to serve the public with thoroughness and honesty. Professional integrity is the cornerstone of a journalist's credibility. Members of the Society share a dedication to ethical behavior and adopt this code to declare the Society's principles and standards of practice.

Seek Truth and Report It   Journalists should be honest, fair and courageous in gathering, reporting and interpreting information.

Journalists should:

- ▶ Test the accuracy of information from all sources and exercise care to avoid inadvertent error. Deliberate distortion is never permissible.

- ▶ Diligently seek out subjects of news stories to give them the opportunity to respond to allegations of wrongdoing.

- ▶ Identify sources whenever feasible. The public is entitled to as much information as possible on sources' reliability.

- ▶ Always question sources' motives before promising anonymity. Clarify conditions attached to any promise made in exchange for information. Keep promises.

▶   Make certain that headlines, news teases and promotional material, photos, video, audio, graphics, sound bites and quotations do not misrepresent. They should not oversimplify or highlight incidents out of context.

▶   Never distort the content of news photos or video. Image enhancement for technical clarity is always permissible. Label montages and photo illustrations.

▶   Avoid misleading re-enactments or staged news events. If re-enactment is necessary to tell a story, label it.

▶   Avoid undercover or other surreptitious methods of gathering information except when traditional open methods will not yield information vital to the public. Use of such methods should be explained as part of the story.

▶   Never plagiarize.

▶   Tell the story of the diversity and magnitude of the human experience boldly, even when it is unpopular to do so.

▶   Examine their own cultural values and avoid imposing those values on others.

▶   Avoid stereotyping by race, gender, age, religion, ethnicity, geography, sexual orientation, disability, physical appearance or social status.

▶   Support the open exchange of views, even views they find repugnant.

▶   Give voice to the voiceless; official and unofficial sources of information can be equally valid.

▶   Distinguish between advocacy and news reporting. Analysis and commentary should be labeled and not misrepresent fact or context.

▶   Distinguish news from advertising and shun hybrids that blur the lines between the two.

▶   Recognize a special obligation to ensure that the public's business is conducted in the open and that government records are open to inspection.

Minimize Harm   Ethical journalists treat sources, subjects and colleagues as human beings deserving of respect.

Journalists should:

- ▶ Show compassion for those who may be affected adversely by news coverage. Use special sensitivity when dealing with children and inexperienced sources or subjects.

- ▶ Be sensitive when seeking or using interviews or photographs of those affected by tragedy or grief.

- ▶ Recognize that gathering and reporting information may cause harm or discomfort. Pursuit of the news is not a license for arrogance.

- ▶ Recognize that private people have a greater right to control information about themselves than do public officials and others who seek power, influence or attention. Only an overriding public need can justify intrusion into anyone's privacy.

- ▶ Show good taste. Avoid pandering to lurid curiosity.

- ▶ Be cautious about identifying juvenile suspects or victims of sex crimes.

- ▶ Be judicious about naming criminal suspects before the formal filing of charges.

- ▶ Balance a criminal suspect's fair trial rights with the public's right to be informed.

Act Independently   Journalists should be free of obligation to any interest other than the public's right to know.

Journalists should:

- ▶ Avoid conflicts of interest, real or perceived.

- ▶ Remain free of associations and activities that may compromise integrity or damage credibility.

- Refuse gifts, favors, fees, free travel and special treatment, and shun secondary employment, political involvement, public office and service in community organizations if they compromise journalistic integrity.

- Disclose unavoidable conflicts.

- Be vigilant and courageous about holding those with power accountable.

- Deny favored treatment to advertisers and special interests and resist their pressure to influence news coverage.

- Be wary of sources offering information for favors or money; avoid bidding for news.

Be Accountable Journalists are accountable to their readers, listeners, viewers and each other.

Journalists should:

- Clarify and explain news coverage and invite dialogue with the public over journalistic conduct.

- Encourage the public to voice grievances against the news media.

- Admit mistakes and correct them promptly.

- Expose unethical practices of journalists and the news media.

- Abide by the same high standards to which they hold others.

The SPJ Code of Ethics is voluntarily embraced by thousands of writers, editors and other news professionals. The present version of the code was adopted by the 1996 SPJ National Convention, after months of study and debate among the Society's members.

Sigma Delta Chi's first Code of Ethics was borrowed from the American Society of Newspaper Editors in 1926. In 1973, Sigma Delta Chi wrote its own code, which was revised in 1984, 1987 and 1996.

Reprinted with permission from the Society of Professional Journalists, http:// spj.org/

▶ RADIO TELEVISION DIGITAL NEWS ASSOCIATION CODE OF ETHICS AND PROFESSIONAL CONDUCT

Preamble   Professional electronic journalists should operate as trustees of the public, seek the truth, report it fairly and with integrity and independence, and stand accountable for their actions.

PUBLIC TRUST: Professional electronic journalists should recognize that their first obligation is to the public.

Professional electronic journalists should:

- ▶ Understand that any commitment other than service to the public undermines trust and credibility.

- ▶ Recognize that service in the public interest creates an obligation to reflect the diversity of the community and guard against oversimplification of issues or events.

- ▶ Provide a full range of information to enable the public to make enlightened decisions.

- ▶ Fight to ensure that the public's business is conducted in public.

TRUTH: Professional electronic journalists should pursue truth aggressively and present the news accurately, in context, and as completely as possible.

Professional electronic journalists should:

- ▶ Continuously seek the truth.

- ▶ Resist distortions that obscure the importance of events.

- ▶ Clearly disclose the origin of information and label all material provided by outsiders.

Professional electronic journalists should not:

- ▶ Report anything known to be false.

- ▶ Manipulate images or sounds in any way that is misleading.

- ▶ Plagiarize.

- ▶ Present images or sounds that are reenacted without informing the public.

FAIRNESS: Professional electronic journalists should present the news fairly and impartially, placing primary value on significance and relevance.

Professional electronic journalists should:

- ▶ Treat all subjects of news coverage with respect and dignity, showing particular compassion to victims of crime or tragedy.

- ▶ Exercise special care when children are involved in a story and give children greater privacy protection than adults.

- ▶ Seek to understand the diversity of their community and inform the public without bias or stereotype.

- ▶ Present a diversity of expressions, opinions, and ideas in context.

- ▶ Present analytical reporting based on professional perspective, not personal bias.

- ▶ Respect the right to a fair trial.

INTEGRITY: Professional electronic journalists should present the news with integrity and decency, avoiding real or perceived conflicts of interest, and respect the dignity and intelligence of the audience as well as the subjects of news.

Professional electronic journalists should:

- ▶ Identify sources whenever possible. Confidential sources should be used only when it is clearly in the public interest to gather or convey important information or when a person providing information might be harmed. Journalists should keep all commitments to protect a confidential source.

- ▶ Clearly label opinion and commentary.

- ▶ Guard against extended coverage of events or individuals that fails to significantly advance a story, place the event in context, or add to the public knowledge.

- ▶ Refrain from contacting participants in violent situations while the situation is in progress.

- ▶ Use technological tools with skill and thoughtfulness, avoiding techniques that skew facts, distort reality, or sensationalize events.

- ▶ Use surreptitious newsgathering techniques, including hidden cameras or microphones, only if there is no other way to obtain stories of significant public importance and only if the technique is explained to the audience.

- ▶ Disseminate the private transmissions of other news organizations only with permission.

Professional electronic journalists should not:

- ▶ Pay news sources who have a vested interest in a story.

- ▶ Accept gifts, favors, or compensation from those who might seek to influence coverage.

- ▶ Engage in activities that may compromise their integrity or independence.

INDEPENDENCE: Professional electronic journalists should defend the independence of all journalists from those seeking influence or control over news content.

Professional electronic journalists should:

- ▶ Gather and report news without fear or favor, and vigorously resist undue influence from any outside forces, including advertisers, sources, story subjects, powerful individuals, and special interest groups.

- ▶ Resist those who would seek to buy or politically influence news content or who would seek to intimidate those who gather and disseminate the news.

- ▶ Determine news content solely through editorial judgment and not as the result of outside influence.

- ▶ Resist any self-interest or peer pressure that might erode journalistic duty and service to the public.

- ▶ Recognize that sponsorship of the news will not be used in any way to determine, restrict, or manipulate content.

- ▶ Refuse to allow the interests of ownership or management to influence news judgment and content inappropriately.

- ▶ Defend the rights of the free press for all journalists, recognizing that any professional or government licensing of journalists is a violation of that freedom.

ACCOUNTABILITY: Professional electronic journalists should recognize that they are accountable for their actions to the public, the profession, and themselves.

Professional electronic journalists should:

- ▶ Actively encourage adherence to these standards by all journalists and their employers.

- ▶ Respond to public concerns. Investigate complaints and correct errors promptly and with as much prominence as the original report.

- ▶ Explain journalistic processes to the public, especially when practices spark questions or controversy.

- ▶ Recognize that professional electronic journalists are duty-bound to conduct themselves ethically.

- ▶ Refrain from ordering or encouraging courses of action that would force employees to commit an unethical act.

- ▶ Carefully listen to employees who raise ethical objections and create environments in which such objections and discussions are encouraged.

- ▶ Seek support for and provide opportunities to train employees in ethical decision-making.

In meeting its responsibility to the profession of electronic journalism, RTDNA has created this code to identify important issues, to serve as a guide for its members, to facilitate self-scrutiny, and to shape future debate.

Adopted at RTNDA2000 in Minneapolis September 14, 2000.

Reprinted with permission from the Radio Television Digital News Association, www.rtnda.org

▶ PUBLIC RELATIONS SOCIETY OF AMERICA MEMBER CODE OF ETHICS

PRSA Code of Ethics: Preamble   This Code applies to PRSA members. The Code is designed to be a useful guide for PRSA members as they carry out their ethical responsibilities. This document is designed to anticipate and accommodate, by precedent, ethical challenges that may arise. The scenarios outlined in the Code provision are actual examples of misconduct. More will be added as experience with the Code occurs.

The Public Relations Society of America (PRSA) is committed to ethical practices. The level of public trust PRSA members seek, as we serve the public good, means we have taken on a special obligation to operate ethically.

The value of member reputation depends upon the ethical conduct of everyone affiliated with the Public Relations Society of America. Each of us sets an example for each other—as well as other professionals—by our pursuit of excellence with powerful standards of performance, professionalism, and ethical conduct.

Emphasis on enforcement of the Code has been eliminated. But, the PRSA Board of Directors retains the right to bar from membership or expel from the Society any individual who has been or is sanctioned by a government agency or convicted in a court of law of an action that fails to comply with the Code.

Ethical practice is the most important obligation of a PRSA member. We view the Member Code of Ethics as a model for other professions, organizations, and professionals.

PRSA Member Statement of Professional Values This statement presents the core values of PRSA members and, more broadly, of the public relations profession. These values provide the foundation for the Member Code of Ethics and set the industry standard for the professional practice of public relations. These values are the fundamental beliefs that guide our behaviors and decision-making process. We believe our professional values are vital to the integrity of the profession as a whole.

Advocacy We serve the public interest by acting as responsible advocates for those we represent. We provide a voice in the marketplace of ideas, facts, and viewpoints to aid informed public debate.

Honesty We adhere to the highest standards of accuracy and truth in advancing the interests of those we represent and in communicating with the public.

Expertise We acquire and responsibly use specialized knowledge and experience. We advance the profession through continued professional development, research, and education. We build mutual understanding, credibility, and relationships among a wide array of institutions and audiences.

Independence We provide objective counsel to those we represent. We are accountable for our actions.

Loyalty We are faithful to those we represent, while honoring our obligation to serve the public interest.

Fairness We deal fairly with clients, employers, competitors, peers, vendors, the media, and the general public. We respect all opinions and support the right of free expression.

▶ PRSA CODE PROVISIONS OF CONDUCT

Free Flow of Information Core Principle Protecting and advancing the free flow of accurate and truthful information is essential to serving the public interest and contributing to informed decision making in a democratic society.

Intent:

▶ To maintain the integrity of relationships with the media, government officials, and the public.

▶ To aid informed decision-making.

Guidelines:

A member shall:

▶ Preserve the integrity of the process of communication.

▶ Be honest and accurate in all communications.

▶ Act promptly to correct erroneous communications for which the practitioner is responsible.

▶ Preserve the free flow of unprejudiced information when giving or receiving gifts by ensuring that gifts are nominal, legal, and infrequent.

Examples of Improper Conduct Under this Provision:

▶ A member representing a ski manufacturer gives a pair of expensive racing skis to a sports magazine columnist, to influence the columnist to write favorable articles about the product.

▶ A member entertains a government official beyond legal limits and/or in violation of government reporting requirements.

Competition   Core Principle Promoting healthy and fair competition among professionals preserves an ethical climate while fostering a robust business environment.

Intent:

▶ To promote respect and fair competition among public relations professionals.

▶ To serve the public interest by providing the widest choice of practitioner options.

Guidelines:

A member shall:

- ▶ Follow ethical hiring practices designed to respect free and open competition without deliberately undermining a competitor.
- ▶ Preserve intellectual property rights in the marketplace.

Examples of Improper Conduct Under This Provision:

- ▶ A member employed by a "client organization" shares helpful information with a counseling firm that is competing with others for the organization's business.
- ▶ A member spreads malicious and unfounded rumors about a competitor in order to alienate the competitor's clients and employees in a ploy to recruit people and business.

Disclosure of Information   Core Principle Open communication fosters informed decision making in a democratic society.

Intent:
To build trust with the public by revealing all information needed for responsible decision making.

Guidelines:

A member shall:

- ▶ Be honest and accurate in all communications.
- ▶ Act promptly to correct erroneous communications for which the member is responsible.
- ▶ Investigate the truthfulness and accuracy of information released on behalf of those represented.
- ▶ Reveal the sponsors for causes and interests represented.
- ▶ Disclose financial interest (such as stock ownership) in a client's organization.
- ▶ Avoid deceptive practices.

Examples of Improper Conduct Under this Provision:

▶ Front groups: A member implements "grass roots" campaigns or letter-writing campaigns to legislators on behalf of undisclosed interest groups.

▶ Lying by omission: A practitioner for a corporation knowingly fails to release financial information, giving a misleading impression of the corporation's performance.

▶ A member discovers inaccurate information disseminated via a website or media kit and does not correct the information.

▶ A member deceives the public by employing people to pose as volunteers to speak at public hearings and participate in "grass roots" campaigns.

Safeguarding Confidences   Core Principle Client trust requires appropriate protection of confidential and private information.

Intent:

To protect the privacy rights of clients, organizations, and individuals by safeguarding confidential information.

Guidelines:

A member shall:

▶ Safeguard the confidences and privacy rights of present, former, and prospective clients and employees.

▶ Protect privileged, confidential, or insider information gained from a client or organization.

▶ Immediately advise an appropriate authority if a member discovers that confidential information is being divulged by an employee of a client company or organization.

Examples of Improper Conduct Under This Provision:

▶ A member changes jobs, takes confidential information, and uses that information in the new position to the detriment of the former employer.

▶ A member intentionally leaks proprietary information to the detriment of some other party.

Conflicts of Interest   Core Principle Avoiding real, potential or perceived conflicts of interest builds the trust of clients, employers, and the publics.

Intent:

▶ To earn trust and mutual respect with clients or employers.

▶ To build trust with the public by avoiding or ending situations that put one's personal or professional interests in conflict with society's interests.

Guidelines:

A member shall:

▶ Act in the best interests of the client or employer, even subordinating the member's personal interests.

▶ Avoid actions and circumstances that may appear to compromise good business judgment or create a conflict between personal and professional interests.

▶ Disclose promptly any existing or potential conflict of interest to affected clients or organizations.

▶ Encourage clients and customers to determine if a conflict exists after notifying all affected parties.

Examples of Improper Conduct Under This Provision:

▶ The member fails to disclose that he or she has a strong financial interest in a client's chief competitor.

▶ The member represents a "competitor company" or a "conflicting interest" without informing a prospective client.

Enhancing the Profession   Core Principle Public relations professionals work constantly to strengthen the public's trust in the profession.

Intent:

▶ To build respect and credibility with the public for the profession of public relations.

▶ To improve, adapt and expand professional practices.

Guidelines:

A member shall:

- ▶ Acknowledge that there is an obligation to protect and enhance the profession.

- ▶ Keep informed and educated about practices in the profession to ensure ethical conduct.

- ▶ Actively pursue personal professional development.

- ▶ Decline representation of clients or organizations that urge or require actions contrary to this Code.

- ▶ Accurately define what public relations activities can accomplish.

- ▶ Counsel subordinates in proper ethical decision making.

- ▶ Require that subordinates adhere to the ethical requirements of the Code.

- ▶ Report practices that fail to comply with the Code, whether committed by PRSA members or not, to the appropriate authority.

Examples of Improper Conduct Under This Provision:

- ▶ A PRSA member declares publicly that a product the client sells is safe, without disclosing evidence to the contrary.

- ▶ A member initially assigns some questionable client work to a non-member practitioner to avoid the ethical obligation of PRSA membership.

PRSA Member Code of Ethics Pledge

I pledge:

To conduct myself professionally, with truth, accuracy, fairness, and responsibility to the public; To improve my individual competence and advance the knowledge and proficiency of the profession through continuing research and education; And to adhere to the articles of the Member Code of Ethics 2000 for the practice of public relations as adopted by the governing Assembly of the Public Relations Society of America.

I understand and accept that there is a consequence for misconduct, up to and including membership revocation.

And, I understand that those who have been or are sanctioned by a government agency or convicted in a court of law of an action that fails to comply with the Code may be barred from membership or expelled from the Society.

© *The Public Relations Society of America, www.prsa.org. Reprinted by permission.*

▶ SOCIETY OF AMERICAN BUSINESS EDITORS AND WRITERS CODE OF ETHICS

Statement of Purpose:

As business and financial journalists, we recognize we are guardians of the public trust and must do nothing to abuse this obligation.

It is not enough that we act with honest intent; as journalists, we must conduct our professional lives in a manner that avoids even the suggestion of personal gain, or any misuse of the power of the press.

It is with this acknowledgment that we offer these guidelines for those who work in business and financial journalism:

Personal investments and relationships:

- ▶ Avoid any practice that might compromise or appear to compromise objectivity or fairness.

- ▶ Never let personal investments influence content. Disclose investment positions to your superior or directly to the public.

- ▶ Disclose personal or family relationships that might pose conflicts of interest.

- ▶ Avoid active trading and other short-term profit-seeking opportunities, as such activities are not compatible with the independent role of the business journalist.

- ▶ Do not take advantage of inside information for personal gain.

Sources:

▶ Insure confidentiality of information during the reporting process, and make every effort to keep information from finding its way to those who might use it for gain before it is disseminated to the public.

▶ Do not alter information, delay or withhold publication or make concessions relating to news content to any government.

Gifts and favors:

▶ In the course of professional activity, accept no gift or special treatment worth more than token value.

▶ Accept no out-of-town travel paid for by outside sources.

▶ Carefully examine offers of free-lance work or speech honoraria to assure such offers are not attempts to influence content.

▶ Disclose to a supervisor any offer of future employment or outside income that springs from the journalist's professional activities or contacts.

▶ Accept food or refreshments of ordinary value only if absolutely necessary, and only during the normal course of business.

Editorial Integrity:

▶ Publishers, owners and newsroom managers should establish policies and guidelines to protect the integrity of business news coverage.

▶ Regardless of news platform, there should be a clear delineation between advertising and editorial content.

▶ Material produced by editorial staff should be used only in sections, programming or pages controlled by editorial departments.

▶ Content, sections or programming controlled by advertising departments should be distinctly different from news sections in typeface, layout and design. Advertising content should be identified as such.

▶ Promising a story in exchange for advertising or other considerations is unethical.

Using outside material:

▶ Using articles or columns from non-journalists is potentially deceptive and poses inherent conflicts of interest. This does not apply to content that is clearly labeled opinion or viewpoint, or to submissions identified as coming directly from the public, such as citizen blogs or letters to the editor.

▶ Submissions should be accepted only from freelancers who abide by the same ethical policies as staff members.

Technology:

▶ Business journalists should take the lead in adapting professional standards to new forms of journalism as technologies emerge and change.

The business journalist should encourage fellow journalists to abide by these standards and principles.

Reprinted with permission from the Society of American Business Editors and Writers, http://sabew.org

Index